Constantinople

From Byzantium to Istanbul

Constantinople

From Byzantium to Istanbul

Text by David Talbot Rice

Photographs by Wim Swaan

 STEIN AND DAY / PUBLISHERS / NEW YORK

Stein and Day / Publishers / 7 East 48 Street, New York, N.Y. 10017

Istituto Geografico De Agostini S. p. A. - Novara 1965
Printed in Italy

Contents

Plates

Jacket illustrations: *front:* The Blue Mosque
back: Mosaic of St John the Baptist in the gallery of Agia Sophia

Title page: Coin of Constantine the Great

Endpapers: Cornice decoration in Agia Sophia

MAP

PLANS

FIGURES

Introduction

NOTHING IS PERHAPS so sweet or enthralling as a first love affair; nothing can cause so many heart-aches. In 1925 I first fell in love with Constantinople—for in those days that was the name the city was still known by in the West—and I hoped to return to this captivating city. In 1927, I found myself there as an archaeological assistant to an expedition sponsored by the British Academy, which was to conduct excavations on the site of the ancient Hippodrome. I began to read the history of the city and to explore its ancient remains. At first the earlier ones, classical or just post-classical, drew my attention; then the later Byzantine ones attracted me, especially the mosaics of Kariye Camii. Only at a much later date did I take an interest in Turkish art, and as a consequence of that, in earlier Turkish history.

The vital importance of the word "continuity" began to dawn on my consciousness. In 1453 Byzantium died, but Ottoman Turkey was born, and it was, after all, to the Ottoman Turks that Istanbul, the Moslem city, owed its being, its monuments and so much of its charm. So I read about the Turks and I looked at their monuments and soon began to value them little less than the Byzantine ones. To understand Constantinople to the full was not possible in a brief space; indeed the consummation of that understanding has occupied much of my time over the past thirty-six years. Now, at length, I can attempt to offer a tangible sign of appreciation by dedicating this book to my early love, the very city which I here attempt to describe and whose story I shall endeavour to recall.

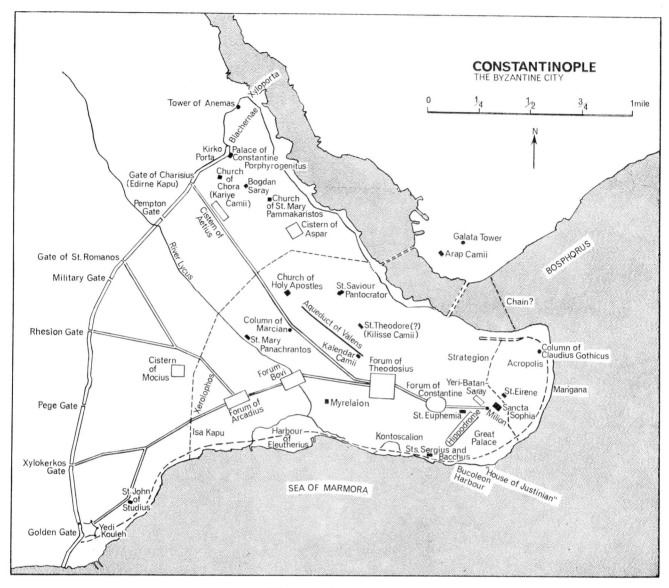

Plan 1. Constantinople: the Byzantine city

Byzantium

IN THE DAYS OF LEGEND when gods were men and men could be gods, the Bosphorus already had a role to play in the story of ancient Greece, for it led to the lands of mystery and imagination, where Jason and his Argonauts sought the golden fleece and where the Cimmerii dwelt in a land of constant mist and fog. Later, when practicalities and material needs superseded the legends, it became one of the greatest trade-routes of the world, linking the classical cities whose cultural heritage we still enjoy with the source of much of their wealth; linen from Colchis, grain from Olbia and other articles of commerce from the whole of the Euxine basin. The Bosphorus was guarded by several cities, or colonies as they were termed, founded by emigrants from the Greek cities—or founded in so far as their existence as static centres of an ordered life was concerned, for even before the days of Greek expansion Thracian tribesmen had settled along the shores at the eastern extremity of Europe.

It would seem that the Asiatic shore was the first to be permanently settled, for there, at the head of the Sea of Marmora, the ancient Propontis, was Chalcedon, a prosperous colony of Megara, established in 685 B. C. Byzantium, on the European shore opposite, was only founded by a later wave of colonizers from the same homeland, under the leadership of Byzas, instructed by an oracle, as legend records, to establish his city opposite that of the blind. The city of the blind was Chalcedon—blind because the colonizers had chosen their site in preference to that of Byzantium. But the name of Byzantium was probably derived from an old Thracian one, rather than being the result of a combination of those of Byzas, and his second-in-command, Antes, as has sometimes been suggested.

Byzantium appears to have been founded around 658; a second wave of colonizers followed thirty years later, and others may well have penetrated subsequently. It took its place as no more and no less than one of the numerous colonial cities of the age, entrepôt for contacts with Thrace, stopping-place and revictualling station for the Black Sea trade. Whether either Byzantium or Chalcedon can have done much to control that trade without maintaining their fleets permanently under arms seems hard to believe, though we do read that dues on corn ships were levied as they passed southwards from the Black Sea. They must have been of value, for Megara established quite a number of colonies in this area, from Astakos in Bithynia, founded in the eighth century B. C., to Pontic Heraklea, the last of them, founded in the sixth. But the agricultural products of Bithynia and Thrace were at first probably the real source of the prosperity of these cities, and the inhabitants of Thrace in particular seem to have been industrious and hard-working. Metals came from the hinterland, both from Asia and from Europe, and their value helped to boost prosperity.

The centuries that immediately followed the foundation of Byzantium appear to have seen considerable progress, and the phase was brought to an end not by wars of jealousy or for economic reasons, which might have been expected since numerous similar colonizing cities, sponsored by rivals of Megara, existed even in the Marmora area, but by the arrival on the scene of the Persians. In 512 Byzantium was involved in wars against the Scythians; in 506 it was attacked and held for a time by the Medes, and in 477, the year after the Greek victory at Plataea, it was liberated by Pausanias. He led a considerable force first to Cyprus, to destroy Persian garrisons there, and then to Byzantium, which was held by a large Persian force; the city only fell to Pausanias after quite a long siege.

Pausanias put Gongylus, an Eritrean and a Persian exile, in charge of the city and sent all the prisoners he had taken back to the Persian commander. Having curried favour in this way, he suggested that Xerxes should marry his daughter and so cement a peace between Sparta and the Persian empire. This was going further than the ephors of Sparta or the representatives of the other Greek cities were prepared to accept and Pausanias was recalled. But he soon returned to Byzantium and renewed from there his contacts with the Persians till he was driven out by the Athenians, who then established their control of the city.

This they retained till 411 B. C. when the Megarian Helixus, assisted by ships of the Peloponnesian fleet, arrived at Byzantium and persuaded the city to revolt against Athens, and it once more became associated with Megara and Sparta. An Athenian effort to recapture it soon after was unsuccessful, and this appears to have occasioned a severe blow to Athens' income, for the tolls on Black Sea shipping which had been collected for her by Byzantium represented an important part of her revenue. She attempted to continue the collection from Chrysopolis on the Asiatic coast held on her behalf by Alcibiades, but this resulted in a renewal of the animosity of the Spartans, who in 410 sent a fleet to support the claims of Byzantium against Chrysopolis.

In 408 Alcibiades attacked Byzantium by land, at the head of a body of Thracian troops, while an Athenian fleet assailed the city by sea. Klearchus, the commander of the Spartan garrison of Byzantium, repelled these attempts, but while he was making a sortie in search of supplies and help, the Byzantines, already showing that opportunism which was to characterize so much of their later conduct, opened the gates of the city in the hope of obtaining favourable terms from Athens. The Athenians, appreciating the value of the city to them, agreed to their conditions and Byzantium once more became part of their tributary. In 403 however it was captured by the Spartan Lysander after the battle of Aegospotami, where the Athenians suffered a crushing defeat.

A few years later, in 400 B. C. to be exact, Byzantium, because of her position more than for any other reason, became the scene of the final act of one of the most impressive and romantic stories of world history, for it was by crossing the Bosphorus just above the city that Xenophon's famous ten thousand made their return to Europe after accomplishing their momentous journey through Asia. The story of the return was however a tragic one, and the part played by Byzantium was not very edifying.

Xenophon's first overtures to procure shipping to transport the army home to Greece were unsuccessful. Eventually however the Spartan commander of the city, Anaxibius, having been bribed by Pharnabazius, who wanted to see the last of Xenophon's troops in Asia, ferried the army over and promised supplies for its forward progress by land. But he treacherously sought to dispatch it without providing these, and it was only thanks to courageous and timely action by Xenophon himself that the troops were prevented from looting the city in revenge for the Spartan's conduct. It was one of Xenophon's greatest actions, for it not only saved the city but also the honour of his army. Thereafter he relinquished his command, being superseded by Koeratades.

In the meantime however, payment of the bribe that had been offered to Anaxibius for conveying the army to Europe was refused by Pharnabazius, and the former ordered Xenophon to take the army back to Asia and attack Pharnabazius. But owing to lack of pay from Koeratades the army had begun to disintegrate and before it could be reassembled Anaxibius was replaced by Aristarchus and the order to march into Asia was countermanded. The army therefore entered the service of Seuthes of Thrace under Xenophon's command, but Seuthes' treatment was little less dishonourable than had been that of Anaxibius, and eventually Xenophon once more led his army into Asia—a sad end to one of the epics of history.

During the next half century the story of Byzantium was little less chequered than that of Xenophon's army. In 393 the city joined a league with Rhodes, Cnidus, Iasus, Samos and Ephesus; in 385 a pact was made with Athens; in 364 the city was won from Athens by the Boeotians; it then became a part of the Athenian confederacy, till in 357 it joined with Chios, Cos and Rhodes in a revolt against Athens. A war, usually known as the Social War, resulted, and in 355 Athens recognized the complete autonomy of all the cities that had allied against her. In 342 however Byzantium was persuaded by Demosthenes to renew its allegiance to Athens and in 340 the city took action with Athens against Philip II of Macedon, the consequence of which was that Philip besieged Byzantium. But with the help of Chios, Cos and Rhodes an Athenian expedition relieved the city and sometime between 339 and 336 Philip concluded a peace with Byzantium. The relief of the siege, believed to have been effected thanks to the divine intervention of Hecate, was commemorated on coins by the symbol of crescent and star, which was to be encountered again many hundreds of years later, for very different reasons.

No great events punctuated the next sixty years of the city's history, but in 279 B. C. large sums seem to have been extorted in blackmail to avoid attack when the Gallic invasions swept over Thrace, to raise which very heavy tolls were imposed on shipping passing through the Bosphorus—much to the annoyance of the Rhodians, whose trade was more affected than anyone else's. It would seem that soon after the tolls were abolished, but whether permanently it is hard to say, for subsequently there is little record of Byzantium until A. D. 73, when the city was deprived of its independence and assigned to the province of Bithynia by the Emperor Vespasian. No doubt the life characteristic of any prosperous trading city of the Roman empire was lived there throughout these years, and this continued till A. D. 196, when the city was besieged by Septimus Severus for having espoused the cause of his rival Pescennius Niger.

The records tell us that Severus tore down the walls at this time, but soon after, realizing the danger of leaving unprotected a city in such a key position, he was responsible for rebuilding them. A few fragments of masonry here and there are all that remain above ground of the Severan city. It is, however, with its refortification by Septimus Severus that the architectural story of Byzantium begins, and it was from soon after that date that it entered the arena of history as one of the world's great cities. Till then its role, as this sketch shows, had been always a subsidiary one, dependent on other and greater powers. But those powers had waxed and waned. Megara, which gave Byzantium birth, had ceded her power to Sparta, Sparta to Athens, and Athens in her turn had declined in face of the rise of Rome. Soon Rome, the city, was to give place to a new capital, Constantinople; Rome, the empire, to a new civilization, and the great days of Byzantium were to begin. But the new role, the new significance, was anticipated to some extent in the time of Septimus Severus, and though little that this emperor built survives, his name is still remembered in connection with a number of sites within the walls that were thereafter to play a major part in the city's topography and architectural history.

The acropolis of the time of Xenophon seems to have been situated on the hill where the inner court of the Saray stands today, and buildings stretched from there to the Seraglio point; a wall built of very large stone blocks which was discovered when the railway was being constructed in 1870 probably belonged to that age; it extended below the kitchens and treasury of the Saray. Nothing more is known, though one day, if extensive excavations were undertaken, further discoveries might well be made. Rather more, though still not very much, is known about the extent of the city, for its walls originally enclosed the whole of the first hill, where the Saray, Agia Sophia and St Eirene now stand. But they were subsequently extended, and the walls that were destroyed by Septimus Severus seem to have included the first two hills, that is to say, the whole area between Seraglio point and a line from the Mosque of Valide on the Golden Horn, past the Column of Constantine, to the shore of the Marmora in the Mangana area. Near where the walls met the sea was a temple dedicated to Aphrodite. According to the records this wall was of large stones, fixed together with iron clamps. No trace of it now survives, nor probably was much to be seen even at the time of Constantine, for its stones were doubtless used when Septimus Severus refortified the city.

The line of the Severan wall can on the other hand be fairly exactly traced. The main entrance was on the summit of the second hill, close to where Constantine later set up his forum; its site is marked today by Constantine's column, the so-called " Burnt Column " of the Turks. The wall probably followed the line of the valley from there to the Golden Horn. Exactly how much land was included within the wall in the direction of the Sea of Marmora is less sure, but the Hippodrome was certainly within this circuit.

The work which had been begun by Septimus Severus was carried on by Caracalla, the city being renamed Antoninia. Both emperors seem to have been responsible for a great deal of construction. Of the buildings which they erected the most important was probably the Hippodrome, though it was not finally completed till the time of Constantine. The Baths of Zeuxippus, which were later to play so important a role in the historical topography of Constantinople, were also in existence; they stood to the south-east of the Hippodrome; the Tetrastoon, which subsequently disappeared, stood to the north. On the Acropolis were temples of Artemis, Apollo, Aphrodite, Zeus, Poseidon and Demeter, while on its eastern slope was a theatre, as well as the Kynegion, which was intended for the exhibition of wild animals. To the north was the stadium, and below, on the Golden Horn, were the ports of Prosophorion and Neorion, with near to them the shrines of Achilles and Ajax. On the slopes of the hill, facing the Bosphorus, was the Theatrum Minor, the site of which is marked today by the column of Claudius II Gothicus, set up between A. D. 268 and 270 to celebrate Claudius's victory over the Goths. According to the historian Nicephorus Gregoras there was originally a statue of Byzas, the traditional founder of the city, at the top of it. Of all these monuments the column and part of the wall of Severus' theatre are the only ones that survive to this day, and as the sites of most of the others lie beneath more recent buildings, most of them of considerable interest and consequence, it is unlikely that any vestiges of them will ever be brought to light, even if a time does come for extensive excavations to be undertaken in the city.

The city apparently prospered as a consequence of its restoration under Severus and Caracalla, till, in 312, it was taken by Maximin. In 323 it was again besieged, this time by Constantine in pursuit of his enemy Licinius who had taken refuge there. Constantine captured the city after a short siege, and history was to some degree repeated, in that the conqueror, like Septimus Severus before him, soon set about restoring the buildings and the defences. But this he did on a far grander and more extensive scale than ever before. Indeed only a very short period elapsed between his occupation of the site and the day in 328 on which he conceived the idea of transferring thither from Rome the capital of the civilized world. A vast work of reconstruction was then put in hand and on 11 May 330 the new capital was inaugurated under the name of the New Rome, soon to be changed to Constantinople, city of Constantine, Christian emperor, heir of the Romans, predecessor of the Byzantines, and supreme ruler of the civilized world. The day was to be kept as a public holiday thereafter till the city eventually fell to the infidel.

Fig. 1. The Column of Claudius Gothicus. From *Beauties of the Bosphorus* by Pardoe, engraving by W. H. Bartlett. Photo: *British Museum.*

Constantinople

CONSTANTINE'S CONSTANTINOPLE

THE ORACLE OF DELPHI was indeed correct; to select in the region of the Bosphorus a site other than that of Byzantium surely suggested blindness. But there were no doubt several causes which led the Roman emperors of the later third and early fourth century A. D. to seek for a site other than Rome as the capital of their empire. The most significant of these, in any case till Constantine's conversion, was the growing importance of the east both in military and in economic affairs. This necessitated the presence of a ruler, whose principal duty was that of commander of the armed forces, close to the scene of action, while the centre of an administration which was becoming daily more concerned with economic problems needed to be near to the principal sources of wealth and supply. Diocletian (284-305) had already begun the move eastward. He had built himself a palace which was at the same time an administrative centre at Spalato, on the eastern seaboard of the Adriatic, and had even thought of Nicomedia on the Asiatic coast of the Marmora as a likely site for the capital. Galerius (305-11) had favoured Salonica, and it is there that many of the principal monuments of his reign are to be found. But not one of these cities was possessed of anything like the same physical advantages as Byzantium, none was at the same time so easily defensible and so centrally placed for purposes of administration and trading; none presented such possibilities for development; none, it would seem as one looks back, could have had such an invincible future before it, and the wisdom of Constantine's choice calls for sincere admiration.

There were revertheless serious rivals to Byzantium. In the west the inhabitants of Rome, the immortal, can hardly have looked with favour on the new upstart in the east. But the atmosphere of the city was no doubt inimical when Constantine had once been converted to Christianity, for it was the hub of a conservative way of life, of the old privileged class and of pagan faiths; it was thus a centre of opposition to all that Constantine stood for. At the opposite extreme stood the cities of the east, where the Fathers of the Church had first taught and where the new faith had made its most rapid progress. Ephesus in Asia Minor or Antioch in northern Syria must have regarded themselves as serious aspirants on religious grounds, while Alexandria in Egypt was one of the principal heirs to Greek culture and had for many centuries been a serious rival to Rome in the economic sphere. Byzantium held no such position. Her history was obscure, her importance secondary, and her claims depended wholly on her geographical, even her topographical, situation. Constantine must have weighed all these considerations most carefully, as others had no doubt done before him, but it was he alone who was granted the vision to crown the choice of Byzas and to confirm finally the wisdom of the Oracle.

The choice was made, the emperor believed, under divine inspiration, though this time it was the Christian faith that directed and not the Oracle of Delphi, just as the city was thereafter to be protected not by Hecate but by the Virgin. Under divine inspiration too he set out to trace the bounds of the new city. Starting from the Sea of Marmora between the spots where the gates of Da'ut Pasha and Psamatia were later to stand, he drew a curving line across the promontory, which reached the Golden Horn near the head of what is today the upper bridge, passing the seventh hill near where the cisterns of Mocius and Aspar were later to be built. The new city was thus four or five times as big again as the old pre-Christian one, but a good deal smaller than the town that was soon to succeed it.

Along the line thus traced by divine inspiration a wall was built. The area outside it, on the seventh hill, was known as the Exokionion and was inhabited at first mostly by men of the Arian persuasion; later, when the Arians were anathematized in the sixth century, it became a fashionable suburban quarter. It was reached at the Marmora end by the gate of the Forerunner, called after a church of the same dedication nearby. There was apparently a statue of Constantine on the top of it. It survived, as did Temple Bar in London, long after the wall of which it formed a part had ceased to exist; indeed, its remains were still there when the traveller Buondelmonti visited Constantinople in 1422. It was called Issa Kapousi (the Gate of Jesus) by the Turks and was finally destroyed in an earthquake in 1508. The area within the gate was known as the Xerolophos, and it was there that the emperor Arcadius built his forum, almost a century later. There were other gates through the wall, notably those on the lines of the three main streets leading along the high ground to the country to the west, and one close to the Golden Horn; close to this was the terminus of a ferry across the water to what is today Galata.

Plan 2. THE HIPPODROME.

17

The land walls were perhaps finished during the reign of Constantine; their continuation along the shores of the Golden Horn and the Marmora was undertaken by Constantius (337-61), who carried on much of the building of the city from where Constantine left off at his death. It would seem that the work as originally planned was all completed during his reign; in any case the walls must have been made secure, for the city successfully withstood an attack by the Goths in 378 which followed upon their victory over the Byzantine army at Adrianople. But the city had already begun to grow, attracting to itself as great cities do a new and increasing population, and early in the next century Theodosius II (408-50) built a new wall enclosing within its circuit the whole of the Exokionion. Constantine's wall was not at once pulled down, for the records state that it was damaged by an earthquake in Justinian's reign and there is a mention of vestiges of it as late as 740. But it would seem to have gradually disintegrated as other constructions arose, and today nothing whatsoever survives above ground.

A defensive wall was a necessity without which no city of those days could permanently survive. But Constantine's building activities were not restricted to such purely utilitarian ends, and work on buildings within the circuit began as early as 328, skilled masons being collected from as far away as Naples, while a general labour force was supplied by 40,000 Gothic Foederati or irregular troops. The city, like Rome, stood on seven hills, and was divided into fourteen regions, ten within the walls, two in the Exokionion, one in the area today known as the Blachernae, and one across the Golden Horn, at Galata. Its plan was based on two main streets which led from either end of the walls to a point of junction slightly to the west of the forum of Constantine, on the summit of the second hill, where his column still stands and which we have already noted as marking the westward limit of the Severan city. From the point of junction to the forum the street was bordered by marble columns, while the forum was oval in plan and had a large marble arch at each end and a porphyry column in the centre. The forum was at first called the Plakoton, or marble paved, but later the name " Forum of Constantine " had been generally adopted. The column at its centre was topped by a statue of Apollo, though this was later replaced by one of Constantine himself; this in turn gave place to one of Julian and then to one of Theodosius. The last was destroyed by lightning in 1081 and the present Corinthian capital was then set up in its place by Alexius Comnenus. The column still stands to mark the site rising from among the tombstones of a small Turkish cemetery; it is known by the Turks as the " Burnt Column " (Çemberli Tash), because it was damaged in a great fire at the end of the sixteenth century. The present rather ungainly base was added by Sultan Mustafa II in 1701 after the old one had been seriously damaged by fire. There are no vestiges above ground of the rest of the forum.

To the east of the forum was another open area, originally known as the Tetrastoon; it was renamed the Augusteon in honour of Constantine's mother the Empress Helena, who bore the title of Augusta. Just in front of the Augusteon was the Milion, from which all distances in the eastern empire were measured. Originally it was a column but later seems to have taken the form of a square building supported on seven marble pillars and standing on the top of a platform reached by steps. There the emperor was later wont to receive the heads of the Factions (see p. 43), but it is doubtful if this custom existed as early as the time of Constantine.

To the east of the Augusteon, down by the sea, the Emperor built a new palace, the Mangana, but it would seem that at this date it was completely separate from the more important palace on the hill above, adjoining the Hippodrome, which later came to be known as the " Great Palace of the Byzantine Emperors "; this was situated on the same site as the present Mosque of Sultan Ahmet. To the east of the Augusteon was the Basilica where the senate met, with statues from Greece

1. The Church of St Eirene. Built by Justinian in 532, it is one of the first churches of the domed-basilica type.

at its entrance. Between the Augusteon and the Great Palace was the Zeuxippus, which had been established by Septimus Severus; it served as a bath, but of a very sumptuous character. Constantine enlarged and improved it and adorned it with a number of statues brought from Greece. To the west of the Zeuxippus and the Palace, on the landward side, ran the Hippodrome (Pl. 29).

The Hippodrome had also originally been set up by Septimus Severus, but it was completed and enlarged by Constantine. Parts of the substructures at the curved end, the Sphendone, are probably to be attributed to Severus; the upper area, where were the seats, was assuredly subsequently modified on several occasions. Constantine brought bronzes and statues for its adornment from elsewhere; they included the bronze column from Delphi, consisting of three serpents intertwined; on it were inscribed the names of the states which had dedicated one tenth of their spoil to the Delphic oracle after the battle of Plataea. The column still stands, without the serpents' heads, on the spot where Constantine placed it, though the ground level has risen considerably since then and its base is now in a pit nearly two metres deep. Michael VI, called the Drunkard, broke off the heads, but they must have been replaced, for they were in place after the Turkish conquest and are indeed shown in several of the miniatures of a volume in the Saray library, the Surnama of Murad III, which dates from 1575; another miniature depicts Mehmet the Conqueror in the Hippodrome casting his mace at the column; according to the accompanying text he broke off the lower jaw of one of the heads; the jaw itself is now preserved in the Museum of Antiquities. When the other heads were destroyed is not known.

The two obelisks which also survive to mark the central line of the Hippodrome were set up rather later; one is a porphyry obelisk bearing the cartouche of Thothmes III which was set up by Theodosius I about 390; the other is associated with the name of Constantine VII Porphyrogenitus (913-59). It takes the form of an obelisk but is built of stone blocks and is not a monolith like the other. Originally it was covered with bronze, but that was torn off by the Crusaders in 1204. An interesting piece of sculpture, now in the Constantinople museum, must also originally have stood in the Hippodrome. It is adorned with reliefs representing Hippodrome races and bears the name of a charioteer called Porphyrius; it must have served as the base of a bronze statue (Pl. 30).

The architecture of the Hippodrome itself is interesting, for there seem to have been no strong protective balustrades as in Rome. These were necessary when bloody contests between beasts and gladiators were the vogue. At Constantinople gladiatorial contests seem to have been replaced by what would appear to have been almost like circus displays or by races. These were extremely popular and became an essential feature of the city's life, the spectators taking sides in support of their champions as members of the " Factions " (*see* p. 43).

The benches of the Hippodrome in Constantine's day were of wood, though later stone ones were substituted which were reached by stairs at the back, leading to gangways between the blocks of seats. Alone of all these secular monuments its extent and its plan can now be fairly clearly distinguished on the surface. But a structure known as the Kathisma, on the seaward side, which formed a sort of Royal Box above and a palace below, has disappeared; it probably stood where there is now an entrance gate to the Mosque of Sultan Ahmet.

The churches which Constantine set up seem to have been rather more scattered than the secular buildings. That of St Eirene stood on the site where the present church stands; it may even have existed before Constantine's day, though he was certainly responsible for altering it, even if he did not actually build it. It was to perish in the Nika riots during Justinian's reign. A larger and more important building nearby, a great basilica dedicated to the Holy Wisdom, was planned where

2. The Aqueduct of Valens.
Built about 370,
it served as the principal source
of water supply until
a new system was developed
by Justinian in the sixth century.

the present Agia Sophia now stands, though it would seem that its construction was in the main the work of Constantine's successor Constantius. It was subsequently damaged during riots in 404 and was finally destroyed in the Nika riots in 532 (*see* p. 43). It is however possible that a circular building which still exists to the north-east of the present cathedral and which served as the Treasury (Skeuophylaction) actually dates from the time of Constantius.

Close to Constantine's land walls, and beside the main road leading to the Blachernae area, the church of the Holy Apostles was built, with beside it a mausoleum for the city's founder, supported by twelve columns, symbols of the twelve Apostles. There he was buried in a great porphyry sarcophagus and the church served as burial place for many of the later emperors. Some of their sarcophagi (Pl. 31), removed at the Latin conquest or when the church was destroyed to make way for the Mosque of the Turkish conqueror Fatih, now stand on the terrace of the Museum of Antiquities, and there is another in the atrium of St Eirene (Pl. 7).

Other churches founded at the time included that of St Mocius, near the walls, and those of St Accacius and St Agathonicus, but nothing of their structures remains. There were also temples. Some of those of earlier times no doubt survived, while temples dedicated to Castor and Pollux and the Tyche or Fortune of Constantinople are superficially mentioned, though no traces survive. But the Tyche remained important for a long time and was frequently represented on Christian ivories like the Consular diptychs for several centuries to come, holding a cornucopia, symbol of the city's prosperity. The foundations of one structure which were discovered some years ago close to the Church of the Myrelaion and which would appear to be of pagan character, may perhaps be assigned to these years; it is a great circular building, in plan very like that of the Pantheon at Rome, and had similar niches in its massive walls. The interior was at some period refurbished as a cistern. Originally it was perhaps a mausoleum, but it is impossible to identify it for there is no mention of it in the texts.

It is not very easy to reconstruct a picture of Constantine's city. The original layout has become so much overlaid by subsequent additions and alterations that it is well nigh impossible to disentangle the vestiges of the past one from another, while the picture is like a palimpsest canvas, the various repaintings inextricably confused. But certain general conclusions may be drawn from a joint study of history, archaeology and topography. Thus the life that was led was still to a great degree Roman. Latin was the language in general use, and even if Christianity was the official faith, a large proportion of the population was still pagan and the ancient temples, especially those on the slopes of the Acropolis facing Galata, where the Gul Hane park now stands, were still in use: pagan worship was only formally forbidden in 416. The larger churches were basilicas, simple three-aisled structures with timber roofs. The main streets were straight and well paved, but it was only later that the various fora were constructed, marking the principal points and making the lines of the streets more varied. The imperial palace must have been on quite a small scale, for the Kathisma can never have been very large and though the building known as the Daphne was already there—it took its name from a statue of Daphne which occupied an important position inside it—the other constructions did not extend over very much of the vast area between the Hippodrome and the sea which the palace complex later came to occupy. Nor can an old supposition that the architecture of this age was mainly of large rectangular ashlar blocks be accepted, for excavations have shown that random work in small stones was usual, as well as the use of square bricks set in very thick courses of hard cement or mortar. The bricks however were probably not quite as large as those that came into use later, especially in the time of Justinian. But the small, tile-like bricks which we know so well in other parts of the Roman world are, when they appear at Constantinople, probably to be associated with the Severan rather than the Constantinian period.

The general arrangement of the city as we know it today can be assigned to this age, for there were to be few major changes in the centuries that followed. The sites of the major buildings have remained unchanged, though there have been numerous additions to them. No doubt Constantine's engineers laid out the general scheme for the water conduits and sewers which still form a honey-comb below the surface of the ground. The line of the principal streets today remains unchanged, though fora and monuments were subsequently erected to mark the junction points or adorn their courses.

The most important of the streets then, as now, ran from the square beside Agia Sophia, the Augusteon as it was called, through the forum of Constantine and thence to what is now the square of Bayazit. There it forked, one branch leading to the gate of St John the Forerunner near the Marmora and the other past the church of the

Fig. 2. Bronze head of Constantine, *Belgrade Museum*. Found at Nish, Constantine's birthplace. The head is exceptionally fine and was probably cast in Constantinople. Photo: *Edinburgh exhibition of Byzantine Art, 1958*.

Holy Apostles, where the mosque of Fatih now stands, to the Adrianople Gate. The section leading from the Augusteon to the point where the two branches parted was the grandest street of the city and later came to be known as the Mese—" middle "—for it virtually divided the city into the Marmora and the Golden Horn quarters.

Two other streets marked not so much the hills as the fringes of the city. The one ran along the Marmora from the region of the Palace to the point where the land walls met the sea; near the walls it no doubt linked up with the more southerly extension of the Mese which passed through the gate of the Forerunner. The other ran from the Palace to the Acropolis, past the Mangana, rounded the point, and then followed the course of the Golden Horn, serving the harbours and passing close to the temples, notably those of Zeus and Poseidon, all of which seem to have been in this area. The strategion or military headquarters, where an equestrian statue of Constantine was set up, also stood on its margin, probably not far from the present railway station of Sirkeci.

There must, by the time of Justinian, have been a good many such statues in the town, but not one of them has survived, though a few fragments which have come there as chance finds can be seen in the Museum of Antiquities. One of the heads there has recently been identified as that of Constantine (Pl. 6), but it cannot be claimed that it is a great masterpiece, and it certainly does not compare in quality with the bronze head of the emperor found at Nish and now at Belgrade. The Nish statue is, however, probably to be regarded as a Constantinopolitan work, for it is in no way provincial. It may well have been made in the royal foundry at Constantinople and sent to Nish, Constantine's birthplace, as a present, much in the way that royal portraits are sent to cities other than the capital today.

The layout of the city was thus quite distinct from that of a typical Roman colonial foundation, with its square plan and streets intersecting at right angles. True, Constantine's forum was originally intended to mark a central point, but it soon became quite subsidiary to other nuclei, like the Augusteon, the Great Palace, the Hippodrome, or the Forum which was constructed by Theodosius where the two main roads from the walls met one another. The essence of the plan was indeed much closer to that of an oriental city such as Palmyra, where the layout was on a longitudinal basis, and where long streets rather than the square plan were the essential feature. In fact in this respect Constantinople was an oriental rather than a Roman town, and anticipated developments in civilization, art and culture, all of which were in the end to become almost as much oriental as they were classical.

THE CITY — VALENS (364-78) TO JUSTIN I (518-27)

LITTLE RECORD SURVIVES of the additions made to the city's architecture by Constantine's immediate successors. Agia Sophia was dedicated in 360, though it had probably been begun under Constantine. It was repaired several times before being entirely rebuilt by Justinian, and only very minor pieces of construction in the lower levels of the walls or actually below ground can be assigned to the original church. Julian (261-63), during whose brief reign there was a reversion to paganism, repaired the Senate House and built a harbour on the Marmora known as the Sigma; it stood near where the church of Sts Sergius and Bacchus was later erected. To Valens (364-78) is to be assigned the aqueduct (Pl. 2) bridging the valley between the third and fourth hills, which is today one of the principal landmarks of the city. It was built in 368, the masonry being of carefully dressed limestone blocks of considerable size, said to have been taken from the walls of the ancient Chalcedonia, the suburb that is now Kadikeuy. It supplied a great reservoir situated beneath the present square in front of the University, bringing the water from the hills beyond the walls. What else Valens built, if anything, we do not know, but he may well have repaired the walls, for the Goths attacked the city during his reign, and he himself died as a result of their victory at Adrianople.

Another monument which is probably to be assigned to these years and which has only recently been discovered is a mosaic floor (Pl. 4), unearthed quite near Valens' aqueduct when the new buildings for the Belediye or town administration were erected in 1955. The theme of the floor, which was of quite a considerable extent, was formal, but included figures of Euphrasius, Eusebius and so on, and H. del Medico suggests that it belonged to a villa which was the property of one Euphrasius and should therefore be dated to 367 or 368. The floor is now in the Mosaic Museum. The cubes are fairly large, the work on the coarse side, and even if the association with Euphrasius is not certain, the situation and the rather provincial character of the work indicate that it must have been done for a private rather than an imperial patron.

Valens' successor, Theodosius I (379-95), the Great, was to leave a more important architectural legacy than any of his predecessors since Constantine. During the forty or so years that separated his accession from Constantine's death, the city had grown considerably in size and prosperity, new streets had been laid out, and new arterial points were called for. Most important of them was a new forum to mark the end of the single street of the Mese and the fork of its two principal westward extensions. It was thereafter sometimes called the Forum of Theodosius and sometimes the Forum Tauri, though it remains uncertain whether this latter name was taken from that of an individual of the period, Florentius Taurus, or from the fact that a statue of a bull stood there. In the middle of the forum was a column set up in 386 to celebrate a victory over the Goths. It had reliefs running up the surface in a spiral like those of Trajan's column at Rome. On the top was a silver statue of the emperor, but it fell in an earthquake in 448 and was replaced in 506 by one representing Anastasius. This too had disappeared before 1204, but the column itself survived till Turkish times; Gyllius says it was then pulled down by Sultan Bayazit II (1481-1512), but others assert it was destroyed by a hurricane in

3

the reign of Selim I (1512-20). Portions of it can still be seen, built into a bath on the right-hand side of the road leading from Bayazit square to Ak Saray.

The western extremity of the forum was apparently marked by a triumphal arch, for two great podia and a number of fragments of columns have recently been unearthed at the spot where it must have stood. The podia present no unusual features, but the columns were adorned with a sort of looped pattern reminiscent of a peacock's feathers or perhaps of the trunk of a palm tree. On one of the fragments are great fingers set horizontally which seem to be grasping the column. It is all most unusual and is far removed from anything familiar in the classical world at the time—or for that matter from anything known anywhere else. A column with a similar " peacock's feather " design up its shaft, but on a rather smaller scale, is built into one of the cisterns, that known as the Yeri Batan Saray, and there is another on the terrace of the museum; it is possible that they formed a part of the same structure, but there is nothing to show what the fingers meant or how they were articulated. The arch was apparently destroyed by an earthquake which did serious damage in the city in 730, for there is a note in the texts that the column of Arcadius was damaged and " The Arch of Tauri " destroyed. In any case the forum seems to have fallen on evil days soon after, for the Emperor Constantine V Copronymus (717-75) transferred the cattle market thither.

Close to the forum, and associated with it, were a basilical hall, a church and a bath, and forming part of its structure were two apse-like niches containing statues of the emperor's two sons, Honorius and Arcadius, who on their father's death succeeded to a divided empire, the one becoming emperor of the West, the other of the East. A short distance to the west, on the road leading to the Gate of the Forerunner, there was another but rather smaller forum, the Forum Bovi; its position is marked by the modern road junction known as Ak Saray, but little is known about it. Farther beyond Theodosius's successor Arcadius built another forum, which was at first called the Xerolophus, and then the Forum of Arcadius. It also had a sculptured column at its centre. The base and the lowest row of the reliefs that decorated it still survive in someone's back garden. Arcadius set it up in 403 to commemorate his father's victories against the Goths and the Visigoths. Theodosius II placed a statue of Arcadius on the top of it, but this was damaged by lightning in 543 and completely destroyed in 740. The column however survived till 1715; Gyllius measured it in 1550 and Banduri made a drawing of it in 1685.

A more just idea of Theodosius I's additions to the city's monuments is today provided by the obelisk (Pl. 29) in the Hippodrome that bears his name than by the meagre remains of his Forum. The obelisk itself is Egyptian and bears the cartouche of Thothmes III; it was set up and the base on which it stands was sculptured in the year 390 at the command of Theodosius. It seems to have been Julian who conceived the idea of transporting the obelisk from Egypt, just as quite a number of others had been taken at one time or another to Rome; but it was Theodosius who actually accomplished the work and had it erected. It stands on four small bronze cubes, one at each corner, above a sculptured base. The base itself is fully worthy of the great obelisk above, for it has taken its place as a key monument in the story of sculpture in early Christian times.

At the bottom on either side are scenes in very low relief which show how the obelisk was transported and set up. At the ends are inscriptions, one in Greek and the other in Latin, recording the event; the fact that the inscription is bilingual is of significance, for it indicates that the native tongue, Greek, was already regarded as equal in importance to that of the official tongue which had been brought by the emperors from Rome; soon it was to supplant the imported language, Latin, entirely. Above these, on the main section of the base, are scenes in much higher relief, representing various activities of the emperor. On one side he is shown be-

4. Mosaic floor of the fourth century, which must originally have adorned the house of one of the more important nobles.

tween his wife, his sons and his courtiers (Pl. 10), presiding at the games in the Hippodrome; on another he watches dancing; on another he receives ambassadors; on the fourth his son Arcadius, who was to succeed him, is shown surrounded by Gothic soldiers. The Goths, under their leader Guinas, were very influential in Constantinople at that time; in 401 the Emperor Arcadius ceded a church to them where they could practise their own faith, the version of Christianity known as the Arian heresy, which was not admitted elsewhere, for Theodosius's regime was strict and there was little toleration of heretics, none at all of pagans.

The sculptures are extremely interesting and may be compared with an outstandingly lovely portrait head of Arcadius (395-408) (Pl. 11) in the Museum. The head is refined and delicate and the sculptor was clearly concerned both with problems of naturalism—for it is obviously a true portrait—and of idealism, for it is also a thing of almost exquisite beauty. No less striking a contrast is offered by the figures which adorn a sarcophagus now in the Archaeological Museum which was perhaps carved half a century or so later. The figures here again are well proportioned and elegant, the style Greek rather than Roman. Other work of similar type was done in Constantinople till around 500; it is usually described as the neo-Attic style.

The reliefs on the base, on the contrary, show a wholly different approach, for the figures are posed frontally, in serried ranks, and the heads are all over-large in relation to their bodies. At one time scholars regarded these features as indicating the decadence of art at that period. More recently they have been accepted as an intrusion of new ideas from the east, where frontality had become hallowed by custom, where expressiveness was valued more than delicacy, and where a convention amounting almost to stylization had supplanted naturalism. In fact the sculptures of the base heralded certain of the changes which within little more than a century were to mark the birth of a new style in art—a style which we know as Byzantine—which was something quite new and distinct, not merely decadent Roman art, as was once supposed.

At the death of Theodosius I the empire was divided, the west falling to his son Honorius (395-423), the east to Arcadius (395-408), a weak ruler, whose policy was controlled by ambitious ministers like Stilico. In the west the age was marked by the rising power of the Huns and other barbarians, which culminated in the sack of Rome in 410 and the transference of the capital first to Milan and then to Ravenna. In the east the growing influence of the Goths was curbed by anti-Gothic riots and when Arcadius was succeeded by Theodosius II in 408, at the age of 7, control fell into the hands of very capable regents, first the Prefect Anthemius, and then the emperor's sister the pious Pulcheria, who founded the Church of St Mary of the Blachernae (where the Virgin's girdle was preserved) as well as several other churches also dedicated to the Virgin. Her outlook was the very opposite of that of Arcadius' empress, who had been denounced by St John Chrysostom on account of her frivolous behaviour and the useless luxury of her court.

Contrary to the attitude which was later so often to prevail in the Byzantine world, the well-being of the state was uppermost in the minds of all and the reign of Theodosius II (408-50) was a period of great prosperity and of very considerable consequence in the story of Constantinople. Abroad peace was maintained with Persia and the barbarians were kept north of the Danube; at home a new university was opened in 425, with teaching both in Latin and Greek; in 438 the laws were codified, and daily life enjoyed a new prosperity and security. So far as incursions were concerned, the city was made doubly secure by the construction of new land walls, which were to make it impregnable to all attack till the Crusading invasion of 1204 and which subsequently protected first the restored Byzantine, and then the Turkish, town almost to the present day. The walls now form one of the most impressive and romantic monuments of the past that we have, for they are in

5. Interior of Agia Sophia from the Gallery. The building was set up by Justinian after the destruction of an earlier building on the site during the Nika riots of 532.

the main well preserved. As one follows their course along the undulating country there are places where one can reconstruct in one's mind's eye almost every move of the Turkish attack of 1453, or visualize the presence of barbarian, Arab or Bulgar hordes encamped in the surrounding country, daunted only by the great triple line of defence before them.

The need for new land walls (Pl. 3) was not due to any inadequacy for defensive purposes of those built by Constantine, but rather to the fact that the new capital, like London or New York today, had proved to be something of a magnet, drawing people to it because of the prospects of employment and security it offered. Artisans were in great demand; special inducements were offered to settlers; much of the population of Thrace had moved within the walls to escape the Goths and even though the dangers of barbarian looting were removed when once they had been driven north of the Danube by the Prefect Anthemius, the demand for space within the city was not reduced.

Anthemius started the new wall in 413. It ran more or less parallel with that of Constantine, but was situated between a mile and a mile and a quarter to the west, and made the complete tour of the walls, both sea and land, a journey of some thirteen miles. The new wall consisted of a single line of defence some thirty feet high with towers at regular intervals of about 180 feet; there were ninety-six of them in all. On the lower floor they formed large vaulted store-rooms; the upper floors communicated with the parapet walk, which was reached by ramps or flights of steps set at right angles to the wall.

In 439 the sea walls were rebuilt under the Prefect Cyrus and presumably between the two periods they were extended to assure the protection of the newly enclosed area along the water fronts, while in 447 extensive repairs were made necessary by a severe earthquake; as many as fifty-seven of the towers of the land walls were damaged by it. The damage was repaired under the direction of the Praetorian Prefect Constantine, and at much the same time a moat was dug outside the wall and between the two a lower curtain-wall was built, with a battlemented parapet walk on the top and towers alternating between those of the main wall. Between the two walls was a terrace fifty to sixty feet wide, called the Peribolos. The moat was of much the same width and there were low walls across it dividing it into sections. As the ground was undulating these apparently formed a series of enclosures which could be filled with water independently though there has been much discussion as to whether they were ever actually filled. The historian Chrysoloras writes as if the moat was permanently full of water, but there is no mention of water in the accounts of any of the sieges and it is possible that the problems of keeping a moat filled at so many different levels proved insuperable.

The whole population of the city was called on to build the first wall, under the direction of the Faction leaders (*see* p. 43), and it is likely that a similar method was followed in the case of the outer wall. That would account for certain variations of technique in building. In the main, however, the same type of masonry was employed throughout. It consisted of bands of brick, set in thick courses of very hard mortar, alternating with bands of small, roughly squared stones; usually there were five courses of brick to ten of stone. Greater variation is to be seen in the vaults which form the roofs of the lower storeys of the towers; here spherical vaults, primitive groin vaults, and barrel vaults of brick all occur; the bricks of the latter were sometimes set longitudinally and laid with the aid of centering, and sometimes transversely, in the manner known as pitching, which could be done without centerings. In certain areas, notably in the region of the Adrianople Gate, stones rather larger than usual were used, but it was only in the Golden Gate itself that really massive blocks—here of brilliant, shining marble—were employed.

There has been a good deal of discussion as to the date of the Golden Gate (Pl. 18).

6. Head of the Emperor Constantine. Several heads of the emperor are known. *Museum of Antiquities, Constantinople.*

It is certainly a separate structure from the walls, and some have suggested that it stood alone, as a sort of triumphal arch like those of Titus or Constantine in Rome, and that it only became incorporated in the defensive scheme when the Theodosian walls were built. Thereafter it formed a sort of citadel in itself. The latter assumption seems on the face of it the more likely, but the words of an inscription which adorned the face of the arch seem to argue against it. This inscription was in bronze letters, and though these have long since disappeared, their character can be deduced from the arrangement of the dowels for their attachment. The inscription can be reconstructed as follows:

> *Haec loca Theodosius decorat post fata tyranni*
> *Aura saecla gerat qui portam construit auro.*

The nature of the inscription precludes any possibility that it was added later; while the phrase " post fata tyranni " does not seem to refer in any way to Theodosius II, it could be interpreted as having reference to Theodosius I; if this were so the most probable date would be between 388 and 391. Perhaps the most likely assumption is that the whole idea of the new wall was conceived by Theodosius I, that the Golden Gate was built, and that for one reason or another work was then interrupted till the regent Anthemius carried it through in 413. It is more likely that so great an undertaking was conceived in the mind of an emperor than in that of a regent, however powerful and competent he may have been, and no emperor would be more likely to have thought on such grand lines than Theodosius I, the Great. And that nothing was done during the intervening reign of Arcadius is not surprising, for he was weak and his advisers were either too ambitious of personal power or too fond of luxurious living to have devoted the funds of the Treasury to such an enterprise.

The Golden Gate itself had a triple entrance, the central arch being wider than the side ones. At its summit were statues, which included bronze elephants, a Victory which fell in an earthquake during the reign of Michael III (842-67), a crowned female, and a statue of Theodosius, as well as a cross which was blown down in Justinian's reign. The gates were walled up at a subsequent date, probably by Isaac II, except for an entrance on a minor scale. On either side of the triple entrance were massive towers, built in the same glistening marble, and between them was a paved court, bounded to the west by a propylaeum, which formed a part of the outer wall set up by the Prefect Constantine. It is a somewhat mean structure in contrast with the great Golden Gate behind, and seems a wholly unnecessary adjunct, in any case so far as defensive needs were concerned, for the Golden Gate must have been well-nigh impregnable. And it must have impeded the progress of the great processions when the emperor passed through it in triumph or entered the city after his inauguration, which was first solemnized at the palace of the Hebdomon outside the walls. The outer gate was, however, adorned with sculptures, and in the seventeenth century the Earl of Arundel asked the British ambassador, Sir Thomas Roe, to arrange for their purchase; after long negotiations he was unsuccessful, and they have now disappeared.

In addition to the Golden Gate, which was reserved wholly for the use of the emperor or a few specially honoured envoys, there were ten other gates, as well as a few smaller posterns or military gates for the use of troops. One, now known as the Yedi Kouleh Kapoussi, stood between the Golden Gate and the sea, while there was another entrance to the north of the Golden Gate, for public use; the present gate is wholly Turkish. The next gate, the Gate of the Pege (Spring) served the public road leading to the Xerolophos and the forum of Arcadius, and was important because the spring itself was regarded with great reverence and was visited officially by the emperor on the festival of the Ascension. It was here that the vanguard of

Fig. 3. The Column of Marcian. From *Beauties of the Bosphorus* by Pardoe, engraving by W. H. Bartlett. Photo: *British Museum*.

the Palaeologi first penetrated into the city at the restoration of 1261. Beyond this was the Rhegium Gate, marking the continuation of the road which had passed through the Constantinian walls at the gate of St Saturnin; its northern fork reached the Theodosian walls at the gate of St Romanus, which stood near a church of that name founded by the Empress Helena. It was just to the north of this that the Turks forced an entry in 1453.

More important than any of these was the Charisius Gate, the name of which was taken from that of the man who was head of the Blue Faction when the walls were built; it was also known as the Polyandrion or Myriandrion and was later called the Adrianople Gate, the Edirne Kapu of the Turks. It stood at the head of the main street leading from the Augusteon to the Forum of Theodosius and thence to the walls past the Church of the Holy Apostles. The area to the north of this gate was particularly vulnerable and attacks were directed against it in a whole series of sieges, notably by the Avars in 626.

A short distance beyond this the wall of Theodosius, which had run in a slightly curving line all the way from the sea of Marmora, today comes to an end, and the fortifications between there and the Golden Horn are all of later date. It is impossible to be sure of the line that the wall followed originally, but it would seem that it turned north-eastward and ran along the eastern spur of the sixth hill, leaving outside the city the whole of the area that was later occupied by the Blachernae Palace, till a new wall was built in 627 (see pp. 62-76). The story of the buildings in this area will be taken up later.

The history of the sea walls is not nearly as clearly defined as that of those on the landward side. There seem to have been many more periods of construction and it is far from clear how much was done by Constantine and how much in the time of Theodosius II. Also they were always less imposing, for the Golden Horn could be shut off by a chain and on the Marmora side winds and currents presented grave difficulties for an attacker. But there was certainly some work done at the time that the outer wall was added on the landward side in the reign of Theodosius. As it stands today, most of the work in the sea walls is however later, and much belongs to the ninth century, especially to the time of Theophilus.

There is some uncertainty as to who was responsible for the outer of the two walls built at the time of Theodosius II, for two prefects are mentioned, Cyrus and Constantine, and some have thought that they must actually have been one and the same man. It would in any case seem to be Cyrus who did much work of a beneficial character, including the introduction of street lighting. He made himself very popular through his work and his benefactions to the city, so much so, one of the historians records, that the emperor became jealous and exiled him to Smyrna, making him a bishop for the purpose. The story seems somewhat unlikely, though it would not be the only instance of the elevation of a distinguished layman to a high position in the Church comparatively late in life.

With the construction of the Theodosian land walls the city took on a form that was not to be altered till very recent times. But there was still room for improving the lay-out within the area enclosed by the walls. The three great open cisterns known as those of Aspar, near the Adrianople Gate, Bonus, near the Mosque of Sultan Selim, and Mocius, at Ak Saray, are built of masonry very similar to that of the Theodosian walls, and are to be dated to the reign of that emperor or soon after. His successor Marcian (450-7) set up a column on the road to the Church of the Holy Apostles. It differed from those of Theodosius and Arcadius in that it had an unadorned marble shaft, with a Corinthian capital at the top. Its base was sculptured and on one side two winged genii still survive. It once supported a statue of the emperor, but this has long since perished. It thus followed the older tradition as exemplified in the column of Claudius Gothicus, and others of the type must have existed even if no record of them has survived; the immense capital (Pl. 15) and a portion of the shaft of one of them have recently been unearthed close to the Turkish kitchens of the Saray.

All these emperors were also responsible for additions to the Great Palace which Constantine had begun beside the Hippodrome. Theodosius seems to have added a section near the sea, while Marcian built what were called his galleries, which are perhaps to be identified with some substructures below the level of a great courtyard which was unearthed by the Walker Trust expedition shortly before and after the 1939-45 war (see pp. 76 and 85). Marcian also erected a number of churches in the city, but none survives.

In addition to the imperial patrons, the more important nobles also built. There were great houses, some on the summit of the fourth hill not far from the aqueduct

7. Porphyry sarcophagus, now in the atrium of St Eirene. The earlier emperors were all buried in the Church of the Holy Apostles. At the Turkish conquest the sarcophagi were removed and are now preserved in various places in the city.

of Valens and some to the west of the Great Palace, but a few walls that have come to light in casual excavations and a few fragmentary mosaic pavements are all that we know of them. But one church which was set up during this early phase of Constantinople's architectural history does survive in a more or less complete state; it is that of St John of Studius (Pl. 16), standing not far from the Golden Gate. It was founded by the Patrician Studius in 463 and is especially interesting because it is the only church in the city of the pre-Justinian period. It was a timber-roofed basilica, with three aisles, the aisles being separated by rather widely spaced columns supporting an horizontal entablature. It thus represents a rather conservative form, for even in Rome the more up-to-date arcades had become quite usual by this time. But there was a gallery above the entablature, with a second row of columns on a smaller scale, and these supported an arcade. There was a single apse, semi-circular within, polygonal without, at the end of the central aisle. There was a transverse narthex at the western end, in accordance with a practice which had already become usual in the east and outside this there was originally an atrium or fore-court; only the narthex now survives. The church is very wide in relation to its length, and it would seem that the proportions of the building, which is nearly square in plan, are to be regarded as characteristic of eastern rather than western Christendom, where basilicas of longitudinal shape were in favour. The architraves and capitals were elaborately sculptured, but these were severely damaged when the building was burnt in 1782. Sculptures of the same type however survive on the walls of the narthex. They are important, for though they follow in the main prototypes of classical character, the low relief and rather schematic designs already herald what was to become typical of the true Byzantine style was developed under Justinian, for example in his church of Sts Sergius and Bacchus.

The role played by the church of St John of Studius and the monastery which was associated with it was no less outstanding in the story of events in Constantinople than was that of the building itself and its sculptures in the history of the city's architecture and decoration. The monastic community was large and noted for its piety, and services continued uninterruptedly throughout the twenty-four hours. The monastery was closed by Constantine v in the days of Iconoclasm, but was re-opened about 787 under the Empress Eirene and in 799 fresh monks were brought from the famous house of Saccudion. Soon the redoubtable Theodore of Studius was at its head, and the monastery became not only the main centre of resistance to Iconoclasm, but also so strict in its discipline that female animals were not allowed within its precincts. Argument wavered to and fro, Theodore always throwing himself into the centre of the discussion, till the community was broken up by Nicephorus i (797-802) because of Theodore's hostility to his actions; it was reformed under Michael (811-13), and, after other vicissitudes, once more became the first in the city under Alexius i Comnenus (1081-1118). The head of St John the Baptist was preserved there and the emperor made a pilgrimage there in great state to attend the service on the Feast of the Decapitation. The church was renowned as a sanctuary and a place of penitence; thither Michael iv fled in 1041 to escape the fury of the populace after the deposition of the Empress Zoe, legitimate heir of the Macedonian line; Isaac Comnenus spent his last days there as a monk; Michael vii (1067-78) retired there, and the son of Sultan Bayazit i, who had become a Christian, was buried there in 1417. It was also noted as the place of education for higher class youths and the fame of its relics drew pilgrims from every region. The building was restored in the middle of the eleventh century by Isaac Comnenus (1057-9) and again in 1290, under Andronicus ii, to repair the damage caused by neglect during the Latin domination; it was probably on the former occasion that a fine floor in opus Alexandrinum was added, a few fragments of which survive, though it was seriously damaged both by a severe fire in the eighteenth century

8. Mosaic of Christ in Agia Sophia. The original decoration was destroyed during the years of Iconoclasm, but new mosaics were set at various period after 843.

which burned all the superstructure and by subsequent neglect. The church was converted into a mosque during the reign of Bayazit II (1481-1512).

The date of the foundation of the monastery of St John of Studius, 463, falls within the reign of Leo I (457-474) who was proclaimed emperor by the army and senate on Marcian's death, and so founded a new dynasty, the Leonine, which replaced the Theodosian. He was ill-educated but practical, and there was at first no marked break in the conduct of affairs. He reorganized the Corps of the Palace Guards, and established the company known as the Excubitors, who were thereafter to play an important role in the affairs of the Palace. In fact the policy of consolidation and reform which had distinguished the rule of the Theodosian dynasty continued. Marcian's reign had been very prosperous materially, and the state of affairs in the east contrasted markedly with that in the west. There the Vandals had settled in Africa after 435; from 441 the Huns had penetrated into the Balkans; in 451 Attila had invaded Gaul and then advanced on Rome. On the death of the western Emperor Valentian III (425-55) there was no obvious successor, and this resulted in the government becoming even more insecure and unsettled. The process of decline and decay which gave its title to Gibbon's great history had indeed already set in in the west. It was to be halted for a time by the arrival on the scene of the Byzantinized Goth Theodoric, who exercised a firm control from the new capital at Ravenna, and it was checked again by the subsequent subjection of Africa and Italy to Justinian. But at his death the rot set in once more and for the next century or more Italy was of little significance. It was not to become important again till Charlemagne was crowned at Rome in 800.

Very many years were however to elapse before any real decline, still less anything like a fall, was to characterize the east. True, there were numerous bad emperors and much misrule, but an empire which was wholly rotten could not have survived the onslaught of enemies from every quarter, including all-conquering Islam. Yet as it was, progress was for a space interrupted by the accession of Zeno in 474. He was unpopular, and the first years of his rule were marked by disturbances and revolts, as a result of which a whole quarter of Constantinople, the Chalcopratia, was burnt, together with the Library of the Basilica, which stood to the west of Agia Sophia, close to where the Yeri Batan Saray cistern is now situated. The basilica was soon rebuilt and stood till 726, when it was again destroyed as a protest against iconoclasm. But in spite of the menace of attack from outside on the part of Vandals, Ostrogoths and Huns from the north and of Arabs and Sasanians from the east, or perhaps to some extent because of it, Zeno weathered the storm, and with the accession of Anastasius I in 491 a phase of progress once more set in which was even more marked in art than in the political sphere, for the year 500 marks the establishment of the new style which we know as Byzantine as clearly as any single date can be said to do. The years around 500 were to constitute the prelude to the reign of the great Justinian, which has been very happily termed the " First Golden Age " of the Byzantine civilization.

The Earlier Years of the Sixth Century

There is good reason to believe that the magnificent ivory in the Louvre (Pl. 20), known as the Barberini ivory, which bears the figure of a mounted emperor on its central leaf, was made for Anastasius around the year 500. The face closely resembles that of Anastasius on his coins, while the scenes shown on the panel at the bottom tally with events in his reign. He defeated the Goths several times shortly before 500 and received an embassy from India in 496; and on one side of the bottom panel barbarian envoys are shown bearing tribute, while on the other an embassy arrives

9. The dome of Agia Sophia. It was described by a contemporary as seeming to be suspended from heaven on invisible chains.

bringing presents of ivory; the figures are to be identified as Indians by the head-dresses they wear and by the great tusks of ivory they carry. But even if the identi-fication of the portrait as that of Anastasius is not accepted, there can be no doubt whatsoever as to the approximate date and the provenance of the ivory; it must have been carved at the end of the fifth or early in the sixth century and it was undoubt-edly a Constantinopolitan product. These great multiple ivory leaves were not unusual; two panels with portraits of the Empress Ariadne at Florence and Vienna may be noted. They are typical of the official court art of the capital at the time and an analysis of their style serves to give a very clear indication of the character of the capital itself. Thus they are impressive, grand and dignified, yet at the same time the rendering of the figures combines with the pomp of Rome something of the idealism of the Greek world and the interest in expression and emotion that characterized the art of Syria and the east. Again the belief in God's supremacy that typified Christian thought at the time is apparent in the arrangement of the panels for there is a bust of Christ, supported by angels, at the top of the ivory, above the imperial portrait.

The symbolism of the Barberini ivory is thus significant. At its centre, on a separate panel, is the emperor himself, the great autocrat, wielding full power, do-minating all and subduing the enemies of the state. But his power was granted him only by the sanction of the senate and the army who proclaimed him. Further he assumed his responsibility only by the grace of God, for he was " Emperor in Christ ", and power was delegated to him as head of the church and the Christian state. The secular authority is indicated on the ivory by the standing figure of a man in military costume at one side; there was no doubt a senator where there is now a blank on the opposite side. The divine will is represented by the figure of Christ, supported by two angels, at the top. Christ is supreme, yet old pagan ideas still survive, for what the warrior bears in his hand is not an angel but a figure of Vic-tory, wholly pagan in conception; the old faith had been abolished and the temples pulled down or converted to Christian use as a result of a decree of Theodosius I, but the old ideas were not completely dead. And just as the emperor was subject to Christ and was therefore shown below him, so his enemies and the representatives of heathen power were subject to the emperor, and appear as tribute bearers at the bottom of the ivory.

But Constantinople was not only heir to the classical tradition; its site had been chosen to no small degree because it was in the east, and eastern links had begun to make themselves felt in art. The conception of the emperor as divine, vice-regent of Christ on earth, stemmed from an eastern rather than a classical source; the diadem which the emperor wears on the ivory was of a type which had been introduced from Persia by Constantine; the bust of Christ above, with the figure in strict frontality, shows the reflection of an oriental rather than a classical conception in art, and it was to penetrate and influence the whole of the east Christian world with increasing effect in the years that were to follow. Ivory, the very material in which the portrait is carved, came from the east, and the trade in this and other materials, notably silk, was soon to become one of the sources and also one of the indications, of By-zantine wealth and prosperity; that source of wealth and power is here symbolized by the representation of the embassy from India. Nor could the region to the north ever be disregarded. On the ivory the barbarian envoys personify the wild tribes which presented a constant threat from the country across the Danube. Yet it was this area that provided the slaves and certain valuable raw materials, without which the life of the capital could hardly have prospered; it also formed a link with the region of the eastern steppe, as the Phrygian caps and the trousers worn by the envoys on the ivory prove, and it was from there that certain rather stylized art forms which were to influence the jewellery and even the carvings of Byzantium

10. In 390 Theodosius I set up in the Hippodrome an obelisk brought from Egypt. On its square base were sculptures showing the emperor in the Hippodrome.

emanated, and from there, or from there by way of Persia, that came some of the ideas and beliefs which made the religious ideas of the Manichaeans a serious danger to Orthodox thought throughout the early centuries of Christendom.

Anastasius was responsible for the construction of a great wall across the peninsula at the point of which Constantinople stood from the Black Sea to the Marmora; it was fifty-four miles long and was situated about forty miles to the west of the city. It was repaired by Justinian in 559, but it was too long to be kept permanently manned or to have been of very much use. On the whole however Anastasius' policy seems to have been one of financial retrenchment and there are no buildings surviving in the city that can be attributed to him. It was however during his reign that the princess Anicia Juliana, whose name we know from a famous manuscript of the works of Dioscorides at Vienna, rebuilt the Church of St Polyeuktos. Some fine capitals and cornices which belonged to it have recently been unearthed close to the cross roads formed by the Ataturk Boulevard and the road from Bayazit to the Adrianople Gate and within easy reach of the aqueduct of Valens. The style of the carving is already much more Byzantine than that of the reliefs that adorn the west end of the Church of St John of Studius.

Another interesting building which is perhaps also to be assigned to this period, vestiges of which were unearthed in the nineteen-forties, is the Martyrium of St Euphemia; they lie just to the north-west of the Hippodrome, where the new Palace of Justice is now being built. The building was of an unusual and rather complicated plan. The layout was semicircular; at the centre of the semicircle was a hexagonal structure with semi-circular niches around it; on either side were two smaller circular chambers. The hexagonal building was presumably the actual martyrium where the saint's bones were disposed; the function of the other structures in uncertain. It is not known when the remains were brought to Constantinople, but the character of the masonry suggests a date early in the sixth century. Some wall paintings which survive in a part of the building are however later additions, and are probably to be dated to the early fourteenth century, rather than the twelfth as has sometimes been held.

The age was a prosperous one, as the character of these works proves, and if there were riots and disturbances, they were due to disputes about religion rather than to political discontent or economic pressure. These disputes had indeed begun to take a serious turn in that they had started to excite very wide interest. They all centred on arguments as to the definition of Christ's nature. The third Council of the Church, held at Ephesus in 431, had been concerned with the interpretation proposed by Nestorius and he with his followers had been declared heretical. His views together with those of the Monophysites were again condemned at the Fourth Council which was held at Chalcedon in 451. But this did not mean the end of either group. Nestorius had a large following in the east and the Monophysites were all-powerful in Egypt, and had many supporters in the east and even in Constantinople. Anastasius was an avowed Monophysite and though his successor, the uneducated Justin I (518-27), seems to have taken no very definite line, Theodora, Justinian's queen, was again a supporter of the movement. An attempt was made to bring the Monophysites and the Orthodox together in 482 which not only infuriated Rome, but also brought division in the capital, with the Patriarch and the church and a large part of the population on one side and the imperial house and the rest of the population on the other.

Justinian when he came to the throne in 527 did not improve the situation, for though he was Orthodox he tended to treat the Patriarch and the higher clergy in the same way that he treated his court officials, that is to say, he demanded complete obedience from them and expected the theological arguments to cease at his command, in the interests of political unity. When they did not he assembled a

Fifth Council of the Church at Constantinople in 553, in the hopes of bringing about a compromise. But as Egypt and the east were ardent supporters either of Nestorius or of the Monophysite persuasion and the west was vehemently opposed to any compromise which was reached in Constantinople as a result of the emperor's influence, the conclusions of the Council were not universally accepted, and the situation remained unsatisfactory; indeed, the disaffection of Egypt and the east probably accounted to a great extent for their readiness to accept Moslem overlordship a century later, when both Syria and Egypt fell to the Islamic conqueror with comparative ease.

There can be no doubt that these religious disputes were at the base of the discontent which simmered gently all through the later years of the fifth and the early ones of the sixth century, but when Justinian's policy of imperial expansion, with the severe burdens of taxation and the tremendous demands on manpower that they involved came to be realized, the discontent took on another guise; it became anti-imperial and in 532 reached a head when the two circus factions, the Blues and the Greens, which had by now virtually become active political parties, joined together with the object of dethroning the emperor. Violent rioting ensued, a puppet emperor was crowned and Justinian might well have taken flight had it not been for the courage of Theodora and the prompt action of the Commander-in-Chief, Belisarius.

The Nika riots, as they were called from the cry " nika ", " conquer ", which the people raised, began with a gathering of the populace in the Hippodrome, where the Factions which supported their respective charioteers and circus performers had their natural home. Originally there had been four of these Factions, the Reds, the Blues, the Greens and the Whites, but well before the time of Justinian they had been reduced to two, the Reds merging with the Blues, the Whites with the Greens. Usually the two were at enmity, not only because their respective supporters showed something of the same enthusiasm for their favourites in the circus as do the supporters of the great football teams today, but because they were also inspired by political ideals, the Blues being basically aristocratic and conservative in outlook, while the Greens were more democratic and liberal. Justinian had originally been in sympathy with the Blues, but on his accession he tried to do without the Factions, with the result that the aims of the two groups were united in opposition: to reduce the burdens of taxation and if need be to depose the emperor.

This rare unity produced an unexpectedly violent reaction, which was soon transformed into mass frenzy. One of the crowd's first actions was to break into the Praetorium and set it on fire. The excitement spread, the mob moved down the " Mese " and attacked the " Chalke ", the building in which was situated the bronze gate which formed the entrance to the Great Palace from the Augusteon. This too was set on fire, and from there the flames spread to the Senate House, and thence to the Cathedral of Agia Sophia, which was burnt to the ground, together with the Church of St Eirene to the north. The next day the mob set light to the Zeuxippus in which a great collection of classical sculpture was preserved. It too was burnt, together with part of the Augusteon.

It would seem however that the parts of the Great Palace lying between the southern section of the Hippodrome and the sea were not touched; it was there that the emperor and his supporters had assembled and there that Theodora made her famous speech urging resistance and decrying flight as being beneath the dignity of an emperor; death came to all in its course, she urged, and the purple would make the finest of winding sheets. Her words rallied the hearts of all, the riots were suppressed, and the emperor's policy continued unchanged. Indeed the burden of taxation must if anything have been increased, for Justinian was faced with the task of rebuilding the city, so much of which had been destroyed as a result of the riots.

Fig. 4. Facsimile of Gold Medallion of Justinian. The original was preserved in the Cabinet des Médailles until the nineteenth century, when it was stolen. From *Art of Byzantium* by D. Talbot Rice (Thames and Hudson).

From the point of view of the city's architectural history, the rebuilding that followed upon the Nika riots produced results even more considerable than those resulting from Constantine's transference of the capital from Rome to Byzantium. Time was to show that Justinian's policy of refashioning the Roman empire along its old frontiers was to have no more than an ephemeral effect; it was doomed to failure, for the old world had gone and a new one was arising. But his work as codifier of the laws and patron of art and architecture was to prove of lasting significance. Here he was not looking back to the inspiration of the past, but forward to the future. Change was in the air, a new style in art was being born, and it was as a result of the devastations of the Nika riots than the architects were given an unprecedented opportunity in the capital itself.

The records tell of important works done by Justinian in the section of the Great Palace where the royal party sheltered during the riots, works which would no doubt have been carried out in any case. And he built religious edifices like the new Church of the Holy Apostles or that of Sts Sergius and Bacchus, in parts of the city which were not touched by the riots. He also built throughout the empire, at Ravenna in the west and at Bethlehem and Jerusalem in the east, and set up mosaic decorations like those which still survive in the Church of the Transfiguration on Mount Sinai. But it was at the very hub of the state that the most important work in the way of building and decoration was done, much of it the direct result of the riots, and all of it within a few yards of the milion, at the end of the Mese, from where the distances throughout the empire were measured. And beside it he built the most glorious work of all, the new Cathedral of the Holy Wisdom, in which the whole building resources of the state were centred, so that it might be completed within the shortest possible space of time. As it happened the work was done by 537, three years before a severe plague seriously reduced the population of the capital: 300,000 souls are said to have perished.

Had it not been for the Nika riots Justinian would certainly have been one of the greatest patrons of architecture of all time. But it was as a direct result of the riots that he built Agia Sophia, which was to remain thereafter one of the most superb buildings of the world. Constantine had transformed Byzantium from a minor colonial city into the capital of the civilized world, though it still had its rivals, Alexandria, Antioch, and the old Rome. Justinian made it the centre of contemporary thought, art and culture, surpassing all others, and in this respect at least endowing it with the forward vision which was to keep the eastern empire great for another seven centuries.

JUSTINIAN'S BUILDINGS IN CONSTANTINOPLE

THREE OF JUSTINIAN's churches in Constantinople survive, Sts Sergius and Bacchus, St Eirene and Agia Sophia (Pl. 28). There are records which enable us to make a fairly accurate reconstruction of a fourth, the Church of the Holy Apostles, and they may be compared with buildings for which he was mainly responsible elsewhere, like San Vitale at Ravenna or the church of St John at Ephesus. The other churches which he built in the capital—and there seem to have been quite a number of them—have disappeared, as have most of the secular works for which he was responsible, with the exception of three or four underground cisterns, the largest of which the Turks have termed the Yeri-Batan-Saray, the " Underground Palace ", though that known as the Bin-bir-Derek or " The Thousand and One Columns " is perhaps more original and unusual. These cisterns—there are forty or more of them in the city—are works of considerable significance, not only for their function—a very important one in a city liable to have its water supply cut off in a time of siege—but also

11. Head of Emperor Arcadius
(395-408),
one of the most beautiful
heads of late Roman art.
Museum of Antiquities, Constantinople.

architecturally, for they are interesting from the point of view of construction and often both very impressive and very beautiful as buildings.

From a purely architectural point of view the Bin-bir-Derek is the finest. Unlike most of the other cisterns, where old material was re-used, its columns were made specially for it, and were of most unusual proportions, being 12.40 metres in height and made up of two sections, joined at the centre by a drum. At the present time the lowest portions are buried in debris to a depth of some five metres. There are sixteen rows, each of fourteen columns, making a total of 224. The capitals are of simple cubic form; they all support arches, and the squares formed by these are roofed by small domes. The cistern is sometimes called that of Philoxenus, a noble who built a house near the site which was raised up on a cistern to get a good view. But the capitals are of a type not used before the sixth century, and even if Philoxenus' cistern stood on the spot, it must have been entirely rebuilt in Justinian's day. A tradition which attributes the work to Anthemius of Tralles, the architect of Agia Sophia, is far more probable.

The Yeri-Batan-Saray (Pl. 17) is in some ways more attractive to the visitor, for it is larger, its roof is supported by no less than 336 columns, and it is still full of water, which certainly enhances its romantic appeal. But architecturally it is less original, for the columns have all been re-used, they are not uniform in size, while the capitals are all of varying types, some fine Corinthian ones perhaps taken from earlier temples, and some no more than roughly shaped. But it is fascinating to think that the cistern is still in use and that its water is conveyed by aqueduct and underground pipes all the way from the Forest of Belgrade far to the north of the Golden Horn.

Here, near the village of Pyrgos, was the most important source of the city's water supply and a number of impressive aqueducts leading across a river valley still survive. Some of them are Turkish, some Byzantine; at least two of them date from the time of Justinian, who made the provision of fresh water for the city one of the first calls on his architects; one is perhaps tenth century (the Eyri Kemer), and two are Turkish. The Byzantine ones were all repaired in Turkish times. The water for the Yeri-Batan-Saray cistern is carried on that usually known as the Cebecikoy aqueduct. It is 170 metres long and consists of two superimposed series of arches, eight on the lower and eleven on the upper tier; the piers of the lower tier are supported by great buttresses on the western side, which were probably subsequent additions. Justinian's other aqueduct, which the Turks call the Mouallak Kemer, was probably built towards the end of his reign; its middle section consists of two rows of arches of unusually wide span, with narrower arches between them. The large sloping buttresses, which extend almost to the tops of the arches of the upper tier, are later additions; according to the chronicler Nicetas Choniates the aqueduct was repaired by Andronicus Comnenus (1183-85), but further work was perhaps done in Turkish times.

It would seem that the source of supply of water in the area of the Forest of Belgrade was one of the innovations to be attributed to Justinian, for in earlier days the water came from the hills to the south of the Golden Horn. And the idea of multiplying the covered cisterns is perhaps also to be attributed to him, for the reserves in earlier times seem mostly to have been kept in open air cisterns like those known by the names of Bonus and Mocius (*see* p. 34). Some of the open cisterns indeed may even have fallen out of use by Justinian's day or soon after. One of them bears the name Filhaneh, which in Turkish means " House of the Elephants "; and it is possible that the cistern was employed as a stable for the elephants used in the Hippodrome even in Byzantine times. The covered cisterns represented a great advance on the old open ones, for the water in them kept fresh and cool and provided a fully adequate reserve even if the aqueducts were cut.

Important and ingenious though these structures were, however, it was in the

12. Mosaic floor of the Great Palace.
It was laid in the cloister-like surround of a great fore court and probably dates from soon after the middle of the sixth century.

47

sphere of religious building that Justinian's most valuable contribution to architecture lay, both in so far as his own capital was concerned, and with regard to architectural history as a whole. Of his three churches that survive in Constantinople, the earliest was that of Sts Sergius and Bacchus. It was situated well to the south of the Great Palace, in an area which was not touched by the Nika riots, and stood on the low ground close to the sea walls. In its original form it shared a common court or atrium with the basilical church of St Peter and St Paul. Both were close to the monastery of Hormisdas, which had been a palace but was richly endowed as a religious foundation by Justinian. No vestiges either of the monastery or of the Church of St Peter and St Paul now survive above ground.

The foundations of the Church of Sts Sergius and Bacchus were laid in 527, the year of Justinian's accession; it was completed in 536. On plan it takes the form of an inner open octagon, its corners marked by piers which support the dome above, and this is enclosed within a square surround, with a projecting apse to the east and an arcaded entrance to the west, which originally gave on to the atrium. The plan is thus closely related to that of the Church of San Vitale at Ravenna, where the central area is also octagonal, though the outer wall is eight-sided and not square as at Sts Sergius and Bacchus. The idea represents a development of what we see in such a church as Sta Constanza at Rome, though there the dome is supported on columns and not by piers. Such an evolution was a natural one, and does not represent any very daring or unexpected development. But the sculpture that decorates the capitals and the cornices is in a wholly new style and marks a very considerable degree of evolution since the period when the west front of St John of Studius was decorated less than a century before. There, in spite of the intrusion of new elements, the work was basically classical—call it evolved or debased, as you will. In Sts Sergius and Bacchus an entirely new style has been reached, where the love of an almost geometrically balanced, stylized pattern has wholly replaced any strict fidelity to nature. The formal ornament made by the leaves and the great inscription on the cornices, the contrasting black and white pattern of the capitals, produce a new but very lovely effect, and the carvings of Sts Sergius and Bacchus betoken, as far as art can betoken, the dawn not only of a new style but of a new outlook, where an abstract idea in the mind has come to count for more than a vision of nature. And the same basic conception characterizes the building itself, for its plan and its elevation are intricate and ornate, while it is gorgeous within, but simple, plain and unadorned outside.

In Sts Sergius and Bacchus the dome topped an octagon and the supporting of its circular base created no major problem; it represented merely the enlargement and ennoblement of an established building form, which is generally termed the centralized type, and of which the Tholos or Martyrium provided the classical prototype. Beside it there stood, in the Church of St Peter and St Paul, an example of the other favourite building type of early Christian times, the basilica, but whether it was long and narrow, like those of Rome, or nearly square, like the Church of St John of Studius, we do not know.

It may have been this chance juxtaposition of these two basic types of building that suggested to Justinian's architects, or even to the emperor himself, the idea of combining the two forms in a single structure, which was to be exploited in the next great church that he built, St Eirene. Or perhaps the idea came from the east, from Anatolia, Syria, or even further afield, where experiments in domical construction had been going ahead for some time. But however it arose, the idea was soon to bear fruit and was responsible for many remarkable developments during the next few years.

The Church of St Eirene (Pl. 1), as we know it today, was begun in 532, to take the place of its predecessor on the site, built perhaps even before the time of

13. Floor from the Great Palace. The compositions tell no continuous story, but show a series of isolated scenes, most of them of a very classical nature.

14. Floor of the Great Palace. This immense floor, measuring some 10 by 70 yards, was unearthed by the Trust expedition in the years before and after the Second World War.

48

13

14

Constantine; it had been destroyed in the Nika riots. On plan the new church was basilical, having three aisles separated by columns. But the central aisle was unusually wide, and the rows of columns were interrupted by built piers (Pl. 23, 24). This in itself was nothing very unusual, for piers had alternated with groups of columns in much the same way in some of the early basilicas in the eastern parts of the Roman empire, like that of St Demetrius at Salonica, probably in order to give greater stability in an area where earthquakes were not unusual. But in St Eirene, the piers were enlarged; they were carried right up through the gallery, and were linked at their summits by four great arches, all of equal size, two spanning the main aisle, and two, at right angles, embracing the columns and arcades below. In this way a great square chamber was constituted, open below on all four sides. In St Eirene another chamber, this time not quite so large, was constructed to the west, so adding to the length and increasing the impression of a longitudinal basilica below. At the eastern end there was a large apse, while the outer walls on the north and south sides were carried up to the level of the arches. In another of Justinian's buildings, the Church of the Holy Apostles, the idea was extended, and five such square chambers were built, a large central one, with slightly smaller ones on its four sides, so producing a cruciform building. This plan was copied in St Mark's at Venice and elsewhere, though apparently the scale was reduced. In the Church of St John at Ephesus two square chambers were built to the west of the crossing, so producing a long cruciform basilica, made up of six square chambers, each of them roofed with a dome.

But first the problem of how to pose a circular dome above the great squares had to be solved. The roofing of the centralized structures like San Vitale or Sts Sergius and Bacchus had presented no very grave problem for the octagon of the plan could easily be made into a circle. In St Eirene it was a square base that had to be converted; it was done by building into the corners, and at the level of the great spanning arches, four spherical triangles. Two of their sides corresponded to the curves of the great arches that topped the piers; the third was given a similar curve at the top and this was prolonged over the summits of the arches, to meet that of its companion in the adjacent space. A circle was thus provided, lying horizontally in mid air, on which the circular base of the dome could be placed either directly or, if desired, set above a vertical drum into which windows could be built as easily as into a wall.

In this way a new type of building was created, the domed basilica, which was to dominate in the Byzantine region from that time onward, and to give to the world the new architectural style which we know as the Byzantine.

St Eirene was to suffer a number of vicissitudes. In 564 its atrium or forecourt and part of the narthex which terminated it at the west were destroyed by fire; in 740 it was severely damaged in an earthquake, and the apse had to be rebuilt; it was repaired again in Turkish times, when the original columns supporting the galleries were extracted, and others of varying size inserted in their place; the original ones were no doubt used in one of the great mosques. The church never became a mosque, like Sts Sergius and Bacchus, but was used as an arsenal until the nineteenth century, when it was transformed into a military museum; it was perhaps for that reason that the mosaics of its apse were left uncovered; they consist of a great cross with a biblical inscription around the top. Some other rather fragmentary mosaics survive at the western end, but all the rest have vanished; the whole wall space was no doubt once originally covered. The church is now empty, and is open to visitors as an ancient monument.

Both of these churches had an important role to perform in the history of the city. St Eirene, being close to Agia Sophia, sometimes even played a part in competition with its greater neighbour. In 857, for instance, two rival claimants

15. Capital found below the ground close to the kitchens of the Saray. Several great columns adorned the city; the identity of the one to which this immense capital belonged has not been determined.

to the Patriarchate were set up; the supporters of one, Ignatius, met in St Eirene, those of the other, the legitimate Patriarch Phoius, in the Church of the Holy Apostles. In 921 the Emperor Leo VI attended a very special service there, arranged to mark the end of a long argument as to the legality of his fourth marriage, which had provoked a schism in the church. Every Good Friday a yearly service for the catechumens was held there, and the church played a part in other ecclesiastical and state functions.

Sts Sergius and Bacchus on the other hand was more linked with the Western World, for it was on more than one occasion placed at the service of visiting Latin clerics. Indeed, early in its history it served as the refuge of Pope Vigilius, while in the ninth century Pope John VIII thanked the Emperor Basil I for returning it to the Latins; they had presumably been deprived of it during Iconoclasm. Pope Vigilius had been summoned to Constantinople by the emperor because of his desire to uphold the decisions of the Council of Chalcedon, which had acquitted from the charge of heresy certain writings on ecclesiastical problems known as " The Three Chapters ". Justinian had allied himself with a group which wished to condemn the writings, and was furious when the Pope refused to fall in with his view. He ordered the Pope's arrest, but Vigilius, who was a large and very powerful man, grasped the pillars of the altar and refused to surrender. The guards endeavoured to tear him away, but he held fast, and the canopy of the altar came crashing to the ground. By this time a crowd had gathered, and their sympathies for the victim forced the guards to abandon their task. The next day Belisarius, the conqueror of Africa, together with Justinian's heir apparent, visited the Pope and persuaded him that it was useless to oppose the emperor; he returned to his former residence. The rest of his time in Constantinople was, so far as the records tell us, spent in peace. But he was forced to pass as many as seven years in the eastern capital.

Though the Latins used the church from time to time and indeed sometimes even claimed it as a right rather than a privilege, the monastery of Hormisdas which lay alongside the church was a wholly Orthodox institution; indeed the monks probably continued to use the church of Sts Sergius and Bacchus while the Latins used the adjacent basilica of St Peter and St Paul. The monastery was important and numbered many distinguished men among its abbots; the most outstanding of them was probably John Hylilas, better known as John the Grammarian, leader of the Iconoclast movement in the reigns of Leo V, Michael II and Theophilus. He was charged by Leo, along with others, to compile a list of quotations from the Scriptures that could be interpreted as condemning icons and representation of the divine or saintly form in sacred art, and prominent supporters of the icons were sent to the monastery in the hope that he would be able to convert them. He acted as tutor to the prince who later became the Emperor Theophilus and was appointed Patriarch by him. His name appears, along with that of the Emperor, on the bronze doors in the south porch of Agia Sophia which were set up by Theophilus in 838, though later, when a son was born to the emperor, an attempt was made to substitute his name, Michael, in place of that of the Patriarch. The attempt was not very successful and the Patriarch's name is still legible below that of the young prince.

As time progressed the ceremonial duties pertaining to the imperial dignity increased in number and importance; one of them was an annual visit to Sts Sergius and Bacchus. The emperor went there in procession, lighted tapers in a number of chapels situated in the gallery, and remained there while a service was celebrated in the church below. When the service was over refreshments were taken and the procession then returned to the palace.

If Sts Sergius and Bacchus and St Eirene were periodically visited by the emperor in state, it was of course at Agia Sophia that the majority of the official functions were held, and no building could have been better suited to house their

16. West front of the Church of St John of Studius. The church was built in 463. Its sculptures represent a transition between a classical and a truly Byzantine style.

pomp and grandeur than Justinian's great cathedral, which stood on the north side of the Augusteon, the main square of the city, which adjoined the Great Palace of the Emperors, and which dominated almost the highest point of the first of the seven hills on which Constantinople was built. There, near enough to the ancient acropolis to inherit the sanctity and reverence which had accrued through the centuries but far enough away for its role as a Christian cathedral to assert its independence, Constantine had begun the building which in the eyes of the emperors of the East and their subjects was to be regarded as the central shrine of Christendom. There, on the same site, Justinian built the new church which was to surpass even Solomon's temple in beauty and grandeur.

The original mosaic decoration of its interior has been removed; the silver iconostasis, the silk hangings, the gold vessels used in the services, the lamps and other adornments have all perished; much of the glory has gone. But the building itself remains, to bear witness to Justinian's discernment and to the architect's genius. Once the centre of the Christian faith, then the principal shrine of Islam, it is now, in these days of doubt and uncertainty, an ancient monument. At first glance some find it disappointing; for outside it is plain and severe, and the various turbehs and other structures of Turkish date which have grown up around it detract somewhat from its impressiveness, while the four minarets which were added when it became a mosque distract the eye. But inside the balance of its proportions exercises on the spectator an effect that is almost physical; something that could be apprehended even by a blind man. No view or photograph can convey this impression. It has to be experienced at first hand, and experienced at leisure. It is something quite independent of the building's historical or emotional association. It is the appeal of mathematics, of pure proportion, and in this, if in nothing else, Agia Sophia stands supreme.

JUSTINIAN'S AGIA SOPHIA

THE CHURCH IS OFTEN called St Sophia, but that is wrong, for it was not dedicated to any single saint, but to "The Holy Wisdom". The Greeks would have us call it Haghia or Agia Sophia which is correct, but in the West few know Greek and the Latin translation of Sancta Sophia is perhaps more readily understandable. The Turkish name, Aya Sofia, is derived directly from the Greek, but Turkish spelling is unfamiliar.

The church which Constantine had founded and which Constantinus completed was dedicated in February 360; it was seriously damaged in 404 and repaired by 415. On January 15th, 532, it was completely destroyed in the Nika riots. Though the church had thus existed for less than two centuries, its fame had been established and its importance had become so considerable that the building of the new structure was put in hand within little more than six weeks after the destruction of the old one; on February 23rd work began. It continued for five years, eleven months and ten days, and on December 26th, 537, the building was dedicated, in the eleventh year of Justinian's reign. It was believed that the work of reconstruction was completed so rapidly thanks to heavenly aid. "Thus by Divine consuel, while angels watched, was the temple built again" wrote Paul the Silentiary in his description of Agia Sophia, and a special degree of sanctity was thereafter always attributed to the building.

Here, as in St Eirene, the conception of a three-aisled, longitudinal building, able to accommodate a large congregation, was subtly fused with that of the centralized building roofed with a dome. On the ground the three aisles are there, separated by columns and by four great piers, even if the piers and their counterparts, the buttresses on the north and south walls, are so large that each of the three side

17. The Yeri-Batan-Saray (underground palace) cistern. It stands not far from the west doors of Agia Sophia, and like the great cathedral was built under the patronage of Justinian.

55

areas takes on the character of a separate chamber rather than a longitudinal aisle. But they provided, none the less, important sections of the church, which could be used in part to house a congregation and in part as subsidiary chapels, while above them the building was so divided that there were galleries of very considerable size which were reserved for the imperial household, something very essential in the principal church of the empire, for it was there that the emperor, his attendants and the court officials had their normal place.

But important though the side aisles and the galleries above them were, it was the great central area (Pl. 5) that was most essential and most impressive. The four great piers, set at the corners of an area which was practically a square, were topped by four great arches, and it was this complex of piers and arches that did the work of supporting the great central dome, (Pl. 9) set at the top of them on a low drum above the four great pendentives. The spaces to north and south, above the galleries, were closed only by curtain walls, pierced by windows and adorned with mosaics. To east and west the building was prolonged by great semi-domes, one at either end, which in turn sprang from massive piers set respectively on either side of the apse and on either side of the western entrance, and they supported not only the great semi-domes on the main eastwest axis, but also smaller ones set in the corners, between the supports of the semidomes and the four principal piers upholding the dome. Recent examination has shown these semi-domes, especially those on the eastwest axis, to be very light constructions, which help very little to counteract the thrust of the main central dome; that was conveyed to the ground through the pendentives, and was compensated at the sides by the four great buttress towers in the north and south walls.

At the west of the church was a long transverse narthex, into which the main entrances opened through magnificent bronze doors—they still survive, though the crosses which stood in relief upon them have been in part destroyed. The narthex gave on to a large forecourt or atrium, most of which has now disappeared, though its limits were ascertained recently in excavations carried out by the German archaeologist A. M. Schneider.

Close to the north-east corner of the church there stood—and still stands—a small circular structure which served as treasury. It has received little attention from travellers and other early writers, but its construction is of a character that would seem to be earlier than Justinian's day and it may well have belonged to the earlier basilica; it is so solid that it could easily have resisted damage in the fire. On the southern side, near the south-western corner, was a square baptistry, which also stands today though it was used by the Turks as a burial place and is now obscured by a mass of minor structures added in late Turkish times; some of them could be removed with advantage. It is to be assigned to Justinian's day.

The plan of Agia Sophia was thus wholly new and original. Other buildings like St Eirene or Sts Sergius and Bacchus in Constantinople or certain churches in Asia Minor may mark the stages in the evolution of the centralized building roofed with a dome which had to be reached before Agia Sophia could have been built, but the ideas which we see realized there had gone no further than a very embryonic stage. A creative genius of outstanding ability was required to bring them to fruition, and such a man Justinian found in the person of Anthemius of Tralles. It is hard to believe that he could have conceived of the plan, worked out its proportions and calculated the thrusts of the immense dome in the few weeks that elapsed between the destruction of the old building and the commencement of the new, even with the forceful personality of Justinian there to urge him; if he did he would have been a striking contrast to the architects of today! One is driven to wonder whether Justinian had not already conceived the idea of setting up a new cathedral even before the destructions resulting from the Nika riots?

A factual account of the construction of the new cathedral has been left for us by the historian Procopius, and it not only serves as a basis for a reconstruction of the building's history, but also adds much to our knowledge of the outlook of people at the time towards art and architecture as a whole. Procopius describes the church as " glorious, extraordinary to those who behold it and altogether incredible to those who are told of it. " It was, he said, distinguished by astonishing beauty, more magnificent than ordinary buildings, singularly full of light and sunshine; its dome was a source of wonder to him, and he thoroughly appreciated the system of thrusts and counter-thrusts by which it was upheld. " The dome does not appear to rest upon a solid foundation, but to cover the place beneath it as though it were suspended from heaven by a fabled golden chain. All the parts are surprisingly joined to one another in the air, are suspended from one another and rest only on that which is next to them, and form the work into one admirably harmonious mass. " He then goes on to describe the details, the gold mosaics, the columns, the varied colours of the marble revetments, producing the effect of a field of flowers in full bloom, and he adds that " whosoever enters there to worship perceives at once that it is not by any human strength or skill, but by the favour of God, that the work was perfected. "

One of the most surprising things about this building was the shallowness of its dome. It stood on a low drum, pierced with windows, but was only about 27 feet in height from its springing to its summit, though its base spanned 104 feet. The thrust of so low a dome—it may be contrasted with that of St Peter's in Rome, which is 100 feet in height from springing to summit, with a span of 137 feet 6 inches—was too great, and on May 7th, 558, the eastern part of the dome fell as the result of an earthquake. It was rebuilt some 20 feet taller, under the direction of Isidore of Miletus, who had worked with Anthemius of Tralles on the original building, for Anthemius himself was then dead.

The newly restored building was then described by several writers with no less enthusiasm than that with which Procopius had described its original appearance; indeed there was little to distinguish it from the first version, for though the dome was higher it still remained surprisingly low in comparison to its span, it still appeared as if supported on invisible chains, and the other changes that had been made were all in the uppermost zone and concerned the buttressing rather than the character of the interior. Of these descriptions those by the historians Evagrius and Agathias are factual and straightforward and are primarily concerned with architectural detail. That of Paul the Silentiary, a court official, is of a very different character, for it is poetic and imaginative, and is of primary interest because of the light it throws on contemporary taste and criticism—though one can discern, throughout it, the outlook of the courtier, for the first eighty lines—it is written in Homeric hexameters—are devoted to an eulogy of Justinian. But the description of the rededication is moving and effective. " At last the holy morn had come, " he writes, " and the great doors of the newly built temple groaned on their hinges, inviting emperor and people to enter; and when the interior was seen sorrow fled from the hearts of all as the sun lit up the glories of the temple. And when the first gleam of rosy-fingered light drove away the shadows, leaping from arch to arch, all the princes and people with one voice hymned their songs of prayer and praise; and as they came to the sacred courts it seemed to them as if the mighty arches were set in heaven. "

He too notes the brilliance and gaiety of the coloured marbles, and compares them to the flower-bordered streams of Thessaly, while the mosaics on the arches are described as being like " the many coloured bow of Iris ". He too describes the wondrous way in which the dome was upheld and the effect it exercised on the spectator; " and it seems that the eye, as it wanders round, gazes on the circling heavens." His description is much fuller and more detailed than that of Procopius; every section of the building is dealt with in detail, and then all the adornments are discussed, the capitals, the floor, the mosaics, the ciborium or altar canopy, the altar itself, with its golden columns and its embroidered curtains, with figures of Christ, apostles, archangels and king, the elaborate system of lighting, the silver iconostasis, and finally the ambo or pulpit. This was regarded as of very special importance and was described at great length. It was of marble, enriched with silver.

From what the Silentiary writes, the general attitude can be clearly deduced. First and foremost in people's minds was the profound sanctity of the building; it was a church, intended for the worship of Christ, and all in it was done to the glory of God. Further, its reconstruction had been accomplished with divine aid. It was recognized that the emperor was to a considerable extent involved—but in his capacity as Christ's vice-regent on earth, rather than as a man or an individual. The great beauty of the building, its proportions and its gorgeous decoration, called forth much praise and it was clearly appreciated for its own sake, as well as for its function and its miraculous associations. Again the genius of the architect was admired and Anthemius was described as " the man most skilled in the mathematical sciences not only of his own day, but of all time."

A great architect Anthemius most certainly was, but at times it seems to have been the emperor who made the major decisions, for example whether to try a particularly daring experiment. On one such occasion, " when the piers upon which the great arch rested, unable to support the weight put upon them, all at once split open and seemed as if they would fall to pieces ", the architects sought the emperor's permission to start afresh. But the emperor, " I know not by what impulse, but probably inspired by heaven, for he is not an architect, ordered them to complete the arch, for it, said he, resting upon itself, will no longer need the piers below." In his foresight and daring the emperor had thus discovered the principles of organic architecture which were to dominate thereafter not only the Byzantine style, but also Romanesque, Gothic and the best of Renaissance building.

Paul the Silentiary speaks of a great cross in mosaic at the centre of the dome, and the fragments of mosaic that survive from Justinian's day on the vault of the side aisles are also non-representational. Whether the rest of the mosaic decoration included figures of divine or saintly character or scenes from the Bible story is unknown; certainly no mention of figures or scenes is made in any of the descriptions, all the parallels drawn being to fields, flowers and meadows. There is however evidence that some medallions in a chamber over the south porch which are now made up of crosses of the iconoclast period did formerly contain portrait busts, and the nature of contemporary work at Ravenna, Salonica, Mount Sinai and in Cyprus suggests that some figural work must have existed, perhaps in the galleries. Apart from these medallions, the decorative work in the side aisles and one great scroll which was perhaps put up when the church was restored in 558 or perhaps added rather later, under Justin II (565-78), the mosaics that are now to be seen are all of much later date, having been set at various periods subsequent to the repeal of the iconoclast ban (843). It may be that the vertical walls of the galleries and the great north and south curtain walls were adorned by Justinian with decorative work which served during iconoclasm and was only subsequently replaced; but the possibility that there were originally figures and scenes there like those in San Vitale at Ravenna, which were destroyed by the iconoclasts, must also be considered. The texts are silent on the subject, but they are silent about a great deal, for though we have several very full records of Justinian's church and its restoration, we know but little of the subsequent history of the building.

It is now more than 1400 years since Agia Sophia was built; 916 years were to elapse between that time and the Turkish conquest, and during that period it has

18. The Golden Gate. The gate formed a part of the land walls as set up by Theodosius II, but may actually have been standing when the walls were built.

18

been calculated that there were twenty-three severe earthquakes, while between 1511 and 1765 ten are mentioned in the Turkish records. The decoration of the church was certainly considerably affected during the Iconoclast struggle (730-843); its contents were looted and the building was converted to the Latin rite after the Crusading conquest of 1204, while at the Turkish conquest in 1453 it was first looted again and then became a mosque. All these events must have occasioned a very

Fig. 5. Interior of Agia Sophia. From an engraving by Fossati.

great deal of reconstruction. What is perhaps most amazing is the fact that the building has undergone so little change.

Certain major restorations are however known. Under Basil the Macedonian (867-886) the great western arch was rebuilt, and he or his predecessor probably added the north and south porches. In October 975 the western semi-dome was thrown by an earthquake and was probably restored by Basil II (976-1025), and Romanus III Argyrus (1028-34) was also responsible for repairs. Andronicus I Palaeologus (1282-1328) strengthened the north and east sides with buttresses, and

19. Capitals in Agia Sophia. These are some of the earliest in the new, rather abstract style developed by the Byzantines.

further repairs were made necessary by an earthquake in 1346, when about a third of the roof fell; some of the damage was dealt with by the Empress Anna, wife of Andronicus II Palaeologus, but the upper part of the roof was only repaired in the following year by John VI Cantacuzenus (1347-54). By the next century the building was probably in a bad state, but the traveller Boundelmonte's statement that much of it was in ruins must surely have been an exaggeration.

One might have expected that the next phase in the building's history would have been one of great disaster; at the city's conquest by the Turks the Janissaries rushed to the building, thinking it to be full of gold, and began to dig up the floor. But Mehmet the Conqueror rode straight there, dismounted at the threshold, placed earth on his head as sign of reverence, and having entered, he stopped in the doorway and gazed for some moments in silence. No more expressive evidence than that could be furnished regarding the effect created by the building's amazing proportions and beauty.

Soon after the conquest the church became a mosque. This meant that the icons were destroyed and also much of the interior furnishing. The mosaics were covered over or removed, but the preservation of the structure was assured. The first minaret was built at the south-east corner by Sultan Mehmet; Selim II (1566-74) built the second, at the north-east corner; the other two were added by Murad III (1574-95). Minor repairs of one sort or another were carried out at various times, but no truly major work was done until a thorough and complete restoration was entrusted to two Italian architects, the brothers Fossati, by Sultan Abdul Mecid in 1847. Then the dome was secured by a chain all round it, the structure was thoroughly overhauled, and the whole interior was redecorated. The Fossati brothers produced a book of very beautiful engravings of the building, and made sketches of those mosaics which had survived before covering them again with plaster as the use of the building as a mosque necessitated. Their drawings remained but little known until 1962, when they were published by Professor Cyril Mango. But an Austrian scholar, Salzenberg, was able to take advantage of the Fossatis' scaffolding and to make copies himself, which were published in 1854. They were not very good and gave little idea of the beauty of the mosaics, and it is only now that they are once more being uncovered under the care of the Byzantine Institute of America that their real quality can be appreciated. But alas, even in the course of the relatively brief period since 1847 earthquakes and damp have claimed their toll, and today there is not as much as there was little more than a century ago. The walls and the more accessible areas have now been dealt with. The pendentives, with their great cherubim, the semi-domes, and even the dome itself, remain to be tackled. The marble revetments too need to be cleaned; this has been done in part at the western end, but the great shields with koranic inscriptions which date from the days of Sultan Abdul Mecid should be removed, for they are a serious disfigurement. Much has been undertaken since 1932, when the work of the Byzantine Institute of America began thanks to the direct sponsorship of Ataturk; perhaps, in the course of the next half-century, all the cleaning and restoration will be accomplished, and the great cathedral restored once more to something like its pristine glory.

The Great Palace of the Byzantine Emperors

THE FIRST OF THE BUILDINGS which were eventually to become the fabled Great Palace of the Byzantine Emperors was set up by Constantine more or less where

the Mosque of Sultan Ahmet stands today. His successors added others until, by the tenth century, the Palace occupied virtually the whole of the area between the Hippodrome and the sea in one direction and Agia Sophia and the sphendone end

of the Hippodrome in the other, an area amounting according to Labarte to 400,000 square metres. Not all of this extent was actually occupied by a palace in the Western sense of the term. There were courtyards, gardens, streets and stairways; there were numerous churches and chapels; there were barracks for the imperial guard and armouries; textile manufactories and workshops for other craftsmen sponsored by imperial patronage; audience halls and rooms for the numerous court officials; and finally the living quarters of the emperors themselves, which seem to have been changed, added to and rebuilt with astonishing frequency. It was from there that, for a long time, virtually the whole of the civilized world was governed; there that its wealth and luxuries were above anywhere else accumulated; there that was centred the fantasy and lavishness of an official life which has never in the world's history been surpassed in grandeur.

We know something of the Palace because it has been mentioned by nearly all the historians and writers; even more because, in the tenth century, the Emperor Constantine VII Porphyrogenitus wrote a long book about it, describing the ceremonies of the court and the various parts of the Palace in which they were enacted. The text of the manuscript is preserved at Leipzig, and though bits of it seem to be copies of earlier texts and other bits are later, it forms a more or less coherent whole, of extreme interest and importance. Thanks to the evidence it provides we know most of the numerous churches that stood within the Palace by name; we know what all the more important buildings were called, and in many cases can gather an idea of what they looked like. Although the Great Palace is perhaps better documented in this way than any other ancient building, it still remains an enigma, for the various attempts that have been made to reconstruct its plan on the basis of these records have nearly all produced different results; indeed above anything else they show how difficult it is to visualize something when no adequate fixed points survive.

Virtually nothing of this once so vast a complex of buildings now stands above ground, and the few excavations that have been made on the site have failed to identify for certain more than a very few of the major buildings described in the texts. Moreover, the whole site is now occupied by modern houses and streets; the few excavations that have been carried out have been very seriously hampered by the presence of existing buildings, and as a result of the construction of the great Mosque of Sultan Ahmet at the very hub of the site, it is probable that quite a good many of the questions that the historian would raise and the archaeologist would hope to solve will never be answered, even if part of the area may one day be investigated by digging where the small houses and squalid streets of the modern town now stand.

The location of one starting point is however roughly determinable, for the Great Palace was entered through a building known as the Chalke or " Bronze House ", and this must have been situated to the south of the large garden which now lies between Agia Sophia and Sultan Ahmet, and probably near its eastern corner——that is, the corner nearest to the sea.

The Chalke could apparently be reached directly from the Mese or central street, without passing through the Augusteon, which was where the garden itself now lies. The great white stone columns which belonged to it were still standing when the Spanish traveller Clavijo visited Constantinople in 1403.

The original structure of the Chalke of Constantine's day was destroyed in the Nika riots; it was rebuilt by Justinian, apparently with a reproduction of the bronze doors which originally gave it its name; it may also have had a bronze roof. One authority states that a bronze statue of Christ was placed there by Constantine, but in a recent study Professor Mango has concluded that no such statue existed; it may have been confused with a mosaic of Christ which was set up over the bronze

21. Panel of incrustation work representing St Eudoxia. It was found in the Church of St Mary Panachrantos and is probably to be dated to the twelfth century. *Museum of Antiquities, Constantinople.*

door, and which was torn down by Leo the Isaurian (717-40), the first of the Iconoclast emperors; it had perhaps been placed there by Maurice (582-602). Justinian adorned the interior of the Chalke with a series of mosaics depicting the campaigns of Belisarius. Basil I (867-86) restored it and used it for judicial purposes, and John I Tsimisces (967-76) redecorated it and apparently turned it into a sort of museum for precious objects. But Isaac Angelus (1185-95) took down the doors and used them for the Church of St Michael at Anaplous, and the building probably fell into ruin soon after.

From the Chalke a passage led to the more southerly part of the Palace. It was sometimes known as the passage or gate of the Scholae and took its name from the Scholae, a detachment of the guard whose barracks were close by. Their duty was to garrison important towns and furnish a guard for the Palace itself. This they did along with two other bodies, the Candidates and the Excubitores. The former were chosen from the Scholae and formed a sort of noble guard who not only looked after the palace, but also occupied a position close to the emperor on campaigns; they wore golden chains as their badge of office. The Excubitores performed a similar function, under the control of the military commander of the Green Faction. Each group had its own living quarters and a great hall or triclinium where the troops ate; such halls as that of the Knights of St George in the Kremlin at Moscow must have ultimately been modelled on them. Nearby was another large hall in which treasures were preserved, and two churches, one dedicated to the Holy Apostles and the other to Our Lord, stood close to the quarters of the Excubitores. Nearby again was the Consistorium where the emperors at one time gave audiences, and where the cross of Constantine and other relics were kept. Adjoining it was a courtyard; it must have stood close to where there is now a sort of raised terrace bounded on the south side by the northern enclosing wall of Sultan Ahmet and on the west by the library of the same mosque. Between it and the northern extremity of the Hippodrome was the Zeuxippus, the position of which was established with reasonable certainty during excavations conducted on behalf of the British Academy in 1928. It was originally a sort of museum containing a number of statues brought from Greece, but was severely damaged in the Nika riots. By the tenth century the state silk weaving looms had been established there. The Numera, which apparently served as a sort of barracks, were also in the same area, but the building was probably separate from the Zeuxippus.

To the south of this complex, almost under the forecourt of the mosque, stood the Palace of the Daphne, which had in early days constituted Constantine's private living quarters. To the west of it was the Kathisma, a two-storied structure, the upper part of which formed a sort of royal box on the eastern side of the Hippodrome. It was reached by a winding stair from the Daphne. Not far from it was the Church of St Stephen, where important relics were preserved, and a building known as the Octagon, which was used as a robing room by the emperors on state occasions. Also in this area, and close to the Hippodrome, was the Triclinium of 19 Sofas which was apparently very magnificent and was used as a dining hall on state occasions: all the vessels used in it were of gold.

To the south of the Daphne, and apparently at a lower level down the slope towards the sea, was the Chrysotriklinos, where after the sixth century some of the most important functions of the palace took place. It was a great octagonal hall roofed by a dome, and with an apse at the eastern end, in which the emperor's throne was placed. It was built by Justin II (565-78), was decorated by Tiberius (578-82) and new mosaics were added by Michael III (842-67). The mosaics on the roof, or it may have been those in the apse, depicted Christ enthroned. Theophilus had made for it an astonishing cupboard called the Pentapyrgion, in which crowns and other imperial treasures were kept. It was made of gold and had five

22

towers or pinnacles—the descriptions of it almost suggest a design by Pugin! Constantine VII Porphyrogenitus (913-59) presented silver doors for the building and in its centre was a rectangular table of gold. In front of the entrance was a vestibule called the Tripeton, and to the north was the Oratory of St Theodore. New living quarters were added nearby by Phocas (602-10). They were probably situated towards the south, for it was in a southward and eastward direction that the Palace tended to expand from the sixth century onwards.

Between these buildings and the Hippodrome was a smaller covered Hippodrome which could be entered from the Daphne and from the Hippodrome itself; it was probably situated more or less where the southern court of the Mosque of Sultan Ahmet now lies. Between it and the Daphne was the Thermastra, probably a sort of passage which took its name from an adjacent bath. Close to it also stood the Church of St Stephen, from the windows of which it was possible to watch games in the Hippodrome. It had been built either by Constantine or Pulcheria, sister of Theodosius II, and was for a time the principal church of the Palace where imperial marriages were celebrated. Both buildings must have been at a high level on the slope, while below, at the same level as the Chrysotriklinos, were a series of other buildings, all of great magnificence.

It is far from easy to reconstruct the picture, however, for a great deal of rebuilding was constantly taking place, and not all the buildings mentioned in the texts were there at one and the same time. Thus in 694 Justinian II built on the site of the Church of the Virgin of the Metropolis, which was destroyed to make way for it, what was termed the Phiale of the Blue Faction; it took the form of a court with a fountain in the middle and tiers of seats at the sides. It was close to the terrace of the Chrysotriklinos, but at a lower level. Soon after it was finished he built another phiale for the Greens. But Basil I (867-86) abolished the phiales, and on the place of that of the Blues he built a bath, the largest and finest in the Palace; the actual fountains he took to adorn an important church which he built, called the Nea. One of them was of Egyptian marble, with dragons carved on it, the other was in a different marble and its cornice was adorned with a frieze of cocks, goats and other animals.

Close to the site of the Phiale of the Greens was the Justinianos, built by Justinian II in 694. It was a large hall, adorned with mosaics, and was used for festivities by the emperors. In 957 the Russian Princess Olga was entertained there. It communicated with the buildings on the upper level and with the Hippodrome by way of the Skyla. It also communicated directly with another hall built by the same emperor, called the Lausiacos, which was near to the portico of the Chrysotriklinos. It was adorned with mosaics by Theophilus.

Somewhere near the south-eastern corner of the palace enclosure stood the Pharos; it was a tall tower, used as a lighthouse and also for signalling by means of fire and smoke. Close to it was a church, that of the Virgin of the Pharos, built by Constantine V (741-75). By the time of Constantine VII it had come to play an important part in the ceremonies; it was no great distance from the Chrysotriklinos. Not far from it was a second church, round in plan, which was dedicated to the prophet Elias. More important was the Church of St Demetrius, built by Leo VI (886-912), where at a special ceremony the emperor presented silver crosses to his courtiers; this took place each year on the day before Palm Sunday.

Moving back towards the north, but at the lower level—that is to say more or less half way between Sultan Ahmet and the sea, where there is now a garden standing above some Byzantine substructures, was an area where the Emperor Theophilus seems to have set up quite a number of buildings. The most important of them was the Triconchos, a large structure with three apses, where the emperor liked to conduct his official business. On its western façade were three doors, communicat-

23. Interior of the Church of St Eirene built under the patronage of Justinian around 52

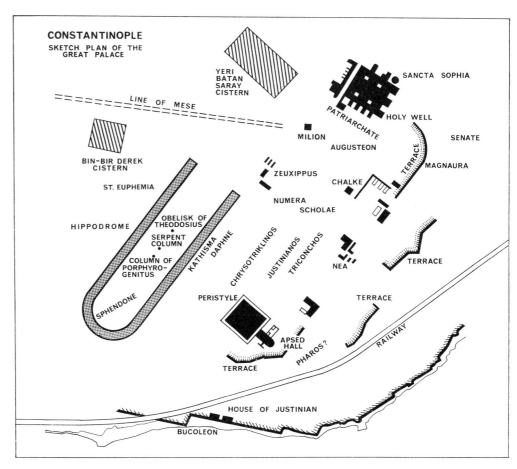

CONSTANTINOPLE
SKETCH PLAN OF THE
GREAT PALACE

YERI BATAN SARAY CISTERN

LINE OF MESE

SANCTA SOPHIA

PATRIARCHATE

HOLY WELL

MILION

SENATE

AUGUSTEON

BIN-BIR DEREK CISTERN

ST. EUPHEMIA

ZEUXIPPUS

TERRACE

MAGNAURA

CHALKE

NUMERA

SCHOLAE

HIPPODROME

OBELISK OF THEODOSIUS

SERPENT COLUMN

COLUMN OF PORPHYRO-GENITUS

KATHISMA

DAPHNE

CHRYSOTRIKLINOS

JUSTINIANOS

TRICONCHOS

NEA

TERRACE

SPHENDONE

PERISTYLE

TERRACE

APSED HALL

PHAROS?

RAILWAY

TERRACE

HOUSE OF JUSTINIAN

BUCOLEON

Plan 3.   Constantinople: sketch plan of the Great Palace

ing with another building called the Sigma which was used for displays of dancing. Theophilus also built nearby a court with a fountain in it, a hall called the Mysterion, which had a strange echo effect within, and a series of gardens and living apartments. None of these buildings played a great part in the ceremonies, but they formed a composite architectural group.

Somewhere in the same area Basil I (867-86) built his famous church of the Nea. In order to do so he took over part of a polo ground, the Tsycanisterion, which had been laid out by Theodosius II, and substituted for it a larger one, on flat ground not far from the sea. It was described as being close to the Nea, so that this famous church must have stood at a low level too, probably not very far from the Pharos. The church itself was set up in 881. It had an atrium in front of it in which the two fountains from the Phiales of the Blues and Greens were erected. The church itself, which was dedicated to Christ, had five domes, and was apparently modelled on that of the Holy Apostles, which Justinian had built, but it was most famed because of the mosaic decoration of its interior. It was either here or in the Church of the Theotokos that a scheme of arrangement of the Bible scenes was devised which was thereafter adhered to in major decorations all over the Byzantine world. Hitherto the disposition of the scenes and figures had followed no special system. According to the new system the interior was conceived as a microcosm of the Christian world, with heaven above and earth below, so that the figures of Christ and the Virgin were set at the summit of the building, the most

70

intimate scenes of their lives on the upper parts of the walls, and the less important ones at a lower level. Nearest to the ground were the figures of saints who would act as intermediaries between earth and heaven. A diagrammatic representation of this decoration would correspond closely to those of the universe that appear in a geographical treatise of the sixth century called *The Travels of Cosmas Indicopleustes*.

All these buildings, from the Kathisma and the Daphne close to the Hippodrome to those nearest the sea, formed a central block in the Palace. There were two other important blocks, one to the north, the other to the south. That to the north was smaller, but rivalled the central one in importance. Its most outstanding building was the Magnaura, which was separated from the central block by a road which ran gently down to the sea from the Augusteon. It must have followed much the same line as the present street which descends towards the sea from the south-east corner of the garden between Agia Sophia and Sultan Ahmet. The Magnaura Palace communicated with Agia Sophia by a passage and was surrounded by gardens and terraces. Its construction was attributed to Constantine, but it had become especially important in the ninth century, for it was there that was situated an astonishing mechanical throne, which could by some invisible mechanism be raised into the air. It was there that the Pope's emissary Liutprand of Cremona, grovelling in reverence on his stomach, on raising his eyes was amazed to see in the dim light the emperor rising into the air. On either side of the throne the Emperor Theophilus (829-42) had made two gilded lions which roared and also a golden plane tree with birds which twittered in its branches. " I am not certain whether the lions were of bronze or wood," wrote Liutprand, " but in either case they were gilt. They beat their tails upon the ground, opened their mouths, wagged their tongues and roared loudly." These marvels were perhaps contrived by Leo the Mathematician, who was a protégé of Theophilus, and was invited by him to teach in the Magnaura. Theophilus also had made two golden griffins and an organ of gold. They were all melted down by his successor Michael to meet his wasteful expenditure. There is also mention of two silver organs, the one belonging to the Blue, the other to the Green Faction. There were superb silk hangings on the walls, golden candelabra hung from the roof on copper chains silvered over, and there were Persian carpets on the floor; on great occasions, however, the floor was strewn with roses.

Constantine's Senate House cannot have been far removed from the Magnaura, but though it was rebuilt by Justinian after the Nika riots it is not thereafter mentioned by the writers; perhaps it was incorporated into the Magnaura. A Chapel of the Saviour apparently stood between it and the Chalke, and close to the south-east corner of Agia Sophia was the Sacred Well, so called because the head of the well where Christ had spoken to the Samaritan woman was preserved there. To the west of this, running along the southern side of the great church itself, was the Patriarchal Palace, and to the north, towards the Church of St Eirene, and perhaps even between St Eirene and Agia Sophia, was the Hospital of Sampson, which was rebuilt by Justinian after the Nika riots. It is however impossible to identify it with any part of the heterogeneous collection of buildings excavated some years ago to the south of St Eirene.

At the very opposite extremity of the Palace was another distinct complex, known as the Bucoleon, which took its name from a sculpture of a lion capturing an ox. It consisted apparently of three separate sections, an upper palace, a lower palace, which was the more important, and a harbour. The palaces were apparently built by Theodosius II, but there is little mention of them till the tenth century. They then became much favoured. Constantine VII Porphyrogenitus (912-59) did some repairs; Nicephorus II Phocas (963-69) enlarged the palace and surrounded it with a wall; he also apparently strengthened the wall that protected the whole Palace area. Alexius Comnenus (1081-1118) lived in the Bucoleon Palace and it was probably there that the famous Porphyria or purple chamber—so called because it was hung with textiles of imperial purple—was situated.

It was in the lower palace that one of the more unpleasant episodes of Byzantine history was enacted, for there Nicephorus Phocas, who appears to have loved it more than any other part of the structure, was murdered by his one-time friend John I Tsimisces (969-76), who crossed over from the Asiatic shore in a boat on a cold snowy night and was admitted into the emperor's bedroom with the aid of Nicephorus' wife Theophano.

The harbour of the Bucoleon was distinct from the palace of the same name. It had a double mole to protect it from the winds in any direction, and served the whole of the Great Palace. There is frequent mention of it in the texts from the tenth century onwards; it was still in use in the thirteenth, but by the fourteenth had begun to silt up. A stair led from it to the terrace near the Pharos and there was a passage to the Nea.

The site of the harbour can still be traced, as can the commencement of the great stair which led from it up to the palace, on the slopes above, and it is very probable that the maritime palace of the Bucoleon is to be identified with the ruinous building which still survives to the north of the harbour and which goes by the name of the "House of Justinian" (Pl. 41). Investigations carried out by the Walker Trust in 1953 proved that none of the present structure belongs to the time of Theodosius II; it is in fact all to be dated to the seventh century at earliest. It is quite possible that we see here the parts which were added to the lower palace by Nicephorus Phocas. We know that his murderers climbed up to the Empress's chamber from a boat; here that could easily have been done, and it may well have been in one of the ruinous rooms that now survive between the sea wall and the railway that the murder took place.

Apart from the British Academy excavations in the Zeuxippus area and the work of the Walker Trust in the region of the Bucoleon, the only large-scale excavations on the site of the Great Palace that have been undertaken were on the terrace immediately below the Mosque of Sultan Ahmet, more or less in the region of the Chrysotriklinos. A large building, longitudinal in plan, and terminating in an apse giving out towards the sea was discovered. It had been built on sloping ground, so that this apse must have stood to a very considerable height, on enormous substructures, whereas the opposite extremity of the building where the entrance lay was almost at ground level. And in front of the entrance was a very large court or atrium, rather like a cloister in disposition, for the centre appears to have been occupied by a court or garden, while around the four sides was an arcade of marble columns; each of these arcades was some ten metres in depth and seventy metres long. They were bounded at the back by a wall of stone, and their floors were paved with mosaics (Pl. 12. 13. 14.). In the course of time these had naturally suffered very considerably, but at one place on the south and over the greater part of the north side they were reasonably well preserved.

The layout was the same throughout. There was a border about a metre wide, both at the back and the front of the mosaics, composed of a great scroll with birds and animals and fruits in its interstices, while at intervals it framed great heads, some of them stylized, others so natural that they look like portraits. The main area, between the borders, was occupied by figures in a very naturalistic style, depicting animals, boys at play, scenes of the countryside, buildings, combats in the Hippodrome and so on. But all were in individual groups, isolated from and having no connection with their neighbouring compositions, telling no continuous story, but harmonizing in a general composition. They were depicted as if silhouetted against a plain white background, without shadows or any subsidiary decoration, or any

24. Interior of St. Eirene. On the ground the plan is that of a three-aisled basilica, (but the roof consists of two domes in echelon). The original columns have at some time been replaced by others which are not uniform in size.

25

26

attempt to put the figures in relief. But though in this respect the conception was formal rather than naturalistic, the treatment of the individual figures, both human and animal, indicated a close observation of nature; so close was it at times that it is tempting to suggest that the artists must have worked from life even if the actual themes were mostly chosen from a repertory of late classical times, showing so far as iconography is concerned close links with the floors of North Africa, Italy or Syria. But one thing distinguishes these mosaics from any others, namely the excellence of the technique, for there is nothing elsewhere which is quite so fine from the artistic point of view; elsewhere the technique may at times be almost as good; in other places the composition as a whole may be more balanced, more carefully thought out; in some places the colouring may be just as elaborate. But nowhere else do the mosaics seem to show quite the same overall mastery as here; nowhere else can one say, quite so confidently, this is a great work of art.

Very considerable discussions have been entered into regarding the date of these mosaics. When the first of them were discovered before the war they were associated with the early days of Theodosius II (c. 410) on the basis of the very classical character of the work. Excavations conducted after the war showed that on archaeological grounds they could not be earlier than about 500, and were more probably later. Authorities who have written on the subject subsequently have suggested an association with Justin II (565-78) or even Tiberius II (578-82). More recently still a date at the end of the seventh century has been proposed, on the strength of similarities in style and technique to the wall mosaics in the court of the Omayyad Mosque at Damascus, which were set up in 715, and on this assumption Dr P. J. Nordhagen has suggested that the building to which they belong is to be identified as the Justinianos, erected by the Emperor Justinian II in 694. Though the evidence of topography favours such a date, the pottery found in the filling below the mosaics suggests rather one around 550 and until further examination can be undertaken a date in the second half of the sixth century seems most likely.

The Years Between Justinian and the End of Iconoclasm

The half century that followed the reign of Justinian, under the rule of the remaining emperors of the Justinianic dynasty, has usually been regarded as the dark age of Byzantine history, redeemed only by the organizing ability of Heraclius, who founded a new line in 610 and took in hand a very disasterous military situation. The empire which Justinian had built up in the West had disintegrated rapidly; Slav and Avar hordes were pouring into the Balkans; Rome's old enemy, Sasanian Persia, was attacking in the east; Jerusalem had been captured by the Sasanians and the True Cross taken to Ctesiphon, and the situation looked very black indeed when Heraclius came to the throne.

But though foreign affairs were far from prosperous throughout the later years of the sixth century, the picture of a completely empty treasury and intense depression at home which some historians have given is not wholly true, and depends to a great extent on the scarcity of literary sources. A study of the art and architecture of the age presents a rather different picture. We have thus seen in our examination of the Great Palace that many of the rulers of this age were responsible for extensive decorations or considerable building activity there—the names of Justin II (565-78), Tiberius II (578-82), and Maurice (582-602) stand out in particular—while their patronage in the minor arts was far from negligible; indeed a large percentage of the dated works that survive from the age before Iconoclasm—notably the silver plates—are to be assigned to the reigns of Justin II, Maurice, Phocas (602-10) and Heraclius (610-41). And if buildings were undertaken and mosaics

25. Mosaic in the south gallery of Agia Sophia. Detail of Christ enthroned between the Emperor Constantine Monomachos (1042-55) and his Empress Zoe

26. The Empress Zoe. Detail of the portrait group in the south gallery of Agia Sophia. The full group represents Christ between the Empress and her third husband, Constantine Monomachos (1042-56).

set up within the Great Palace, similar work was probably done elsewhere, though it must be admitted that there are virtually no records of foundations made in these years and there are few buildings surviving in Constantinople that can be definitely dated to them.

There are however reasonable grounds for assigning to the period two of the churches which still survive in the city. The first is St Andrew in Chrisei, now the Mosque of Hoca Mustafa Pasha. It has undergone numerous alterations, but its original plan, with central dome on four piers, with arcades on two columns between them to the north, west and south, was reconstructed by van Millingen. The capitals are of a late sixth century type, similar to those in Agia Sophia, but rather less undercut. The church was converted to the worship of Islam by Mustafa Pasha, who held the office of Grand Vizier under Selim I (1512-30).

The second church stands near the aqueduct of Valens; it is known by the name of Kalendar Camii and is probably to be identified as the Church of St Mary Diakonissa. It is a cruciform domed church with very fine sculptures and superb marble revetments inside. Authorities are divided as to its date, but the late sixth or early seventh century seems most likely.

The northernmost of the two structures that form the double Church of St Mary Panachrantos, transformed into a mosque as Feneri Isa Camisi, was built by Constantine Lips about 907. Investigations carried out in 1928 by Theodore Macridy suggested that Lips's building had replaced an earlier one, sculptures from which had either been re-used or broken up for building material. Fragments recovered included portions of a very remarkable arch, with figures of the apostles set radially upon it. It probably formed part of an altar canopy or ciborium. The nature of the sculpture suggested a date a little after Justinian's time. Recent excavations undertaken by the Byzantine Institute of America however, have disclosed no traces of an earlier building, and textual evidence for its existence has been shown to be lacking. It must therefore be concluded that it never existed. Comparative study has also shown that the sculptures are to be assigned to a much later date. The ornamental sculpture of the tenth century church is more oriental in style and suggests a comparison with the great marble pillars outside St Mark's at Venice, also from Constantinople.

It is improbable that any great architectural enterprises in Constantinople are to be associated with the name of Heraclius (610-41), even if a number of fine silver vessels do bear his name—he was too much occupied with stemming the tide of enemy aggression in Africa and the East, and in 626 also at home, to have thought much of such things; he would even have been ready to move the centre of control to Carthage had the inhabitants of Constantinople not raised such violent objections. But it was nevertheless he who was responsible for building in 627 a new wall from the Blachernae Palace to the Golden Horn, a region which seems never to have previously been adequately defended. The need for stronger defences here was brought home in 626 when an army of Avars, Slavs, Bulgars and Gepids, under the command of the Avar Khan, attacked the city while a Persian force occupied Chalcedon on the Asiatic shore. Heraclius and the main army were away in Lazica, but the Patriarch rallied the defence, the Byzantine fleet was able to disperse the invaders, and the Persians were chased back to Syria.

Heraclius's policy was however very soon to exercise a far more profound effect on the city's history than did this piece of construction. Had it not been for his military activities the Sasanians might well have been in a position to renew their attack and even to capture the city as they captured Jerusalem in 630, and had it not been for his policy of dividing Asia Minor into "themes" or military districts and settling troops there in reward for their services, but with obligations of further service, the far more dangerous expansion of the Arabs, spurred on by the militant faith of Islam, might have carried Asia Minor before it as it carried Syria, Pales-

27. Mosaic of the Virgin and Child now in the Church of the Orthodox Patriarchate at Constantinople. It probably dates from about 1065.

tine, Egypt and North Africa around 640. As it was, the provinces in Asia Minor stood firm, and the attack on Constantinople, when it did come, was for the Arabs a costly failure.

The first sign of Arab intentions was the building of a fleet, for all their early conquests had been overland. It was tried out in raids on Rhodes, Cos and other islands in 654, and in 655 proved its prowess in a victory over the Byzantines, which nearly resulted in the capture of the Emperor Constans II (641-68), but internal problems prevented the Caliph Moawiyah from following up this advantage. In 663 however his troops penetrated into Asia Minor and they raided there every year for fifteen years; in 672 his fleet captured Smyrna, and in 674 an imposing fleet appeared off Constantinople. But it made little progress and was forced to retire to Cyzicus for the winter. In the summer, and for several summers thereafter, Constantinople was under siege, but little impression was made, and in 678 the fleet withdrew, baffled, having suffered severe losses, thanks to some extent to the employment of a new weapon by the Byzantines, namely the famous Greek fire. This was the first occasion on which the Arab forces, which had conquered from Spain on the one hand to Afghanistan on the other, had been halted. It was a landmark in the history not only of the city, but of the world.

In 710 an insurrection broke out against Justinian II and the Armenian Bardanes (711-13) appeared with a fleet off Constantinople; Justinian was deposed and killed and Bardanes was proclaimed emperor. This did not represent a real attack on the city, for the outcome had really been decided by the defection of the army in Asia and the inhabitants of Constantinople were ready to follow its example. But soon a more serious threat was to arise, for in 711 the Bulgar Tervel was ravaging the suburbs of Constantinople and the Arabs once more took the field and arrived with a large army and fleet before the walls of the capital. By then a new dynasty, the Isaurian, had come to power, and its founder, Leo III (717-40) had to face an assault only six months after coming to the throne.

As on the previous occasion, it was the sea walls that bore the brunt of the attack, and we hear now for the first time of the use of a chain across the entrance to the Golden Horn, to prevent enemy shipping from penetrating up it. Thanks partly to the strength of the walls, partly to the use of Greek fire, and partly to the weather, which, when winter came, decimated the Arab forces, the attack was once more a failure.

But the Arabs had still to be evicted from Asia Minor, where they raided yearly, and it was not till 740 that the emperor was able to inflict a serious defeat on them there. It was an important success, for Asia Minor was the source of the empire's manpower, most of its minerals and much of its food, and without it Constantinople was a head without a body—and the city appears to have been in a poor way, for the records tell us that it had hardly been possible to repair the walls after damage in an earthquake in 740 owing to lack of manpower. Trade with the East, and more especially with the grain-producing lands of Egypt, had been interrupted by the Islamic conquests. It began again in the eighth century and a trading treaty with the Arabs was signed in 717; a century later contacts had become so close and so numerous that Leo V (813-20) issued an edict forbidding travel to Egypt and Syria.

The final result of these attacks on Constantinople was, as we have stated, to be attributed to three things, the strength of the walls, the use of Greek fire and the weather—and the third of these was to play an even more vital role in 860, when a Russian fleet was dispersed by a storm. Today this would be attributed to chance. To the Byzantine it seemed to be the result not merely of fate, but was rather attributable to the fact that the city was held to be under the special protection of the Virgin. It was believed that it was her intervention that had brought the storms,

28. Agia Sophia seen from the roof of Sultan Ahmed; the domes in the foreground belong to the library of Sultan Ahmed. The four minarets were added to St. Sophia after the Turkish conquest.

and had helped to save the city. In 672 and 865 a sacred icon depicting her had been brought forth and intercession was made through the icon; in 718 such a line of approach would have been impossible, for in 726 Leo the Isaurian imposed a ban not only on the undue reverence which tended to be accorded to icons but also on the use and the making of icons of any type, and instituted his new policy by tearing down from above the great bronze doors of the Chalke the famous mosaic of Christ, which was probably the most highly reverenced image in the city; it was destroyed, it would seem, in 730.

At much the same time Leo closed the university, which had been assimilated into the Patriarchal school apparently since the time of Heraclius, because it was a centre of anti-Iconoclast thought. But schools seem to have been numerous and active throughout the period and Theophilus (829-42) reopened the University, especially for the consideration of mathematical problems; the ingenious devices he installed in the palace prove the advanced state of thought in this direction. At the same time the classics were admired and studied and there was great activity in the copying of classical manuscripts.

The Iconoclast period (726-843) was one of quite outstanding interest in Byzantine political history, for there was rivalry between potential emperors, division of opinion with regard to the icons, and disputes between emperors and patriarchs. John the Grammarian, abbot of the monastery of Hormisdas, close to Sts Sergius and Bacchus, was one of the most distinguished of the supporters of Iconoclasm; John of Damascus and later Theodore, abbot of the monastery of St John of Studius, were equally ardent as upholders of the icons, and it was in Constantinople more than anywhere else that the disputes raged. But it was not, so far as we can tell, an age in which the city saw any very great changes. If churches were built—and the records show that several were founded between 726 and 843—they were not adorned with figural mosaics or paintings, and such evidence as there is suggests that the outlook of the Iconoclasts was puritan in the sense that they not only avoided figural decorations, but also preferred simplicity to ornateness. The richly carved cornices and capitals, the brilliantly coloured marble revetments, which had been so much admired and which were included whenever expense permitted in the preceding age, were apparently avoided, in favour of simple interiors and plainness in decoration. Attention must however be drawn to the mosaics that adorn the court of the great Mosque of Damascus, set up by the Caliph at Walid in 715, with the aid of craftsmen borrowed from the Byzantine emperor at Constantinople. The compositions there are on a large scale and cover considerable areas, but they are entirely figureless, being composed of trees, views of hill-towns and the countryside and fantastic architectural compositions. They constitute the most effective example of non-figural and also non-abstract art that we know. This is exactly the sort of decoration that one would have expected to find sponsored by a patron of strict Iconoclast tendencies, and even if it was produced before the ban came into force in the Byzantine world, may be described as an Iconoclast work of art. It is a masterpiece of an artist who must have been schooled in the Byzantine capital.

One major event beset the capital in these years, an attack by the Bulgar chieftain Krum (c. 803-16) in 813. The rise of the Bulgars was to a great extent facilitated by Charlemagne's victory over the Avars which removed the Avar threat; it was carried forward by the energy and determination of Krum, who was able to capture in turn a series of towns which the Byzantines had fortified as a bastion to protect Constantinople. In 809 Sardica was overrun and in 811 Krum won a signal victory in which the Byzantine army was cut to pieces and the emperor, Nicephorus I, killed; Krum made a drinking cup of his skull, an ignominy which was not quickly forgotten and which had a most serious effect on Byzantine prestige—

29. The Hippodrome. A race course was first set up on the site by Septimus Severus, it was enlarged by Constantine and served throughout the Byzantine age. The site remains little changed, though the level of the ground has risen. It is called by the Turks the At Maydan or Place of Horses.

30. This relief, on which chariot races in the Hippodrome are depicted, once stoo din the Hippodrome itself. *Museum of Antiquities, Constantinople.*

indeed so much so that when in 812 he offered terms to the Byzantines after capturing Mesembria and a large booty, many were in favour of accepting the offer. But others, Theodore, Abbot of the Studios monastery at their head, urged rejection, and the Byzantine forces decided to make a stand at Versinikia near Adrianople. But the troops from Asia Minor refused to fight and Krum won an easy victory. He followed it up by capturing Adrianople. Meanwhile at home the discontent marked by the disloyalty of the troops from Asia Minor at Versinikia had come to a head, the Emperor Michael I (811-13) had been deposed and a new emperor from the east, Leo V, the Armenian (813-20) had come to the throne. Within a few months of his accession Krum's forces appeared at the walls. But the walls daunted him; he proposed a parley to which he went unarmed, and during which he was attacked. He succeeded in escaping, and thereafter, though he devastated much of Thrace, the city was safe. But the state of the walls in the region of the Golden Horn gave rise to anxiety. Heraclius had constructed a wall there in 627, but it did not seem strong enough and Leo erected a second one in front of it. It cannot have been a simple duplication, as we see in the Theodosian wall, for the effect was to produce a sort of citadel or strong point which was called the Brachionion. The exact line of these walls cannot now be traced, for the whole area was much altered when the Blachernae Palace was built (*see* p. 95). Before that however both Michael II (820-29) and Theophilus (829-42) added towers and other defences to Leo's wall.

The strength of Leo's wall must have been called to question before that, however, for in 821 the city was besieged for nearly a year by a usurper called Thomas, a champion of the supporters of icons against the more active Iconoclast policy which had been instituted by Leo the Armenian. He had been crowned by the Patriarch of Antioch in opposition to Michael II, and had gained the support of certain themes in the east, as well as of the fleet. But the discipline and good leadership of Michael's forces gave the legitimate emperor the advantage and ultimately broke Thomas's power, though not before Michael had had to call to his aid the Bulgar leader Omurtag (814-31); friendly relations had now been established with Krum's successor. But by the next century hostilities had broken out again, and Simeon of Bulgaria (893-927) captured Adrianople in 914 and in 918 was devastating Greece. But he never actually attacked Constantinople; perhaps the strength of the city's defences daunted him, for with the additions made by Leo, Michael II and Theophilus there was no weak point, and the reputation of the city's defences must have been an important factor for peace in the years that were to follow. We have already mentioned the activities of Theophilus (829-42) in the Great Palace, both as a builder and as a contriver of ingenious mechanical devices, and the work he did on the walls must have been considerable, especially with regard to those along the Golden Horn, where almost every tower bears his name. Damage had no doubt been wrought by Krum's attack in 813, and perhaps also by Thomas, and before that the walls at the Saray Point had been battered by a pile-up of icebergs from the Bosphorus in the severe winter of 764.

Another event of Theophilus's reign which happened to have been very fully described by a contemporary writer was his triumphal entry in 831 through the Golden Gate after a successful campaign against the Arabs. It must have been typical of many similar triumphs. He was met at Chalcedon on his return by his empress and by the Praepositus and Master of the Soldiers, who had been responsible for the defence of the city during his absence. There was a pause of a few days at Chalcedon so that the prisoners could catch up with him and then he went by boat up the Golden Horn to the Blachernae and thence on horseback to the Golden Gate itself where a pavilion had been prepared. Other processions, especially those at the emperor's accession, started from the Palace of the Hebdomon, a few miles

31. Detail from the front of a sarcophagus dating from the fifth century. The figure which still retains the character of a classical orator actually represents an apostle.

32. The so-called palace of Constantine Porphyrogenitus. It formed a part of the Blachernae Palace, near where the walls meet the Golden Horn. As it stands today it mostly dates from the time of the Palaeologue emperors.

to the west, on the shores of the Marmora. It was at the Golden Gate that the true triumphal entry began. There a great procession was formed, with the booty and the prisoners in front, the senators and all the court and military officials behind and finally the emperor himself, on a magnificent white charger. At the gate the Praepositus and the Master of the Soldiers awaited the emperor and presented him with a golden crown, and the procession moved off along the main street which had been decorated with hangings and strewn with flowers. At the milion the senators and other officials all dismounted, but the emperor continued on horseback to the sacred well at the south-east corner of Agia Sophia. There he dismounted and entered the church for a short service of thanksgiving. Then he walked across the Augusteon to the Chalke, where a throne had been prepared on a dais, with a great gold cross and a golden organ beside it. The officials of the city then received him officially and presented him with golden armlets, and he made a speech in which he gave an account of the campaign. He then mounted again and rode past the Zeuxippus to the Hippodrome and from there retired to the palace itself.

Theophilus's work of repair on the walls was to be brought to the test within a comparatively short time, for in 860 an attack came from a new quarter, Russia. It was beaten off, but the date is significant, for it marked the beginning of a relationship which was to prove of the very first importance in the history of the Orthodox Christian world. A century or so later Russia adopted Orthodox Christianity and if Constantinople was the second Rome, Moscow eventually succeeded to the heritage as the third.

But in the meantime events were moving fast at home. During the regency of Theodora, one of those powerful female personalities which the Byzantine ruling house not infrequently threw up, Iconoclasm had been brought to an end in 843 and in 856 the Emperor Michael III took over control of the state. A new university was opened in the Palace of the Magnaura, while one of the most distinguished intellectual figures of the whole of Byzantine history, Photius, was appointed to the Patriarchal throne. He was much admired and respected, and the violent opposition of the Pope to his appointment only served to accentuate in the East the resentment against the West which was eventually to lead to a final split between the Orthodox and Latin churches. They were similarly accentuated in the West by the excommunication of the Pope by the Synod of Constantinople in 867.

THE SECOND GOLDEN AGE

DURING THE REIGN of Michael III (842-67), the first of the post-Iconoclast rulers, a young peasant from Macedonia, made his way to Constantinople and took refuge, as a penniless wanderer, in the Church of St Diomed not far from the Golden Gate; standing near to the walls it was no doubt the first church he encountered. That peasant was, before many years had elapsed, to come to the throne as the Emperor Basil I (867-86), founder of the famous Macedonian dynasty, which was to rule in Constantinople during what eventually proved the most truly Byzantine and also in many ways the most prosperous era of the long-lived Byzantine empire. It was an age of great brilliance and importance, when Byzantine art blossomed to its fullest flower and when the supremacy of Constantinople as a centre of art and culture not only within the Byzantine world, but also in Europe as a whole, reached its zenith. It was, as Kondakov called it, a Golden Age, and Constantinople, wherein were concentrated the state's greatest splendours and riches, was its unrivalled centre, the sovereign city to which the West turned for inspiration and from which the Slav world inherited the basic essentials not only of its art but also of its whole culture. At no phase in the city's history, either before or after, was the adjective "sump-

33. Nativity, from the mosaics of Kariye Camii. These mosaics date from around 1310. They have recently been cleaned on behalf of the Byzantine Institute of America and probably constitute the finest series of mosaics that the world knows.

tuous ", which has often been associated with Byzantine art, so applicable, not only to the art, but also to the life that was lived and the thought that lay behind it.

It would seem that at this period the other great cities of the state had lost much of their importance. Alexandria and Antioch, Constantinople's greatest rivals in early days, had of course succumbed to the Islamic advance shortly before the middle of the seventh century. Rome and the towns of Italy had become completely divorced from the Byzantine world. In any case their significance had greatly decreased with the rise of the Carolingian empire in northern France and southern Germany, and in the ninth century Aachen stood for much more than Rome except in the purely religious sphere. In the East the cities of Asia Minor, which had played so forceful a role in the days of the early Fathers of the church, had now lapsed into local centres of little significance. Only Salonica in Greece stood out as a creative centre in art and thought, though it was never a serious rival to the capital.

Around the middle of the ninth century, when Basil I came to the throne, the emperor was the principal pivot around which cultural life revolved. But as the centuries passed the power and importance of the great families began to increase, and when the Macedonian dynasty ended in 1059, the empire passed in turn to members of the greatest of these families, first to those of the Ducas line, then to the Comnenes, and finally to the Angeli. But though these families drew their wealth from the countryside, they were absentee landlords, who exploited their estates in order to finance their life in Constantinople, and we hear little of links with provincial towns. By the twelfth century if not before the leading members of these families had become patrons of art and architecture in their own right, and any new ecclesiastical or monastic foundations that were made were just as likely to be indebted to the great courtiers or aristocrats as to the emperors themselves.

But if there were changes in the twelfth century, the age between 843 and the conquest of Constantinople by the Latins in 1204 began with a courtly pomp and circumstance which had perhaps never before been equalled and which was centred entirely around the person of the emperor and his principal residence, the Great Palace. We know of it from a series of vivid and enthralling contemporary accounts. The first of these is that of the Arab traveller Harun-ibn-Yahya, who was in Constantinople between 881 and 886. He noted the magnificent courts of the Palace, paved in marble, the golden tables in the great hall (presumably the Chrysotriklinos), and the wonderful mosaics on the walls; but most of all he was impressed by the guards and their magnificent uniforms and the seats and cushions covered in silks and brocades. He noted three separate corps of troops, black men, Khazars, and Turks, so it would seem that the main army was already to some extent a mercenary one; happily there was still plenty of money to pay the troops.

Liutprand, Bishop of Cremona, tells us rather more about the court ceremonial and actual living conditions. He went twice to Constantinople as the emissary of Otto II, once in 949 and again in 968. On his first visit he was received by the emperor in the palace and was much impressed by its wonders, especially the mechanical throne (see p. 71). At the second visit, when Nicephorus II Phocas had come to the throne, he was treated with great disrespect and unkindness by the emperor, and his account is a sad and plaintive one, ending with an attack on the customs officers who rifled his baggage when he left. But he was on both occasions immensely impressed, though somewhat shocked, by the services in Agia Sophia, which were far too dramatic for his tastes.

The fullest account of all is that compiled by the Emperor Constantine VII Por-

34. Christ, between the Virgin and St. John, detail from a mosaic of the 12th century in the gallery of Agia Sophia

89

phyrogenitus, which we know as the *Book of Ceremonies*. It deals in detail with the day to day activities of the emperor's official life. These activites were centred around the Great Palace, though processions to churches outside its limits are described and there is mention of other luxurious structures.

Constantine VII was also responsible for another volume, called *The Book of the Prefect*, in which he was concerned with the system of administration; it is of particular value to historians. There was too a good deal of excellent historical writing, like that of Leo the Deacon in the tenth and Psellos in the eleventh century, and this age was to see the birth of new types of literature in the romance of Digenis Akrites or the Alexiad of Anna Comnena. It is perhaps true that undue stress was laid in the literary world on oratory and expression, but a knowledge of the classics was widespread and the calumnies that have sometimes been heaped on the Byzantine world as lacking in literary competence are wholly unjustified. Quite a number of the emperors were well read, indeed learned, even if a few were almost wholly self-educated.

Basil I, the founder of the Macedonian dynasty, falls into that category, for he came to the city as a penniless wanderer, but he later became a great patron of art, and thought along original lines. He seems to have been the first of the emperors since the time of Constantine to build a residence quite apart from the Great Palace, namely that of the Mangana. It lay beside the Marmora, not far from the point where the present walls of the Saray meet the sea. An arsenal had been built there by Constantine, and it had apparently remained in use till Basil picked on the site, to build in its place a magnificent palace, five storeys high and very resplendent. Alexius I (1081-1118) redecorated parts of it, used it regularly and died there. Manuel I Comnenus (1143-80) also lived in it, but after that it seems to have been relegated for use as offices by the civil service, though Alexius II (1180-83) and his mother were for a time imprisoned there by Andronicus I (1183-85). It was then demolished, either by Andronicus I or by Isaac II (1185-95) to obtain materials for a new building. But the substructures remained and were excavated by the French shortly after the First World War.

Those excavations disclosed the vestiges of several other buildings. Close to Basil's palace were the foundations of a small church, which the excavators suggested was perhaps to be identified with that of the Virgin Panachrantos; it belonged to a monastery first mentioned in 1073, distinct from the foundation of Constantine Lips elsewhere in the city (*see* p. 76). It passed tot he Latins and after the restoration in 1261 became a nunnery. Whether so small a church could have served a monastic community is open to doubt. Adjoining the church, at its northern end, was another and larger one, which with a greater degree of probability was identified by the excavators as that of St George of the Mangana; it was founded by Constantine II Monomachus (1042-55), the emperor who is represented beside the Empress Zoe in a mosaic in Agia Sophia (*see* p. 99). The monastery attached to this church increased in size in the twelfth century and the church itself was repaired at least twice, for it was much revered as the repository of important relics. These included the blood-covered mantle worn by Christ at the Crucifixion, the lance that pierced his side, and the reed and sponge. Close to the church the foundations of a large octagonal baptistry were unearthed; plaques with sculptures of animals in low relief were built into it.

Nearer to the sea, and separated from these buildings by the line of the railway, during the construction of which all of them were seriously damaged, was yet another church, which was identified by the excavators as that of the Saviour. Its façade gave on to the actual sea, forming a part of the walls, and was adorned with ornamental brickwork of great beauty. It too was a comparatively late foundation. Forming part of the walls in this area is a tower, known as the Mangana Tower,

35. The Miracle of Canaa from the mosaics of the Kariye Camii. At the same time that these mosaics were being set Giotto was working in the famous Arena chapel at Padua.

and it was from there or from a point not far distant—the records are somewhat at variance—that a chain was stretched across to bar entry into the Bosphorus. The other end was secured on the small island where the building known as Leander's tower now stands. There was presumably a castle there in Byzantine times; the records mention constructions by Michael Comnenus.

This complex of buildings is interesting not only in itself, but also as an indication of the immense building activity that went on all through the Second Golden Age, both under the patronage of the emperors and also under that of the nobles and presumably the church itself. During the tenth and eleventh centuries this activity was in close accord with the political prosperity of the state, for the empire was large and the economic situation prosperous. Later, as the frontiers were withdrawn and trade fell more and more into the hands of Italians, first the Amalfitans and Pisans, and then the Venetians and Genoese—a treaty which gave great advantages to Venice was concluded in 1082—the luxury of the court and the expansion of building within the city became something of an anomaly. That Basil I should have built a new palace, more commodious and more up to date than the old one, parts of which were already some 500 years old when he came to the throne, was reasonable enough. That Manuel Comnenus (1143-80) should have done so when the finances of the empire were in a parlous state and when enemies were threatening from every quarter indicates the ostrich-like obstinacy which had penetrated the minds of so many of the later rulers, heralding the collapse which was so soon to follow.

The external events of the Macedonian age were closely reflected in the history of Constantinople itself. Six times during this age the strength of the city's defences were tested. In 860 a Russian fleet descended the Bosphorus and troops landed and devastated the countryside at a moment when the emperor, Michael III (842-67), together with the mobile land force, had moved against the Arabs. He returned rapidly, forced his way into the city amidst great acclamation, and rallied the defence. The Russians were defeated, it was believed thanks to the intervention of the Virgin, never-failing protectress of the city.

The Russians appeared on the scene again in 907 with a large fleet commanded by Oleg and forced a trading agreement on the Byzantines which favoured merchants coming from Russia. Around 920 the city was threatened by Simeon of Bulgaria, and in 941 a Russian force once more arrived, landed on the Asiatic coast, and wrought some havoc. But in 988 relationships with Russia took on a new character, for Basil II (976-1025) called on the Russians to aid him against a rival claimant, Bardas Phocas, who had revolted and who was leading a two-pronged attack, by sea and land, against the Byzantine capital. The Russians sent a body of Varangians to Basil's aid, and under his leadership they crushed the revolt. This was the first appearance of the Varangians, but they had come to stay, and thereafter the Varangian guard survived as the most trusted and stable military force in the state. At a later date Saxons and other Norsemen were to join the body; Harold Hardrada is said to have been amongst them.

It was perhaps as a result of this threat that Basil II (976-1025) undertook certain repairs to the walls, but they were not to be put to the test for many years, for in spite of the growing importance of rival states in east, west and north, and of the more or less continued weakness of the rulers who followed Basil, no power arose which was strong enough to penetrate to the capital. Only in 1090 did the barbarous Petchenegs set siege to the city by land while the Moslem Emir of Smyrna attacked from the east. During the winter 1090/91, which was very severe, the inhabitants were in dire need, and it was only because Alexius I (1081-1118) called on another barbarian tribe, the Cumans, to aid him, that the Petcheneg threat was dispelled; in fact the Cuman attack on the Petcheneg rear was so effective that the Petcheneg army was virtually annihilated.

36. Mosaic of Christ in Kariye Camii. The mosaics are distinguished by a new intimacy, delicacy and humanism.

93

Like the twentieth century, the " Second Golden Age " was a period of great prosperity and rapid change, when vogues and fashions counted for much. Indeed, the architectural style of the " Second Golden Age " was quite distinct, as was that of interior decoration (Pl. 21), and the old churches, especially those of basilical type, with their flat walls and simple roofs, must have seemed just as outmoded as did the non-figural decorations of Iconoclast times. In the churches a new figural art, based on that first developed by Basil 1 in one of the churches in the Great Palace, was what was demanded, while in architecture small churches with vaulted aisles and a central, and perhaps also several subsidiary domes, were looked on as the most suitable setting for the new decorative schemes. Basil's Church of the Nea was regarded with great admiration; it was in a new and wholly up to date style, and nothing was spared to make it the most beautiful church of its day. Treasures were presented, and special carpets were woven at the country estate of a rich landowner, former patroness and now friend of the emperor, the widow Danielis.

A great many churches were built and others were redecorated in accordance with the new system from the tenth century onwards. Virtually nothing survives of these decorations except for some mosaics in Agia Sophia which are not wholly typical. Of the actual churches one of the least altered is that usually termed the Mirelaion, an eighth century foundation, which was entirely rebuilt by Romanus 1 Lecapenus (919-44) and was thereafter sometimes called the Monastery of Romanus. Romanus himself was buried there, as were other members of his family. A convent was associated with it; Romanus's sister took the veil there, and the wife and daughter of Isaac Comnenus (1057-59) also retired there. The church is a comparatively simple single-domed structure, but it stood above a crypt almost as tall as itself and a portion at least of this must have stood above ground, giving the appearance of a two-floored church like that of St Francis at Assisi. Immense substructures of this type must have been an important feature of Constantinopolitan architecture. In the Great Palace, which was built on a slope, they were essential in order to provide a level platform; here, where the ground is more or less flat, the substructure was used to bring the floor of the church up to the same level as that of the top of a great cistern which lies to the west of it, contrived within the walls of a large circular building dating perhaps from before the time of Constantine (see p. 22). When the church became a mosque after the Turkish conquest it was altered but little, except for the addition of a minaret at the south-western corner, but its mosaics were removed, either then or as the result of severe fires which damaged the building in 1784 and again in 1902.

The same emperor, Romanus Lecapenus, was also responsible for restoration to another important foundation, the monastery of Manuel, which had been founded by a general of that name during the reign of Theophilus (823-42). Photius, the greatest of all the Patriarchs, had also been responsible for reconstruction there. The only part of it which now survives, at present used by the Turks as a mosque under the name of the Kefeli Mescidii, cannot have been the church of the monastery; it was more probably the refectory.

The number of churches, monasteries and convents founded during these years at Constantinople must have been enormous; just as many churches were redecorated, and large numbers were also rebuilt. Even when the size of the empire had been very considerably reduced, when the Seljuk Turks held most of Asia Minor, and when the Slavs were setting up independent states in the Balkans, the lavish patronage continued and there seems to have been no diminution in activity even in the later years of the twelfth century. In spite of political setbacks, and the avaricious conduct of the tax collectors, it was a prosperous age, and the Spanish traveller Benjamin of Tudela, who visited Constantinople in the eighties of the twelfth century, noted how easy life was in the Byzantine world in contrast with the

West, for all could work in peace whereas in the West, militant feudalism had resulted in perpetual absence of the male population on military duty.

One of the finest churches of Comnene times is probably that of the Saviour Pantokrator, now known as Zeireck Kilisse Camii. It was founded by the Empress Eirene, wife of John II Comnenus (1118-43), who took the veil there shortly before she died in 1126. John granted it a charter as a monastery in 1136, and Manuel Comnenus (1143-80) further enriched it and was eventually buried there. After 1204 the church was appropriated to the Latin cult, but from 1261 reverted to Orthodoxy and received numerous benefits from the Palaeologues, many of whom were buried there. The building actually consists of three churches side by side. The northernmost is the earliest; it has a single dome which originally stood on four columns, but these were removed for use in some mosque and piers were built in their place. The central church has two domes and an extremely fine floor of very elaborate " Opus Sectile, " which has recently been restored by the Byzantine Institute of America. The southern church is similar to the northern one, but is larger and more elaborately decorated. The middle church was probably used for sepulchral purposes and is perhaps to be assigned to Manuel Comnenus, while the northern one probably belongs to the original foundation of Eirene.

This was an age in which the church played a very significant role indeed. The literature of the period was almost wholly theological; historical writings were few and those of a purely literary character almost non-existent, while, on the constructive side, church building and church decoration were the most important arts. But though it would be absurd to pretend, as certain scholars seek to do, that secular building or secular art were as important as those of a religious character, secular art did exist. Many of the superb silks which constituted one of Byzantium's most famed products, were wholly secular in theme and intention; there were secular vessels in precious metals as well as pottery, and many of the famous ivory caskets which have survived were no doubt designed for secular use too. In architecture, even if churches outnumbered other foundations, there were secular buildings other than royal palaces, though none of the houses of the nobles have survived and there are few records concerning them.

Basil I, as we have seen, concentrated his building activities on the Mangana; Manuel Comnenus was to build another new palace, the Blachernae, at the opposite end of the town where the walls meet the Golden Horn. But additions were still made to the Great Palace, the most important of which was the construction of a building called the Mouchroutas or " Persian House "; it was in the oriental style, with stalactite niches in its roof, and was probably inspired by a Seljuk model. As a result of their victory at Manzikert in 1071 the Seljuks had become firmly established in Asia Minor, and from about 1100 onwards had been responsible for the construction of some very remarkable mosques, colleges and caravanserais, decorated in a very distinctive style. There was a good deal of give and take between them and the Byzantines; much of their pottery, for instance, was clearly influenced by Byzantine models, and the " Persian House " represented the return influence. It was probably built in the early twelfth century, but there is no record as to which of the emperors sponsored the work.

The Blachernae Palace was begun about 1150 when Manuel Comnenus decided to transfer thither the centre of court life and administration. A small palace had been set up there by Anastasius I, but it was not important, and was really only used by the emperors when they went to visit the shrine of St Mary of the Blachernae where the Virgin's veil was preserved. It had been first endowed by Pulcheria, sister of Theodosius II, and then by Marcian; in 627, when Heraclius built his addition to the city wall, the palace was taken within the enclosure, and certain improvements were made. but under Michael Comnenus a much more considerable building programme was inaugurated. The city walls were extended, and it seems likely that a number of buildings, of some of which the substructures still survive, originally belonged to the palace; the most important of them are those known as the Prison of Anemas and the Towers of Anemas and Isaac Angelus. In any case the Blachernae Palace was both comparatively large and very sumptuous. It was there that Isaac Angelus received the Latins in 1204 and the records tell of the amazing luxury in which he lived: the richness of the rooms, their silk hangings, the gold plate and other treasures, and the gorgeous costumes which the courtiers wore even in the midst of a siege, when much of the treasure had already been dispersed. The Latin emperors at once took possession, but when they left in 1261, the place was very dirty and in a terrible state of dilapidation.

Apart from the walls, one building alone of all those that once existed on the site remains standing; it is the so-called Palace of Constantine Porphyrogenitus, known to the Turks as Tekfur Saray (Pl. 32). There is considerable doubt as to its exact age. It certainly has nothing to do with Constantine VII Porphyrogenitus (913-59), and the presence of monograms of the Palaeologues and other late details in the construction have suggested that it may be Palaeologan (1261-1453). Indeed, the Arab historian Ibn Batutah uses the name Tekfur for Andronicus III (1328-41). But it is more likely that this emperor, or some other Palaeologue, was responsible for repairs done as a result of neglect under the Latins, and that the original structure formed a part of the building enterprise of Manuel Comnenus. Its ornamental façade, with its lovely geometric patterns in brick and coloured marbles, must have been very striking, and attests the oriental influence which had begun to exercise a very considerable effect on Byzantine decorative art from the tenth century onwards.

One other building which stands in this region, though not within the precincts of the Blachernae Palace, may be noted; it is the small ruinous church now known by the name of Bogdan Saray. There is reason to believe that this is all that remains of the Church of St Nicholas, founded soon after 1066 by an English member of the Varangian guard who had fled to the East after the Norman conquest of 1066. The church served for a time as the chapel of the Varangian Guard. It then became the chapel of the Hospodar of Wallachia, who was a sort of High Commissioner of Rumania in Constantinople whilst his country was under Turkish control. However, English citizens who died in Constantinople seem to have continued to be buried there for many centuries, their tombs being mentioned by travellers as late as the nineteenth century.

THE MOSAICS OF AGIA SOPHIA

OF THE NUMEROUS mosaic decorations which were set up in Constantinople during the Second Golden Age the only ones that survive are a series of panels in Agia Sophia; they do not depict scenes from the Bible story, like the complicated narrative mosaics of Basil I's church, but represent individual figures, and most are in one way or another connected with the emperors. But they do indicate the developments of style over the whole of the period, and for this reason they are of special interest.

Almost as soon as the Iconoclast ban was lifted in 843, the redecoration of the church began, and some badly damaged mosaics adorning a chamber above the south porch, which show the Deesis and figures of the Apostles, saints and dignitaries of the church, appear to have been set up as a sort of memorial to the meeting of the Council that reached the decision to return to figural art. They date perhaps from around 850. Very soon after the apse was decorated, for fragments of an

37. Mosaic of the Virgin and Child in Kariye Camii, c. 1310. The figure is situated at the southern side of the apse. The child's head was until recently obscured by plaster, but has now been cleaned by the Byzantine Institute of America.

38

inscription survive in which the names of Michael and Basil are mentioned, and this must have reference to the year 867. Associated with the inscription were a figure of the Virgin in the Apse and those of two archangels, one on either side of the vault in front of the apse; one of the archangels has perished, the other is in reasonably good condition. Stylistically it is close to work at Nicaea, and there seems no reason why the figure should not be dated to the same year as the inscription. The Virgin in the apse raises something of a problem, for the rendering of the face is in a distinct, much less austere, style, and this has led the authorities to propose for it dates which vary between 867 and the fourteenth century. In a sermon preached in Agia Sophia in 868 the Patriarch Photios mentioned a figure of the Virgin in the apse and some have held that he was speaking of this very mosaic. Others interpret the text as referring to a standing figure, whereas the Virgin that is there now is seated, and they think that the mosaic must have been redone. The suggestion of a fourteenth century date which has been proposed by some scholars is however quite impossible; indeed recent investigations undertaken on behalf of the Dumbarton Oaks Institute prove beyond question that all the work in the apse is of the same period and belongs to around 865.

Also to be assigned to the ninth century is the panel in the lunette over the main western entrance of the church, which depicts an emperor prostrate before Christ, who sits on a bejewelled throne. The emperor is in the attitude of extreme reverence and self-abasement, known as proskynesis, which was adopted by emperors before Christ and by courtiers before their emperor. On either side are medallions, one bearing the Virgin, the other the head of an angel. They have reference to a prayer for the dedication of a church where the protection both of the Virgin and of a lance-bearing angel are sought. Agia Sophia was always believed to be under divine protection, as accounts of its construction prove, and in later days an enchanting legend to explain this grew up. The workmen who were constructing the church, it was said, had stopped for a meal, when an angel appeared and asked a boy, who was guarding the tools to fetch the overseer. The boy agreed to do so if the angel would guard the site while he was away. The emperor, realizing that the angel had come to enquire after the progress of the building, forbade the boy ever to return, so that the angel, adhering to his word, would remain always on guard.

There has been some discussion as to the date of the mosaic, some suggesting that the emperor depicted is Basil I (867-86), but the identification originally proposed by Whittemore that it is Leo VI the Wise (886-912) is more likely, for portraits of the emperor on his coins are very similar to that on the mosaic. It is however probable that the half-length figures of bishops and fathers of the Church, some of which survive on the two great curtain walls or tympana to north and south, were begun in the reign of Basil I even if some of them were not completed till the time of Leo VI.

The most recently to be uncovered of all the mosaics, a portrait in the north gallery of the Emperor Alexander, who reigned only for about one year, dates from 912-13—other work which has now perished may also have been done for him. The next mosaic (Pl. 22) in point of date is that in the lunette over the south door; it represents the Emperors Constantine and Justinian presenting respectively models of the city and the church to the Virgin, who sits enthroned in the middle with the Child on her knee. The setting of the mosaic is to be dated to the reign of Basil II (976-1025) who was probably the most competent and effective ruler of the Macedonian dynasty.

The next two panels, taken in chronological order, can be dated exactly thanks to inscriptions and to the identity of the figures they portray. The first is that on the eastern wall of the south gallery, usually known as the Zoe panel (Pl. 8.25.26); it depicts Christ enthroned in the centre, the Empress Zoe to his left and the Emperor

38. Mosaic of the Virgin and Child in Agia Sophia.

99

Fig. 6. Mosaic of the head of an Archangel in Agia Sophia. This is one of a pair of Archangels that adorned the vault in front of the apse. It is dated by an inscription to the year 858. Photo: *Dumbarton Oaks Research Institute*.

Constantine IX Monomachus (1042-55) to his right. The royal figures, in their rich, heavy robes, present an admirable picture of the pomp and grandeur of the court life of the age and correspond closely to the picture of it presented in Constantine VII Porphyrogenitus's *Book of Ceremonies*. The strangely anxious expression of Christ is distinct, and accords less readily with what we know of the rather hieratic tendencies of the religious art of the period. But it does show clearly how mosaic technique was changing, not only because the cubes are smaller than was usual in earlier work, but also because they were now set in a series of bands following the contours of the outline in the face or of the bones below; the manner is quite distinct from that of the Constantine and Justinian panel done about a century earlier. Still more interesting is the contrast of the wholly linear rendering of Christ's face and the much more painterly treatment of the imperial figures. Even though the emperor was Christ's vice-regent on earth, he was nevertheless mortal and his features were depicted according to a convention which differed from that followed in the case of the Almighty.

Constantine Monomachus was Zoe's third husband and it was through this marriage that he had come to the throne. The whole story is strange and intriguing. The great Basil II, Slayer of the Bulgars as he was called (976-1025), had been succeeded by his brother, Constantine VIII (1025-28) who when he died left three daughters but no son. The eldest had become a nun, and the heritage of the empire fell to the two others, Theodora and Zoe. From his death bed however Constantine VIII arranged a marriage between Zoe, then aged 50, and Romanus Argyrus, governor of the city and a member of one of its oldest aristocratic families, and thanks to his marriage to Zoe he came to the throne as Romanus III (1028-34). As a ruler he was weak and as an individual vain, and in so far as internal affairs were concerned yielded to the pressure of self-seeking nobles, who exploited the state finances at the cost of the peasant holders. Meanwhile Romanus rapidly tired of the ageing Zoe and she of him, for she had developed a new zest for life and found a peasant's young son from Paphlagonia, Michael, more to her taste. So Romanus died in his bath and Michael came to the throne as Michael IV (1034-41). But the story was repeated, in that·Michael then lost interest in the woman who had brought him to the throne and had her liberty curtailed. He was to prove a very capable if somewhat ruthless ruler. But in 1041 he returned fatally ill from a Balkan campaign and Zoe was persuaded to adopt a nephew as heir; he came to the throne as Michael V (1041-42), and immediately banished Zoe and her sister to a nunnery. The two

Fig. 7. Cloisonné enamels from the crown of Constantine Monomachus (1042-1055) now in Budapest. The same Emperor is shown with the Empress Zoe on one of the mosaics panels of Agia Sophia. Photo: *Budapest Museum*.

old sisters were however very popular; the action caused an uproar, Michael was deposed and blinded and Zoe and Theodora attempted to rule jointly, but their incompetence and dislike of one another soon proved this course to be impossible and Zoe, at 64, eagerly embarked on a third marriage with the eminent senator Constantine Monomachus. He ruled till 1055, outliving Zoe, and was succeeded by Zoe's sister Theodora who ruled alone till her death one year later.

Constantine was weak and ineffective as a ruler, but very efficient at emptying the treasury. Yet it must be said in his defence that he was a keen supporter of the church and a generous patron of the arts, and in addition to benefactions at Constantinople he founded the famous monastery of Nea Moni on Chios. Some lovely cloisonné enamels which formed his crown are now preserved at Budapest. But he goes down in history not for this so much as for the fact that the final split between the Latin and the Orthodox churches came about during his reign. It had for long been inevitable, but was accelerated by the personality of the Patriarch, Michael Cerularius, a one-time politician who looked for power and advancement in the church. The immediate argument arose on points of dogma, and the Pope, hoping for Constantine Monomachus's support, excommunicated the Patriarch. The Patriarch, with the Eastern church behind him, then excommunicated the papal legates who had laid the bull bearing the Orthodox Patriarch's excommunication on the altar of Agia Sophia. At the time little notice was taken of either event, for squabbles between the two churches had been constant. Only later did it come to be realized that the situation in 1054 marked a climax from which there was no return, however much a pope in the West or an emperor in the East might desire it.

Something of the strange and complicated tale of succession during those years is reflected in the mosaic panel of Zoe and Monomachus for it is clearly obvious that the inscription above Constantine's head has undergone a change. Whereas the main part of it is in fine beautifully balanced letters, similar to those that give Zoe's name, the letters at the beginning and the end of the emperor's inscription are sketchy and careless (Pl. 25. 26). Whittemore, who uncovered the mosaic, put forward the ingenious explanation that the inscription originally referred to Zoe's first husband, Romanus III, and that the name of Constantine was substituted when Zoe remarried; as there was no room for his second name, Monomachus, it was put somewhat untidily into the rather restricted space at the end. Whittemore found that the letters of Romanus's name on the same scale as the rest of the inscription would fit happily into the available space at the beginning. He thought that the heads of the figures were also renewed at the same time: this suggestion is very probable in the case of Constantine, but less likely with regard to the other two figures, in spite of the fact that there are signs of repair around them. Constantine Monomachus was Zoe's third husband; whether a similar substitution of portraits was made in the case of her second husband Michael IV, the Paphlagonian, we shall never know.

The panel that stands next to that of Zoe and Monomachus again represents an imperial pair, John II Comnenus (1118-43) and his consort Eirene, with the Virgin and Child (Pl. 38) between them. John's portrait, though many tesserae have fallen, is grand and impressive and does full justice to the grave, upright character of the emperor who was known as John the Good and who has been generally acclaimed as the greatest of the Comnenes. He was clever, competent and energetic and his untimely death as the result of being hit by a poisoned arrow while on the way to attack Antioch was a great blow to the state at a time when a strong and determined ruler was more than ever necessary. In addition to the ever-present problems raised by Slav desires for independence in the Balkans and Moslem inroads in Asia Minor, the empire was confronted by the rise of the Normans in Sicily; the

39. Exterior of Kariye Camii from the east. The arcading and masonry are typical of good later Byzantine work; the flying buttress is a later addition.

Crusading kingdoms in Syria and Palestine seemed an even more irritating thorn in the flesh, and Venetian trading demands presented a most serious threat from the economic point of view.

The face of Eirene, the empress, shows less character, for in the fashion of the day she wears heavy make-up, her eyebrows are shaved and her cheeks rouged, but broad face attests her foreign origin, for she was a princess of Hungary, renowned for her beauty. Both the portraits of the living persons may once again be contrasted with that of the Virgin, which is a devout religious image, profound and peaceful, and contrast can also be seen in the simplicity of the costume; here there was no need for a gorgeous imperial panoply.

The mosaics must have been set up about 1118, when John came to the throne. In 1122 their son Alexius was proclaimed co-emperor, and it was probably in that year that his portrait was added on a pier to the left of Eirene. The linear stylization which characterized mosaic work of the Second Golden Age has here been carried much further than in any of the other mosaics in Agia Sophia, and is very effective in conveying the sad, sickly appearance of the young prince who was to survive for another ten years and to die before his father.

The last of the mosaics in Agia Sophia in point of date is also the finest as a work of art; it is indeed quite outstanding, and is to be numbered as one of the most glorious products of Byzantine, or indeed any art that we know. It represents a theme which became extremely popular in later Byzantine iconography, which is known as the Deesis and represents the Virgin and St John the Baptist on either side of Christ, interceding with him for the sins of the world. The conception of the scene itself denotes a new outlook, distinct from the hieratic approach of earlier times, for thoughts of mankind and the troubles of this world lie at its root rather than problems of theology or liturgy. But the tendency towards humanism that characterizes the theme has been carried even further in the rendering. Christ is no longer conceived as the Almighty, the jealous god of the Old Testament and the Semitic world, but rather as Jesus, the man of sorrows (Pl. 34), tender, compassionate, considerate. Here, practically for the first time in Byzantine art, the idea of Christian love is uppermost; seldom, if ever, has it been more effectively rendered, and the same note of humanism and compassion distinguishes the other two figures, those of the Virgin and St John.

There has been considerable argument among scholars as to the date of this panel. Whittemore, who first published it, wished to assign it to the end of the first quarter of the twelfth century; others have compared it to the mosaics of Kariye Camii in the city (see p. 121 ff.) which are firmly dated at around 1310, maintaining that the degree of humanism which distinguishes the mosaic had not begun to develop before the very end of the thirteenth century. Whittemore had on the other hand contended that the progress towards humanism had reached just as advanced a stage in the famous icon known as the Virgin of Vladimir, now in Russia, but which is known to have been painted in Constantinople about 1125. He held that the nature of the epigraphy of the inscriptions was quite incompatible with a later date. Moreover it was also suggested that so imposing and majestic a monument was more in accord with the grandeur of the Second Golden Age, even at its end, than with the newly established power of the early Palaeologues, who had only just succeeded in driving out the Latins. Recent research has undoubtedly shown that the progress towards a more humanistic outlook had begun well before the thirteenth century and that from this point of view the style of the Deesis panel would not preclude a date in the twelfth century. Both dates are indeed possible, and the arguments still rage with the authorities divided; on the whole however the earlier date seems to the writer the more strongly supported. But whatever its date, the Deesis panel stands out as a wholly worthy addition to Justinian's great cathedral.

40. Detail of a mosaic of St George in Kariye Camii. The church is usually known by its Turkish name although originally it was called the Church of the Chora.

FOR VERY MANY CENTURIES the great walls, set up by Theodosius and repaired by so many emperors, had served to protect the city, as no other city had been protected throughout history. They had been assailed once by Avars and Persians (626), twice by the Arabs (663 and 717), thrice by insurgent forces (710, 821 and 988), once by the Bulgars (813), twice by the Russians (860 and 907) and once by the Petchenegs (1090-91); and on countless other occasions their very strength had daunted would-be assailants from making the attempt. Indeed, the reputation of the walls of Constantinople had been almost as responsible for discouraging aggressors as their strength had been in resisting actual attacks. In 1204, for the first time in nearly 800 years, they were to be breached, though treachery from within, indecision among the defenders, and dissension in the highest quarters were more responsible for the fall of the city than the actual fighting or the force of the attack. The story of the Latin conquest is thus really more one of the decadence of the Byzantine emperors of the later twelfth century than of Latin prowess; at long last the title of *Decline and Fall* that Gibbon chose for his great history was to be truly justified by events.

Ever since the days of Manuel Comnenus (1143-80) the state of affairs had been rapidly deteriorating in the Byzantine empire. This emperor had been succeeded by his son Alexius I (1180-83), and as he was only twelve, power had been exercised by a vain and insignificant relative, also called Alexius Comnenus, favourite of the emperor's mother. Their pro-Latin policy had aroused considerable opposition, and this came to a head in an anti-Latin revolt in 1182, which brought to the throne a cousin of Manuel's, Andronicus I (1183-85), whose policy had always been intensely opposed to the Latins. His entry to the city was followed by numerous executions of the pro-Latin faction. The unfortunate young emperor was strangled and Andronicus was crowned.

The new emperor set out to reform the state, and in this he was to be admired, for reform was highly necessary; corruption was rife, the people were oppressed by unjust and covetous officials, and power had got into the hands not of the most efficient, but of the most unscrupulous. His methods were harsh and cruel, for he knew no means other than brute force, and Andronicus's struggle against the privileged turned into a reign of terror. It united the feudal aristocracy against him, and the atmosphere of the time, the trend of historical progress was on their side, not on that of a cruel, violent despot, however just his aims. Further, his reforms completely failed to take into account the need for defence; a rising of the Slavs, and Latin advances into Greece were met with no opposition. In 1185 Salonica fell to the Normans, and a force set out against Constantinople. It was destined never to make an attack, but public feeling was aroused and only two years after his welcome as saviour of the city, Andronicus was torn to pieces by an infuriated and terrified mob, urged on no doubt by the agents of his opponents. The throne fell to Isaac II Angelus (1185-95), through his mother the daughter of Alexius I Comnenus.

Isaac made no attempt to curb the mismanagement of the state, the dishonesty of the officials or the extortions of the tax collectors. It was said of him that he sold government posts like vegetables in a market, and vast sums were squandered on useless spectacles, such as his wedding, whilst the provincial population was at the point of starvation. The one bright spot was in military affairs, and though there were retreats and ignominies, such as the treaty which led to the foundation of the Second Bulgarian Empire in 1187 and to permission being granted to Frederick Barbarossa to cross Byzantine territory in 1190, the military situation was on the whole not unsatisfactory. Steven Nemanja of Serbia was defeated in the

same year and Isaac, who was a gallant soldier even if a poor emperor, might have redeemed the position had he not been deposed and blinded by his brother Alexius in 1195. Alexius was a vain weakling, and under his rule the empire's fate was sealed. Serbia and Bulgaria united against him, and by his treatment of his brother he had sown the seeds of opposition at home.

Seen from within, the Byzantine empire was thus in a sorry state. Hopes for its future were not improved by the attitude of the west, for since the very early days of the Crusades the western leaders had looked at Byzantium with suspicion and very covetous eyes—with suspicion because as often as not the Byzantines seemed to favour the Moslems rather than themselves, and with covetousness because the accounts of the luxury and fabulous wealth of Constantinople, spread by all who had visited the capital, had greatly whetted their appetites for plunder. Further, the great trading cities of Italy were determined that the commerce of the Levant should all come their way and not revert to the Greeks. Plans for capturing Constantinople had been discussed by Louis VII at the time of the Second Crusade and Henry VI had considered it; Barbarossa had very nearly attacked the city himself, and might well have done so had his conduct been less honourable. But though there may have been pious and disinterested men among those who assembled at Venice in 1202 to mount the Fourth Crusade, disinterestedness was not uppermost in the minds of the majority. Those from the West were far more interested in prospects of loot or in obtaining land for themselves than in fighting the infidel for altruistic reasons, while the Venetians made no efforts whatsoever to conceal their real objective—the advancement of Venetian power, political and commercial. This was made abundantly clear at the outset, when they demanded help in the capture of Zara as their price for transporting the armed forces to the East. To those whose thoughts were directed along such channels the arrival of the young Alexius Angelus, son of the blinded Isaac, came as a boon, for he sought the support of any who would come to his aid in deposing his uncle; moreover he made promises of great financial rewards when once the throne had been restored either to him or to his blinded father.

In 1202 Zara was taken; in 1203 the expedition reached Constantinople, and the first troops landed in the region now known as Beshiktash, near where the Bosphorus and Golden Horn meet, captured the defences and cut the chain defending the Golden Horn. Their boats sailed in and the troops landed again at its inner extremity near the present Eyub, where it was crossed by a stone bridge. They then occupied the hills facing the Blachernae. At the same time the walls along the Golden Horn were assailed from the water and had almost been captured when there was a revolt in the city in favour of Isaac and the attack was called off. Alexius III fled with as much of the imperial treasure as he could collect; Isaac was freed, and his son was crowned as Alexius IV (1203-04). The part of the city that is now called Stambul remained in the hands of the Greeks, the Latins confronting them from Galata on the northern side of the Golden Horn. But Alexius's reign was to be brief. The Latins, as soon as they found that his promises of payment were valueless, had no use for him, and the population rapidly turned against him because he had brought the invaders. In January 1204 there was a revolt and Murtzuphulus, the son of Alexius III who had been so much despised, was crowned as Alexius V. This did not suit the Crusaders, who had received no money from Alexius IV, and in March they and the Venetians made a pact to divide the city between them. As the attackers were virtually there already and the defenders were far from united, the capture of the city presented little difficulty. The walls of the Golden Horn were once more assailed in the region where the Phanar now stands, bridges being thrown from the poops of the ships, across which the knights rushed and threw open the gates. Within a short time the town was

43. West front of a church now usually known as Kilisse Camii. It is probably to be identified as the Church of St Theodore Tyro. The sculptured slabs are to be dated to the twelfth century.

in Latin hands. It was subjected to pillage for three days and to a sacking which has gone down on record as one of the most profitable in all history.

The looting was accompanied by a series of terrible fires, which devastated the part of the city between Agia Sophia and the sea and also spread to the populous quarter to the west of the Hippodrome. Numerous houses and churches in this area were destroyed and it seems likely that what remained of the Great Palace was also seriously damaged. It had already been in the main deserted and its treasures removed to the Palace of the Blachernae; those which had not been removed by Alexius III were to astound the Crusaders when they took over possession.

Constantinople had long been recognized by the Latins as possessing more of the sacred relics of Christendom than any other city in the world. They had been assembled there since the days of Constantine. Helena and Pulcheria had brought much, and as other holy cities like Jerusalem, Bethlehem, or Edessa, where the sacred mandelion was preserved, fell to the Moslems, their holy treasures too were sent to Constantinople, and there, in the royal workshops, they were enshrined in sumptuous bejewelled frames of gold and silver, enamel and precious stones. A few of the relics may have reached the West at one time or another as gifts, but the majority had remained in the Byzantine capital. Some of the precious mounts may have been taken off by Alexius III or melted down to pay the Crusaders and Venetians by Alexius IV; but no doubt the actual palace treasures had been drawn on for these purposes, while those dispersed throughout the various churches of the capital must have remained, and there was hardly one of the churches that did not boast of some precious possession. Much certainly also remained in the emperor's possession, for the Latin writers speak with astonishment of the riches that confronted them in the palaces. There was much at the Blachernae, and the store in the Bucoleon received special mention from the chroniclers; it would appear to have become a sort of depot as and when the rest of the Great Palace fell into ruin.

If the treasures in gold and silver tempted the more worldly, the cult of sacred relics at the time was such that the prospect of acquiring for this or that church or monastery in the West a relic such as the toe of some saint, let alone a spine from Our Lord's crown of thorns, was enough to entice even the most pious away from the Holy Land towards the Byzantine capital, and the conduct of the pious was little better than that of the rabble.

So far as the major relics were concerned, a division had been agreed on previously; three-quarters were to be the share of the Venetians, one-quarter that of the Franks; other treasures, less famous, were apparently to be divided in the proportions of two to the new Latin kingdom, three to the Venetians and three to the Franks. This however, did not take into account the mass of loot purloined by the common soldiery, whose rapacity even the guards posted at such major centres as Agia Sophia were unable to control, or the objects that were destroyed in passion because they proved to be of copper gilt and not gold. Only after three days was the orgy of private looting and destruction halted, but this gave place to the official and systematic removal of works of a major importance which had escaped the first frenzy, or which, like the famous bronze horses of St Mark's at Venice, were too large for individuals to remove. These were collected at a central point so that the agreed division could be made.

It would seem that the newly elected Latin emperor, Baldwin I (1204-05), succeeded in acquiring quite a considerable share for, following the custom of his Greek predecessor, he was lavish in the distribution of gifts at his coronation; no doubt he hoped in this way to buy the support which he sorely needed. His empire consisted, by the terms of the treaty of division, of one-quarter of the Byzantine territory. Half of the remaining three-quarters went to Venice, the other half being distributed among the knights as fiefs of the emperor. But the territories were in

44. Fresco of the Anastasis or Descent into Limbo, in Kariye Camii. The main church of Kariye is decorated with mosaics, but in a side chapel there are paintings in a similar style and of much the same date.

many cases to prove difficult to hold, the knights unruly, and the lot of the Latin emperors was no easy one. Very soon movements of independence in Asia Minor and the Balkans became embarrassing, and within a few years no less than three claimants to the throne had arisen, all of whom were Orthodox and boasted legitimate descent from an imperial or princely family. The Lascarids of Nicaea were eventually to achieve supremacy amongst them, and Michael VIII (1258-82), the heir of the first Lascarid, Theodore I (1204-22), was to return triumphant to Constantinople in 1261.

It is no easy matter to reconstruct a picture of Constantinople or the life that was lived there during the period of Latin domination (1204-61). Many of the churches were converted to the Latin rite, but few, it would seem, were destroyed; how far the practice of Orthodoxy was able to continue is not very clear, but it may be assumed that in most cases where there is no mention of conversion the churches remained Orthodox. The Great Palace had already been to some extent evacuated in the days of the Comnenes; it had also no doubt been seriously damaged in the fires that followed the capture of the city, and the numerous churches within its periphery were probably not serviceable. During the Latin regime the whole area fell further into decay and the parts that survived were at best occupied by squatters. The Latin emperors themselves lived in the Palace of the Blachernae, and in spite of Baldwin's efforts to ape Byzantine usage, it would seem that the standard of living rapidly declined, for when the Greeks returned there were bitter complaints of the state in which the rooms were left.

The more patriotic and spirited among the Greeks no doubt left the city, to join one of the Orthodox claimants to the throne, in the Epirus, at Nicaea, or even in far distant Trebizond, where a cadet branch of the Comnene line had established itself shortly before the Latin conquest. But others must have remained in the city, and some of the more or less feudal Byzantine nobles—pronoias they were called—may have given their allegiance to the Latins. The life of the multitude cannot have changed greatly, for work had to be done and the Latins needed servants and followers if no more. The Venetians would have seen to it that trade continued, for trade was their very lifeblood. The fact that a few manuscripts survive which were written in Greek in Constantinople during these years serves indeed as proof of the continuance of normal day-to-day life of Orthodox citizens of standing. Manuscripts were even illuminated in the typical Byzantine manner, though it cannot be claimed that any of the work was of very great artistic merit. On the other hand no major works of art in the Byzantine style were produced and there is but little in the way of architecture, sculpture or painting that survives that can be assigned to the Latins. The little that exists is all to be found to the north of the Golden Horn in the region known as Galata, which had even before the conquest been the Latin quarter of the town and which was to remain so even under the domination of the Turks.

The most interesting of the Latin buildings is undoubtedly that now known as Arab Camii, not far from the head of the upper bridge. According to tradition a mosque was set up on the site by Moslems at the time of the Arab siege in 715; what happened after that is not known, but in 1232 a large hall-like building in a Western style was erected by the Dominicans and dedicated either to St Paul or St Dominic. It remained in Latin hands till after the Turkish conquest when it became a mosque. Most of the more important Latins were buried there, and when it was restored in 1913 a mass of flagstones bearing inscriptions and coats of arms were removed; most are now in the archaeological museum.

Though its lower storey is Byzantine—it has been associated with Zeno (474-91)—the Galata Tower is also virtually to be counted as a Latin monument, being situated in the centre of the Genoese quarter. The Genoese added a storey to it in 1352

45. East front of the Church of St Mary Panachrantos, known to the Turks as as Fenari Issa Camii. The church is a double one of various dates: the east end was reconstructed in the fourteenth century.

Fig. 8. The Galata Tower. From *Beauties of the Bosphorus* by Pardoe, engraving by W. H. Bartlett. Photo: *British Museum*.

and in 1446 it was again heightened, but the height was reduced by Mehmet the Conqueror and in 1791 it was refurbished by Selim I after being damaged in a fire; the top storeys with their roofs and arcades must belong to this period, so that its appearance is now partly Latin and partly Turkish; it could never be mistaken for a Byzantine structure.

The monuments are thus silent. If in Syria and Palestine the Crusaders built fine churches and superb castles in a Western style and produced an art of book illustration which is quite distinctive, or if in Cyprus or the Islands they and the Venetians left an architectural heritage which was to survive for many centuries, the Latins who ruled in Constantinople left virtually nothing, nor is there any record of any work being undertaken by them. The Mongols, if best known to history for the pyramids of skulls they built at the gates of the cities they conquered, were nevertheless great patrons of art, and in Iran and Turan some of the finest works we know were done at their expense. We remember the Latins who ruled in Constantinople for more than half a century only for the efficiency with which they looted the city. But we must today be thankful for that, for much of their loot has been preserved in the West; if the treasures had remained in Constantinople they would undoubtedly have perished during the Turkish conquest in 1453.

THE PALAEOLOGUE AGE

MICHAEL VIII PALAEOLOGOS had been made co-emperor with the young John Lascaris at Nicaea in 1258. In 1259 he succeeded in overcoming a strong coalition which had been formed against him; in 1260 his general Strategopoulos, whose task was to watch the Bulgarian frontier, found Constantinople unprotected and in July 1261 he captured it, almost without a fight. In August Michael entered the city in triumph, amidst great rejoicing, and was crowned for a second time in Agia Sophia. He was the first emperor of the Palaeologue dynasty, which was to prove the longest

46. The Çinili Kiosk. This is the earliest building set up by the Ottomans after the conquest of Constantinople in 1453 which still survives.

in duration in Byzantine history. It is perhaps surprising that it lasted as long as it did; what is more surprising is that it proved to be a very vital and creative period in Byzantine history, even more so in the story of Byzantine art.

The empire had been reduced to little more than the city and the territory in its immediate proximity; its treasures had all been ravished and its people were far from prosperous; its trade had fallen almost wholly into the hands of the Venetians and the Genoese; it has been calculated that its population had declined from a possible 800,000 in the twelfth century to some 50,000 in the fifteenth century, and in 1348 it was even further reduced by a terrible plague, the Black Death. Yet cultured life continued; the city once more became the centre of a creative thought and a vigorous art, and in the fourteenth century saw a revival which was in its way comparable to the Renaissance in Italy though it was quite distinct from it. This revival was not confined to Constantinople alone, but embraced also the Despotate of Mistra in the Peloponnese, which was the empire's only independent outpost, the city of Trebizond, where a line of the Comnene family ruled in independence till 1461, Salonica and the new Slav states of Serbia and Bulgaria. But Constantinople was the main source of inspiration; it was from there that ideas in thought and art principally emanated, and it was there that the most important monuments of the age were set up.

The number of churches which were built, repaired or lavishly decorated in these years seems at first glance surprising in contrast to the gloomy picture of the political history, which consists of a list of incessant struggles for power and acts of treachery, of repeated attacks and the dire problems of paying for the army to repulse them, of the progressive loss of territory and of the increasing poverty of the state that resulted. But it would seem that the situation of the nobility was less serious than that of the rulers, for the patrons were individuals more often than emperors, and it may also be concluded that the dilapidations resulting from Latin rule were so considerable that a great deal of rebuilding and reconditioning was necessary.

The architecture of the age is easily distinguished from that of earlier periods; it is lighter and more delicate, more decorative and more colourful; one might perhaps describe it as the Baroque phase of the Byzantine style, though the style did not lend itself to the full exuberance that characterized the work of the later sixteenth century in Italy. The elaborate blank arcading that was so popular in the late Byzantine period with its multiplicity of niches, shows nevertheless something of the same love of ornament for its own sake that we see in Baroque, as does the ornate decorative brickwork. The whole style was indeed somewhat fanciful. So far as architecture is concerned, two very typical examples may be cited, the east end of St Mary Panachrantos (Monastery of Constantine Lips; *see* pp. 76 and 90) and a chapel at the south-east corner of St Mary Pammakaristos (Fetiye Camii). Both are typical of the age and both show work of real distinction. The former church was restored in the late thirteenth century by Theodora, wife of Michael VIII, and she was buried there in 1304; it was also used as the burial place for a number of other members of the imperial family. The graves were excavated by Theodore Macridy on behalf of the Museum of Antiquities in 1928, but they did not contain any treasures or works of art.

The Church of St Mary Pammakaristos had been built, or in any case redecorated, by John Comnenus and Anna Delassena around 1050; the southern chapel was added by the wife of Michael Glabas around 1305; her husband had already done some repairs to the church itself at the end of the previous century. Later from soon after 1453 till 1591, it served as the Patriarchate, then it became a mosque and once more underwent very considerable alterations. Today it is very difficult to work out the building's original plan or to trace exactly which portions belong

47. The Castle of Rumeli Hissar on the Bosphorus. It was built by Sultan Fatih in preparation for the great attack on the Byzantine capital in 1453.

to the mid-eleventh century. A very fine mosaic icon which is now preserved in the Patriarchate must have come from the church, for it was probably presented by John and Anna before her death in 1067. It would appear to have escaped the looting of the Crusaders and to have passed into the possession of the Patriarchate when the church of St Mary Pammakaristos was taken over to house the Patriarch soon after the Turkish conquest.

A number of other churches show work which is characteristic of the fourteenth century, as for instance parts of that called by the Turks Kilisse Camii (Pl. 43), which is usually identified as the Church of St Theodore in the Karbounaria quarter, though this identification is not certain. Other buildings are noted in the texts as undergoing repairs, such as the Church of St Anastasia, mentioned in a Chrysobul of John Palaeologos in 1342, which is perhaps to be identified with Hoca Atik Mustafa Camii, or the famous Gul Camii, once the Church of St Theodosia, where an immense congregation gathered for a vigil of prayer on the night of the conquest in 1453. A monastery of St John the Baptist which was enlarged in 1381 is perhaps to be regarded as the present Bogdan Saray, while the charming Church of St Mary of the Mongols formed part of a convent founded early in the fourteenth century. Its central dome is supported on four exedrae. The building is doubly romantic, first because it is the only Byzantine church in the city which has ever since remained in Greek hands, and secondly because of the strange life of its founder, the Princess Maria Palaeologina, daughter of Michael VIII and sister of Andronicus II. She was promised as a bride to the Mongol Khan Hulagu, and left for the east in 1265, but Hulagu died, and she therefore married his son Abagu; he was poisoned in 1281 and his widow, who had remained a Christian, returned to Constantinople, founded a convent, and built a church for its use. After the Turkish conquest the church was granted to the Greek architect of the Mosque of Sultan Mehmet the Conqueror, Christodoulos, and the gift was confirmed by Bayazit II (1481-1512) in respect of Christodoulos's nephew who was the architect of Bayazit's own great mosque.

Delightful though some of the architecture of this age is, however, the mosaics of the period are most important. They survive in three churches, though originally there were no doubt many others. The least well preserved are those of Kilisse Camii, where mosaics survive in the domes of the exo-narthex, a structure of later date than the church itself. The mosaics were partly cleaned by M. Nouridis in 1937; those of the southern dome depict the Virgin and Child surrounded by prophets, and those of the central dome show prophets and functionaries of the palace. The work is probably to be assigned to the end of the first quarter of the fourteenth century.

The mosaics that adorned the funerary chapel of Michael Glabas in St Mary Pammakaristos (Fetiye Camii) dating from around 1305 are of a higher quality and better preserved. The chapel was an exquisite little building inside as well as out, with four finely carved capitals on marble columns to support the dome, but a spanning arch was at some date inserted in the place of those on the north side, destroying the mosaics in the pendentives and under the voussoirs of the arch at the same time. The mosaics however survive on the south side and in the dome itself. The Pantocrator there and figures of the apostles and prophets in the drum have been known for some years, and the Byzantine Institute of America recently undertook their cleaning. At the same time the chapel was reconditioned and other mosaics were discovered at the east end and on the south side. They are all small in scale, but very delicate and lovely and bear much the same relationship to the great works of the Second Golden Age that the panels of the Sienese school bear to the great canvases of Florence. Like the Sienese, it is a rather exquisite flower, but a strikingly lovely one none the less, and, as in the Sienese school, there is real variety, if within narrow limits, for the style of these mosaics is quite distinct from those in Kilisse Camii or from the more or less contemporary ones at Kariye.

It is however in the Church of St Saviour in Chora, better known perhaps by its Turkish name of Kariye Camii, that the best work of the Palaeologue age is to be found; and here (Pl. 35. 36. 37. 40) is a monument no less fine and no less important in the story of art than the Arena Chapel at Padua, which was frescoed by Giotto at the very same date that Kariye was being adorned, the church and its two exo-narthices with mosaics and a side chapel or pareccleseion with wall paintings. The whole has also recently been cleaned and conserved by the Byzantine Institute of America and the work has been superbly done.

The foundation of the first church on the site has been attributed to Justinian, or even to an earlier date and the name, Chora, if it is to be interpreted as "in the fields", bears out the supposition that there was a shrine there before the Theodosian land walls were built. However, this interpretation of the word has been questioned, for it may well have a mystic significance. Christ on the mosaics is given the title of Η χώρα Των ζώντων which means perhaps something like "the spiritual support of the living". There are no vestiges whatsoever above ground of a building of such an early date, though recent excavations have disclosed the substructures of a wall which may be as early as the sixth century. A general called Priscus was however imprisoned there in the days of Heraclius and he is reported to have done a good deal of rebuilding. In 712 the Patriarch Kyros was also confined there and in 740 another Patriarch, Germanus, was buried there.

The associated monastery was prosperous in the ninth century, but by the year 1000 the church was in ruins. It was restored around 1081 when the Patriarch Cosmas retired there, and when the Blachernae Palace became popular in the early twelfth century the Church of the Chora was again repaired because of its proximity to the royal dwelling. The work was done by Maria, wife of Andronicus Dukas and mother-in-law of Alexius Comnenus (1081-1118). The central square of the church and the northern half of the upper narthex are probably to be assigned to this date. Further work was carried out by Isaac Comnenus, who wished to be interred there, though he was in the end buried elsewhere. Finally the church was fully restored around 1310 by a leading court official, Theodore Metochites, for it had fallen into a terrible state of disrepair during the Latin occupation. It was he too who was responsible for the magnificent mosaic decoration; his portrait as donor is included above the entrance to the narthex. Later in his life he fell into disgrace and retired to the monastery of the Chora as a monk. The exo-narthex and the chapel which runs along the whole of the southern façade of the church probably date from this time, together with the wall paintings that decorate it. Dr P. A. Underwood, who was in charge of the work of reconditioning undertaken in the 1950s by the Byzantine Institute of America, thinks that the wall paintings may well be by the hand of the very master who was responsible for the layout and design of the mosaics; this may be questioned, but they are certainly the work of the same school.

The lower portions of the walls in the central body of the church are covered with slabs of marble; now that they have been cleaned and polished they show how impressive this type of wall revetment can be. Over the door is a lovely mosaic of the Dormition of the Virgin, and on either side of the apse are tall panels, Christ to the north, the Virgin and Child to the south. The rest of the mosaics from this part of the church have perished, for at some date the dome and adjacent areas must have been extensively repaired. There was no doubt a great figure of Christ Pantocrator in the dome and some of the major feasts probably occupied the pendentives of the dome and the adjacent areas; the Dormition of the Virgin is all that remains of this cycle; the other scenes would have been drawn from those of special consequence in the Christian religion, the so-called "feasts", which include the Annunciation, the Nativity (Pl. 33) the Presentation, the Baptism, the Transfiguration, the Raising of Lazarus, the Entry into Jerusalem, the Crucifixion, the Anastasis or Descent into Limbo (Pl. 44), the Ascension and Pentecost.

The whole story of the life of Christ and of the Virgin is, however, told very fully on the vaults and domes and on the upper portions of the walls of the two narthices. The series includes the life of Christ, in considerable detail, from the Annunciation onwards, and is followed by the life of the Virgin. The former begins at the north end of the outer narthex, and then passes to the southern dome chamber of the inner narthex; the life of the Virgin begins at the northern end of the inner narthex and occupies all of it but for the southern dome chapel.

The outer dome chamber of the inner narthex is of larger proportions than the rest, and on its eastern wall there is a great composition of Christ and the Virgin— a sort of curtailed Deesis. The greater size of the chamber would seem to have been contrived in order to provide space for this composition; which had grown in importance in the later years of the Second Golden Age, till it had become one of the most favoured scenes in Byzantine iconography. The two figures of Christ and the Virgin are of outstanding beauty, majestic and impressive yet intimate and full of sympathy. They have been compared to the great Deesis panel in Agia Sophia, and there is undoubted similarity; but somehow the Kariye figures are rather more effeminate, rather less monumental, and though both compositions are in the spirit of the last phase of Byzantine art, that of the so-called Revival style, the Agia Sophia mosaic has not progressed quite as far along the path of evolution.

The Kariye panel is of additional interest because of two figures included below on a smaller scale. One of them wears the black robes of a nun, and is designated in the accompanying inscription by the name of Melane; she is no less a person, apparently, than the Princess Maria Palaeologina, whom we encountered as the founder of the church and convent of St Mary of the Mongols and who was married to the Mongol Khan Hulagu. She became a nun in 1307, so that the mosaic must be of later date. On the opposite side is the portrait of Isaac Comnenus, son of the Emperor Alexius. It must be a posthumous portrait, for firstly the style is wholly distinct from that usual in twelfth century work, as a comparison with the John panel in Agia Sophia shows; there the cubes are laid in lines following the contours of the face, whereas here the treatment is far less linear. Secondly the cleaning showed that the plaster of the setting bed on this side overlaps that on the opposite side, so that any possibility of an older composition having been left when the portrait of Melane was added is precluded; and we know that the Melane portrait must date from after 1307. The portrait of Isaac must therefore have been included long after his death, in order probably to commemorate his earlier association with the church.

The most striking feature of the other mosaics, which tell the story of Christ's and the Virgin's lives, is their tremendous vividness. True, the figures are considerably elongated in comparison with Western standards in art, and the architecture of the backgrounds is conventionalized rather than representational. But the scenes are none the less real for all that. The gestures and poses are expressive and full of human interest and emotion; there is nothing hieratic or restrained about the art and the artist must have taken an intense delight both in the world around him and in the way he depicted and interpreted it. Such a scene as the Numbering of the People (Pl. 42) shows this; the busy recorder, the rather bored guard, the timid Virgin, the anxious St Joseph; all are extremely expressive, and the same is true of the figures in all the smaller scenes, which occupy more confined areas on the soffit of an arch or some similar position. With their rich colour and the scintillating effect created by the glass cubes, these mosaics form a superb decoration and make of the church a veritable jewel. But in the expressiveness of the figures and the beauty of the compositions they go further than that, for the result is great art. The mosaics of Kariye indeed constitute one of the truly outstanding artistic products of the early

48. The Mosque of Sultan Suleyman seen across the Golden Horn from the Galata tower. The mosque, perhaps the finest in the city, is distinguished by its four minarets.

122

48

fourteenth century, an age in which men no less great than Giotto, Duccio and Masaccio were all working.

The wall paintings of the pareccleseion are no less important. They may lack the scintillating brilliance of the mosaics, but on the other hand the colouring is even more subtle and varied, and there are niceties of detail especially in the faces and in the rendering of the high lights made possible by the use of the brush but denied to the manipulator of cubes, however skilful. The supreme loveliness of the blending of hues in the costumes, where the high lights are picked out in subtle reflexes, is for instance something that remains unsurpassed—in this case also, unsurpassable—in wall painting and fully compensates for the jewel-like beauty of the mosaics.

The pareccleseion was intended for funerary purposes. In the walls are niches which contained tombs, some decorated with paintings, one with mosaics, though they are in very poor condition, and one, the tomb of Michael Tornikes, with very accomplished and lovely decorative sculpture. In accordance with this purpose the scenes depicted on the walls and the paintings on the vaults above are mostly connected with the future life. Christ's descent into Limbo, which was the usual Byzantine way of representing the Resurrection, fills the apse; nearby are details from the Last Judgement, and above the Judgement itself and the Second Coming of Christ. Saints who prophesied regarding the future life were selected for depiction on the walls. Only in the dome, which occupies the central bay of the chapel, corresponding in position with the main body of the church itself, is there a theme of a more general character, namely the Virgin above and angels below, separated by bands of very lovely decorative work which at a first glance one would tend to assign to fifteenth century Italy.

The mosaics of Kilisse Camii, Fetiye and Kariye were all set up under private sponsorship, while the other churches of the fourteenth century that we know were similarly endowed. The nobles and even the merchants of the age seem to have been prosperous enough, even if the state was impoverished and the emperors not in a position to pay even for works which would assure the peace of their souls. Indeed through most of this age, with new enemies growing up to right and left, it was only thanks to military efforts that they were able to retain independence, and every penny that could be raised was needed to pay the troops, most of them by now mercenaries who would not fight unless money was regularly forthcoming.

So, from the social point of view, the fourteenth century had seen the accomplishment of the rise of the nobles which had begun in the twelfth century, if not before. Now they counted for more than the emperor as patrons, and a similar change of emphasis is to be discerned in the sphere of church life. At the outset the emperor was everything, the very centre of the state; now he was, as often as not, a rather pathetic figure, seeking support and alliances in the West, even at the cost of the union of the Orthodox with the Latin church, which the great ecclesiastics at home were not for a moment prepared to countenance. It is a strange contradiction of earlier Byzantine history that, during the fourteenth century, which was in many ways one of the most important in the story of Byzantine art, the imperial power had so far declined as to be in many ways almost a negligible factor.

During the last fifty years or so of Byzantine history, however, the centre of thought and art moved to some extent to the Peloponnese, to the little city of Mistra, where George Gemistos Plethon lived and sought to bring about a Greek Renaissance, and where Constantine, the last Byzantine emperor, ruled as despot till he was called to the imperial throne. There, at Mistra, the art which reached such great heights at Kariye left its most outstanding heritage, and there, if we are to judge by the monuments that survive, the Palaeologue revival progressed furthest. The fate of Constantinople was really sealed by the end of the fourteenth century. Even as

49. Interior of the Mosque of Sultan Ahmet.
It is also known as the Blue Mosque because of the prevailing colour of its tilework.

early as 1355 the Venetian ambassador there was advising the Doge to take over the city, while in 1390 Sultan Bayazit I virtually took control of the government when he supported the claims of John VII to the throne. True, John's reign was brief, but his successor Manuel was at first confined to the Ottoman court as an hostage. Soon after he succeeded in escaping, and Ottoman activities were diverted by the arrival of the Mongols on their eastern frontier and in 1402 Bayazit was defeated and captured by Tamerlane. This saved Constantinople, for Bayzit's successor Mehmet I devoted himself entirely to the reorganization of his own state, made necessary by the defeat, and this gave Manuel II (1391-1425) a period of respite. He was a dignified, gallant figure, who inspired admiration wherever he went—and he even visited France and England in the course of his travels in search of aid. The West, however, failed to respond and Manuel was thrown back on his own resources. In 1422 Murat II (1421-51), who had reverted to a more aggressive policy when he succeeded to Mehmet I, set siege to Constantinople. He was however forced to withdraw when his brother rose against him, and the Byzantine capital was once more granted respite.

Manuel's successor John VIII (1425-48) was somewhat more successful in his efforts to obtain Western help, for in 1443 a Crusade set out from Hungary against the Turks and at first met with considerable success. A truce was concluded which was favourable to the West in 1444, but the Crusaders broke it the next year, and as a reward for their perfidiousness were signally defeated by the Turks in the battle of Varna. Thus encouraged, the Turks advanced against the Morea which the despot Constantine had consolidated as a small but prosperous Greek state; but with the death of John, Constantine, Despot of the Morea, was called to the Byzantine throne, while on the Ottoman side Murat II was succeeded by Mehmet II (1451-1481) who came to the throne with one principal idea in mind, the capture of Constantinople.

The adjoining countryside was already his, and he was able at once to build the fortress of Rumeli Hissar (Pl. 47) on the European shore of the Bosphorus, only a few miles away from the city. He then assembled a great army, perhaps twenty times as numerous as that of the defenders, and a powerful armament of artillery, bringing specialists from Europe to build and operate it. The siege began on April 7th, 1453. Yet, in face of the vast army and a continued bombardment by cannon of enormous size which the walls had never been designed to withstand, the defence held, and indeed gained ground. On April 20th four Genoese boats came to the aid of the defenders and won an engagement at the mouth of the Golden Horn before reaching safety within the boom which the Byzantines were able to maintain. However, during the night of April 21st the Turks accomplished the astonishing feat of transporting part of their fleet overland from the Bosphorus near Top Hane to the Golden Horn, along a specially constructed causeway, and to their amazement the Greeks found the Turkish vessels riding at anchor close to their walls on the morning of April 22nd. This increased the danger of their position considerably, as it necessitated manning the sea wall in that area when their forces were already inadequate for the defence of the land walls.

It was not until May 29th that the Turks were ready for the final attack, after the walls had been battered for nearly seven weeks by their great cannon cast specially for that purpose. Then a general attack was mounted from three points, the first just to the north of the Charisius (Adrianople) Gate, the next near the Pempton Gate and the third near the Gate of St Romanus. It was in the two latter areas that the most violent fighting took place. Twice the Turks attacked, and twice they were repulsed. Then the gallant Justiniani, who led a body of 700 Genoese, was fatally wounded and, with their leader gone, the Genoese broke. At the same time Mehmet made a violent third attack, throwing in his most formidable

50. The Mosque of Sultan Suleyman. It was built by Sinan, the most famous of all the architects working for the Ottoman sultans, between 1550 and 1557.

troops, the Janissaries. Their efforts were aided by an oversight, for a small gate, the Kirko Porta, was found undefended. There the Janissaries penetrated, and the defenders were overwhelmed, the emperor falling at the walls amidst his troops. So the defence collapsed and the city fell.

A great phase of history had come to an end. It was not because of gunpowder, though that helped; not because the Turks were invincible, good fighters though they were; not because the Greeks lost heart. The truth of the matter was that the fall of the city had become inevitable as a result of the loss of the empire of which it was the natural head. It could have survived only if the advances of the Turks in Western Asia Minor and Eastern Europe could have been checked a century earlier. Without its hinterland the city could not survive; with it, its role was that of a capital, and within a few weeks of the Conquest the city had once more assumed its old role, but under new masters, of Eastern race and of a new faith. The next great chapter in its history had begun.

Fig. 9. Medallion of John VIII Palaeologos, by Pisanello. Photo: *Victoria and Albert Museum.* Crown Copyright.

51. The Mosque of Sultan Ahmet
from Agia Sophia.
Though built early
in the seventeenth century
the mosque is one of the most
lovely in the city,
with its thin pencil-like
minarets which are especially
well proportioned.

Istanbul

The Fate of the Christians under Turkish Domination

Stepping out of the railway station or driving in from the airport, the traveller who pays a visit to Rome even today comes into practically immediate contact with manifestations of Roman civilization. They assert themselves throughout the whole area that was covered by the ancient city and even, in the form of streets or aqueducts, dominate much of the surrounding countryside, while except perhaps in the region of St Peter's the monuments of later ages tend to take a rather secondary place. At Istanbul the situation is exactly the contrary, for there vestiges of Byzantium are far from obvious; they are often obscured and most have to be sought out with care, while the buildings of Turkish times dominate both the streets and the skyline. The most important of them are the great mosques, and from the days following the Conquest onwards there was hardly a sultan or a leading minister of consequence who did not endow the city with at least one such building in perpetuation of his name.

Sultan Mehmet the Conqueror (Pl. 63) set the fashion, for he not only sanctioned the conversion of a number of churches to the faith of Islam—the transference of eight is recorded—but also caused a number of new mosques to be built; the most important of them is the one bearing today the name by which he was usually known to the Turks, Sultan Fatih. He chose as its site that of the Church of the Holy Apostles which had been erected by Justinian and had served as the burial place of a large proportion of the Byzantine emperors thereafter. It was there, at an even earlier date, that Constantine had been buried in a great mausoleum, its dome upheld by twelve columns, one for each apostle; there stood the great porphyry sarcophagi which now grace the terrace of the museum; they were placed in Justinian's magnificent five-domed church, prototype of St Mark's at Venice and of many another building in the Christian West. The church was decorated with a magnificent array of mosaics depicting a complete cycle of New Testament scenes. Indeed it vied with Agia Sophia in fame and glory, and having taken over the one, Mehmet no doubt thought that the other, associated as much with the Byzantine monarchy as with the Christian faith, would be better suppressed.

At first however Sultan Mehmet does not seem to have considered this site, for the church was handed over to the Greek Patriarch Gennadios almost immediately after the conquest, in place of Agia Sophia. The quarter was apparently very sparsely populated and after three years Gennadios asked permission to move; he was

given instead the Church of St Mary Pammakaristos; the Patriarchate was established there, and there it remained till 1498; the nuns who were in possession of the
church at the time were transferred to that of St John the Baptist in Trullo nearby;
both remained in Christian hands till they were made into mosques by Mehmet
Pasha, Grand Vizier to Murat III (1574-95). Guarantees of good treatment were
given to the Patriarch, for the Turks were not ill-disposed towards the Christian
minority, and it would seem that quite a considerable number of the original Greek
inhabitants survived the Conquest, even if the nobles were mostly exterminated and
other important personages exiled. Some 50,000 were, it is reported, enslaved, and
these no doubt mostly remained in the capital. According to Chritovoulos, a Greek
who wrote an account of the siege and the immediately succeeding periods, the Conqueror gave government and other posts to some of the prisoners. Indeed, when
the first frenzy of destruction and looting had subsided, it would seem that the sultan
treated the conquered comparatively reasonably. Within a few years he was trying
to tempt people, Christians as well as Moslems, to settle in the city with offers of
grants and assistance. Just as many of those who took advantage of his offer seem
to have been Christians as Moslems. Violent and ruthless though his character
was, the sultan is also reported to have regretted the destruction and the looting,
and to have compiled plans for the rebuilding of the city almost as soon as the fires
which had devastated large areas of it had been quenched.

Chritovoulos's history, which is the best source of information for this age, covers
the seventeen years that immediately succeeded the conquest. The very fact of its
existence serves to indicate that the Greeks, once the fighting was over, were not
treated unfairly, and that they themselves were reasonably content is suggested by
its dedication, which reads as follows:—

> " To the supreme emperor, king of kings, Mehmet the Fortunate, the victor,
> the winner of trophies, the triumphant, the invincible, Lord of land and
> sea, by the will of God, from Chritovoulos, the Islander, servant of thy
> servants."

He did however apologize to his fellow Greeks for having written it!

The book is divided into three parts. The first is an account of the actual siege,
the second describes the efforts to repopulate and rebuild the city, while the third
is devoted to describing Sultan Mehmet's conquest of the Peloponnese. The manuscript itself, which is in the library of the Saray at Istanbul, bears the date 1470.

Chritovoulos's attitude was fair and broadminded; he was ready to forgive the
cruelties of war and battle and to acknowledge the merits of the new regime in so
far as they were apparent. Indeed, the Greeks at first had little cause for complaint
regarding their treatment by their new overlords, except for the practice of taking
the best of the youths at an early age to be converted to Islam and made members
of the Corps of Janissaries—but it must be remembered that the youths so treated
represented a very small percentage of the total Greek population. The really
serious causes for complaint came later, when the firm control of the earlier sultans
weakened, and greater power fell into the hands of local governors, many of whom
were both incompetent and corrupt. It was then that the population as a whole
began to suffer, but the Christian elements suffered to a greater degree than the
Moslems.

Most serious, probably, was the instability and uncertainty of their position. There
was probably little active oppression, but there were continued difficulties, and as
time went on, dishonesty and mismanagement prevailed. If a Christian business
man sought to better his position, he became a target for the tax collector; if a
farmer increased his flocks they only tempted thieves and he could get little redress;
if he improved his land, the local governor would as likely as not seize a part of it.
Moreover there was a total lack of confidence in the law, for it was virtually impos-

Ianiffaire allant à la guerre.

L 3   fo. 137

Fig. 10. A Janissary. From *Pérégrination Faites en Turquie* by Nicolay, 1567.
Photo: *British Museum*

sible to procure any redress. The system of administration thus led inevitably to inactivity and laziness. The dangers that befell the ambitious or progressive were sufficient to discourage all but the most ardent, while the creed of Islam offered no spur to any activity on the part of the Turks other than to take advantage of their Christian subjects. The ultimate result was stagnation, and the stagnation was made all the more inevitable by the increasing incompetence of so many of the later sultans.

Mehmet himself had great plans for the future. He was ready to lead his armies to the capture of Rome as he had captured Constantinople; he drew out plans for the city with something of the same zeal that Constantine had shown, and he put much of the actual work in hand. His successors built; Islam flourished; mosques which were amongst the finest in the world were erected and decorated and a peak of glory was reached under the great Suleyman the Magnificent. But the state thereafter declined and the Greek Christians, who could have added so much to its prosperity had they been given the opportunity, were hindered and discouraged. " Riyas," flocks, the Turks called them and like flocks they were treated. Flocks were something necessary and useful, but they also had to be confined and guarded, lest they should stray from their appointed pastures.

It is not easy to draw up any very exact picture of the situation that confronted

52. The interior of the dome
of the Yeni Camii.
The mosque stands near
the head of the lower bridge
over the Golden Horn.

132

53

54

the Christians at any one time between 1453 and the nineteenth century. At first they retained their churches and much of their freedom, but as time went on they were slowly and progressively deprived of both, so that towards the last years of the empire only one of the many hundreds of Byzantine churches that survived in Constantinople was still in Christian hands, namely St Mary of the Mongols. All the others had either been confiscated for employment as mosques or destroyed. Agia Sophia was the first to be taken over by Islam, for it was the normal practice immediately after a town was captured for prayer to be said in the most important and impressive building available; it served as an official indication of the conquest. In the case of Agia Sophia, though most of the Christian adornments were destroyed, some were retained as being sacred to Islam also, like the doors said to have been made from the wood of the ark. The sacred well, covered by a stone from the well of Samaria, was resanctified to Islam, for it was believed that it was able to cure palpitations, while the miraculous powers of the famous sweating column were attributed to a Moslem saint instead of to the Christian St Gregory. And in addition other legends grew up associating the building with Islamic history and tradition.

Similar Moslem associations became attached to other churches when they were taken over. Thus St Thekla became Toklu Mescid around 1586, the name being that of a later Moslem healer, derived perhaps from Thekla. The miracle-working properties of the Christian Saint Andrew of Crete were again transferred with his church, St Andrew in Chrisei, to two Moslem women, Fatima and Zeinab, when it became a mosque in 1520; their graves were supposedly discovered there. The church of St Theodosia was desecrated immediately after the Conquest and the bones of the saint scattered. It was then used as a naval store till the reign of Selim II (1566-76) when it became a mosque. When it was restored in 1832 the saint's tomb was also restored but was named the tomb of the Apostles of Christ.

Most of the churches were, however, simply transferred as structures without any special associations. The Church of St John of Studius, the oldest surviving church in the city, was thus taken over by the equerry of Sultan Bayazit around 1500; the Christian name of the Church of Sts Sergius and Bacchus was still in use in Gyllius' time, though it had become a mosque at some previous date, as had the lovely building known as Kalender Camii, which is probably to be identified as the Church of St Mary Diaconissa. Several other churches had been taken over before 1500, such as the churches of the Pantocrator around 1470 and St Mary Pammakaristos in 1496. Within the next century there were many more conversions, most of them made on behalf of individuals, such as that of St John in Trullo by Mehmet Pasha around 1591. By 1600 there was probably hardly a Byzantine church left in Christian hands.

This is only one side of the picture. The Greeks and other Christians were not always prevented from building, and certainly by the eighteenth century they probably preferred the new, more up-to-date structures they were allowed to set up to the old Byzantine ones. The earlier churches that they built were comparatively simple three-aisled, or even single-aisled buildings with a wooden roof, for the use of domes and leaded roofs was reserved for mosques, but by the nineteenth century some quite large and impressive churches had been set up; for example, that of the Trinity near Taksim in the quarter of Pera or the Church of St George, built in 1720 as the new seat of the Patriarch, which forms a part of the Phanar, the Patriarch's residence; it is a hideous but impressive affair of red terracotta dominating a whole quarter of Istanbul from its situation on the slopes above the Golden Horn. In Greece and in some of the country districts there were restrictions as to the size and impressiveness of churches, but this does not seem to have been the case on Mount Athos where the monks were more or less autonomous. Buildings of considerable size were sometimes also set up at other places, as at Trebizond, where

53. The Turbe or mausoleum of Suleyman the Magnificent. Its stands close to the Sultan's mosque and was also designed by the architect Sinan.

54. The tomb of Roxelana. Roxelana, Sultan Suleyman's favourite wife, was buried in a mausoleum similar to that of the Sultan, standing close beside it.

there was a large and extremely prosperous Greek community until the exchange of populations took place after the First World War.

Again from the time of Gennadios onwards there was always a Greek patriarch at Constantinople, and he acted not only as head of the Orthodox church within the Empire, but also as leader of the Greek community. Many of the patriarchs were men of great ability and consequence and they occupied a prominent position in the state. They exercised a certain degree of judicial independence so far as the Orthodox subjects in the empire were concerned, and had direct access to the sultan in that connection. But the position of Patriarch, if influential, was also dangerous and of the hundred and fifty-nine men who occupied the post between 1453 and 1918, six were murdered, twenty-seven abdicated and one hundred and twenty-five were removed from office. It must be remembered however that under some of the sultans the post of Grand Vizier was even more dangerous, and Sultan Selim I is reported to have executed no less than seven grand viziers in eight years.

If the patriarchs suffered in this way their Christian flock was subjected to even severer treatment. Conquered peoples were enslaved; strong and intelligent youths were often forcibly converted to Islam; the famous Corps of the Janissaries was thus mainly formed of Christian youths taken over at an early age, while quite a number of the leading administrators of the state were also Christians who had been converted. There was in fact a continual drain of the best blood and brains to Islam.

With the passing of the centuries the mismanagement of internal affairs led to the growth of bribery, corruption and sloth within the community as a whole; indeed, a slave mentality tended to develop, which in the nineteenth century earned for the Greeks in Turkey a reputation for sharp practice and dishonesty rivalled only by that attached to the Armenians. It would however be wrong to blame the Turks entirely for this. Bribery and corruption had been rife in Byzantine times, especially in the years immediately preceeding the Latin conquest, and though those vices seem at that time to have mainly effected the more influential classes, the reputation of the Byzantine was never very high in the Western world. Even allowing for inevitable Western prejudice, the Byzantine Greeks cannot be completely absolved in this respect, though it was certainly in Turkish times that the servile attitude and a certain oriental laxity and laziness of character developed in addition to sharpness of practice.

Yet, in spite of these characteristics, the Greeks managed to survive. There were periods of oppression, yet if there were massacres they were not always confined to the Christian population. Selim I is thus said to have caused the slaughter of 40,000 Moslems of the Shia persuasion, so in fact his Moslem subjects fared, if anything, worse than the Christians. Mehmet IV is also reported to have massacred 36,000 of his subjects in five years, most of them Moslems. The phases of oppression in fact depended on the eccentricity of the ruler more than on any set principles, and if at times they were severe, these periods were also intermittent.

With the progress of thought in the eighteenth century, Christians throughout the empire began to think of independence, and from around 1800 they began to fight for it, the Slavs supported by Russia, the Greeks by the Western powers and especially Britain. Not surprisingly these revolts called forth reprisals, and in 1821 a massacre of Greeks took place in Constantinople in reprisal for Greek gains in their War of Independence. The aged Patriarch Gregorius was dragged from the altar whilst celebrating mass and brutally murdered, while twelve bishops and numerous priests were slaughtered by the mob. However, these were intermittent tragedies, and throughout the eighteenth and nineteenth centuries many Christians were able to develop businesses and even to live in considerable prosperity; they were appointed to important posts in the Turkish government service, and there are few among the upper class Greeks who do not regard the life they led in Istanbul

55. Detail of the tilework in the gallery of the Mosque of Sultan Ahmet. The tiles of this mosque are mostly blue and white; those of the previous century usually show more elaborate colouring.

previous to 1914 with considerable nostalgia. Large quarters of the city, especially Pera between the Bosphorus and the Golden Horn, and Kadikoy on the Asiatic shore, were almost wholly Greek; most of the commerce was in Greek hands, and the houses in which the richest members of the community lived were large and luxurious.

Such evidence as there is suggests that even immediately following the Conquest many of the finer secular buildings had been in Christian hands. A few of them survive to this day on the shores of the Golden Horn. They have sometimes been claimed as Byzantine, but they more probably date from the century after the Conquest and are to be attributed to Christian traders. The finest were no doubt set up by the Venetians and Genoese—one of them is known as the old Venetian Legation—but later at least some among them passed into the hands of Greek merchants, even if they were not built by them. Their private houses were often equally fine, though they were situated either in the suburbs to the north of the Golden Horn or on the Asiatic shore rather than in the old Stamboul which had been Byzantium.

Fig. 11. Old Turkish houses on the Bosphorus. From *Beauties of the Bosphorus* by Pardoe, engraving by W. H. Bartlett. Photo: *British Museum*.

The European traders from the outset enjoyed a very privileged position. Their trading quarters in Galata and along the shores to the south of the Golden Horn had been firmly established in Byzantine times and very soon they were granted similar privileges by the Turks. As the warlike activities of the Turks declined, opportunities for trade increased, and further important concessions were granted. New competitors entered the field, so that, by the sixteenth century the French and the English played a more important role than the Venetians and the Genoese. These Western colonies on the whole did much to improve the position of the Greeks, who found employment in their establishments and who worked in close association with them. It was not until the later eighteenth or even the nineteenth century, that the Greeks were able to enter seriously into the field of external trade themselves.

Although the most important element of the Christian " raya " population—that is to say, Christians who had been conquered by Islam as opposed to merchants

56. The Miramar Mosque. This mosque is also the work of the great architect Sinan and stands close to the walls of the city, beside the Adrianople Gate.

from the West—were Greeks, the Armenian population was by no means negligible. In any case, until the eighteenth century much of their ancient country lay within the frontiers of Turkey; only then, with the progress of Russian conquests in the Caucasus, did part of it pass to Russian rule. There had no doubt always been an Armenian colony in the capital; by the nineteenth century it probably numbered around 200,000, and of the four patriarchs of the Armenian church one had his seat there. The native land of the Armenians, lying as it did at the junction first of the Persian and Byzantine empires and later at the meeting point of Persia, Turkey and Russia, had always been a battle ground, but its people were peaceful and industrious, and even though it was a mountainous land, lying at a high altitude, it was rich and fruitful. It suffered, like the rest of the Turkish empire, from neglect; it was exploited in the seventeenth century by Persia and its people were oppressed by both overlords, but it was really only with the nineteenth century and more especially during the reign of Abdul Hamid (1876-1909) that oppression of the Armenians became a matter of organized policy and the atrocities that shocked Europe became the accepted custom. Till then the Armenians, like the Greeks, lived a life of varied prosperity under Turkish rule, which was hampered more by the incompetence or dishonesty of individual officials than by organized oppression, and at times individual Armenians enjoyed reasonable security and prosperity within the realm.

The Grand Seraglio

ALTHOUGH THE TALE of the Ottoman sultans is a somewhat depressing one, for so many of the later ones were incompetent, ineffectual, cruel or even mad, that of the Saray, the palace where they lived, is curiously romantic and enthralling. For so many years it was forbidden territory, penetrated only occasionally by some intrepid explorer; it was a curiosity known only from hearsay and reports, which created an additional air of mystery. Indeed as late as the nineteenth century it was forbidden even to pass beside it on horseback or carrying an open umbrella. Till then, the rooms of its harem, centre of intrigue and allurement, had been visited by none; the inner courts had been almost equally impenetrable, for even the most favoured of ambassadors had never penetrated beyond its gate, and few who had once lived there, even among the Turks, were permitted to leave its sacred precincts; only the two outer courts were slightly more familiar, in that a few favoured foreigners, such as ambassadors and their entourage, had been admitted so far and no farther, to pay their respects to the sultan.

The idea of the Saray—a royal palace made up of a series of detached buildings set in or around courtyards—must have been to some extent inspired by the Great Palace of the Byzantine emperors, which was somewhat similar in layout. The actual architecture was distinct however; there was less—indeed little—need for the large banqueting halls or audience chambers which formed so characteristic a feature in the Great Palace, there were no churches and there were of course a number of innovations such as the inclusion of the harem.

So far as we can tell the Osmanli sultans had not built much in the way of secular buildings at Bursa where their capital was situated before they captured Constantinople; two great congregational mosques, some madrassas, a number of fine baths, and the tombs of the early sultans represent the most important of the contributions that were made there to architecture. But when once the sultans had settled in Constantinople the outlook changed, and one of Mehmet II, the Conqueror's, earliest actions was to erect a palace which came to be known as " The Old Saray ". Work actually began in 1454. It stood near the Mosque of Bayazit, where the

57. Interior of the Miramar Mosque. The decoration has been much overpainted in unpleasant colours; the quality of its design, however, remains.

Seraskerat, now part of the university, was later to stand. Nothing of the palace now survives and it never played a role in the life of the city or the sultanate comparable to that of the Saray which now stands on the point of high land to the north of Agia Sophia, the site of the ancient acropolis. Work on this site actually began around 1460, but it only became the chief palace under Suleyman (1520-66). It was for long known as the Yeni or New Saray, though in the nineteenth century the name of Top Kapu Saray (Canon Gate Palace) became associated with it, and today it is sometimes even called the " Old Saray " to distinguish it from the new palaces on the Bosphorus, but the name is both inaccurate and misleading. Most of the numerous buildings of which it is composed are, however, of later date, for virtually every sultan added to it or altered one of the existing buildings, and most of the original ones were damaged or destroyed in a series of fires; the most severe of them took place in 1574 and 1665. The only structure which remains unchanged is, indeed, a pavilion which is outside the main palace enclosure and which now serves as a part of the Museum of Antiquities. It is known as the Çinili Kiosk or Tile Pavilion (Pl. 46) and dates from between 1465 and 1473. Its tiles are closely similar to those of the Yesil Camii or Green Mosque at Bursa, its plan similar to that of Islamic secular buildings elsewhere like that at Palermo known as the Ziza. It is a structure of considerable beauty, particularly with regard to the detail of its ornament. The formal rather severe patterns of its tiles are closer to those of the Seljuk period than to the more delicate painted tiles of Ottoman times, and have a vigorous quality that clearly reflects the character of the earlier sultans.

The Saray as a whole occupies a very extensive area, and is delineated by a high defensive wall extending more or less in a straight line from the Golden Horn to Agia Sophia, and thence, after making a turn of almost a right angle, to the Marmora; Agia Sophia itself is just outside the perimeter, St Eirene just within it. The more private and restricted part occupies the high ground at the extremity of the point and is comparatively restricted in size—especially when one reads the accounts of the great mass of people who lived and the number of institutions which were housed within its precincts; there were for instance twelve mosques, ten immense double kitchens, two bakeries, a flour mill, several hospitals and a military school, to mention but a few of the larger ones.

The wall that delineated the outer area was built by Mehmet II to form a sort of inner citadel, but the rapidity and force of the Turkish conquests never put its strength to the test, though it did once or twice afford protection at the time of palace revolutions. It was originally pierced by twelve gates and defended by battlements and a tower every 150 yards. Along the seashore the old Byzantine walls were heightened and strengthened by a number of Turkish additions. The most important of the gates was the Bab-i-Humayun, close to the north-east corner of Agia Sophia. It still survives, though its appearance has been changed, for originally there was a room with windows above it, used by the imperial treasury, and there were four little towers at the corners. It was by this gate that the sultan entered and left on state occasions, there that visitors were admitted. General access to the palace was gained though this gate, and for this reason inspection of visitors was undertaken by a permanent guard of fifty men. The other gates were primarily used by palace officials or for bringing in goods, and took their names from the principal nature of their use; there was thus a Fish (Balik) Gate, a Wood (Odun) Gate, where the fish for the royal kitchens or the wood for the fires was introduced.

Within this first court there was a great park on the lower ground to the west, where the Gul Hane park now lies; the higher ground was occupied by numerous offices such as the mint, the main bakeries—in that reserved for the sultan's use only the very finest white flour was employed—a hospital, and similar institutions. Here also were the stables, housing some 4,000 horses under the control of the

58. Detail of the tilework in the Mosque of Sultan Ahmet. The tiles which cover the walls of this and of so many other buildings were made at Isnic, the ancient Nicaea, some fifty miles away on the Asiatic coast.

Master of the Royal Horse. Even in this great outer court, though it must have been a hive of activity, thronged with people, rules of behaviour and silence were strictly imposed and the travellers who visited it speak with awe of the quietness and tranquillity of the atmosphere.

From this outer court the Saray proper was entered by the Orta Kapu (Pl. 68) or middle gate, originally known as the Bab es Salaam, beyond which only the sultan could pass on horseback. It gave on to the Court of the Divan, some 460 feet long and 360 wide at its widest. Its name was derived from a large hall on its north-western side where the Council of State (the Divan) met four times a week. The building still survives, with a colonnade along its façade; there are similar colonnades at the ends of the court, that is to say, along the walls that separate it from the outer area on the one side and from the third or inner court on the other. The Hall of the Divan was probably built in the time of Sultan Suleyman, but it was damaged by fire in 1574, and redecorated under Ahmet III (1703-30). Today the tower at its end is the most prominent landmark in the Saray. Here the ambassadors of foreign powers were received by the Divan, and, if thought proper, presented eventually to the sultan, in a special room, the Throne Room (Arz Odasi), just within the bounds of the third court. The day on which the Janissaries received their quarterly pay was usually chosen for the visit, and such ambassadors as have left records speak with awe and admiration of the impression that this event made on them.

The Janissaries had originally been conscripted from the share of one-fifth of the prisoners which fell to the lot of the sultan; later, around 1362, the drafting of Christian youths to the Corps from areas conquered by the advancing Turks was instituted by Murat I. At first the Corps was quite small, but by the sixteenth century it numbered some 12,000 men and by the eighteenth century more than 100,000. While the sultans still went to war the Janissaries were probably the finest troops in the Western world; when settled life in the capital became the rule their discipline and efficiency rapidly deteriorated, and they became a constant centre of trouble. Admittedly, some were always occupied in maintaining order in the provinces and these perhaps showed some efficiency, but the majority, and they were no doubt the most influential, remained in the palace and on days of parade made a very brave showing.

The Divan itself must have been little less impressive, if only because of the magnificent costumes worn by its members and the dignified grandeur with which Turkish ceremonies (Pl. 62) were conducted. The chamber, though it now appears somewhat grim, must also have provided a suitable setting. It was large and high, its roof supported on columns, and at one end, up above, there was a hidden window through which the sultan could watch and listen; it was contrived by Suleyman I. He could reach the chamber in which it was situated by means of a private passage from the harem. Next to the Divan was the Defter Hane, where official documents were prepared; it was burnt in 1574 and redecorated around 1725. Further on was the Inner Treasury, now used for the Saray's fine museum of arms; it dates from the time of Mehmet II, Fatih, so that it represents one of the earliest structures in the Saray. It is, however, far less impressive than the row of ten enormous kitchens (Pl. 67) on the opposite side of the court. Each of these is a double structure of two adjoining square chambers, both roofed by domes, though only one of each pair was furnished with a chimney. The ten tall chimneys constitute one of the most destructive landmarks in the area of the Saray when seen from the Sea of Marmora. They were built by the famous architect Sinan after a fire had damaged the original kitchens in 1574. Once they served to prepare two meals a day for the many hundreds of inmates in the palace, as many as 2,000 in the time of Mehmet IV, as well as for the Janissary guard of some 4,000, and the members of the Divan on days of session. In the eighteenth century up to two hundred sheep, one hundred lambs, forty calves, eighty geese and two hundred chickens were required each day. A part of the immense and spectacular collection of Chinese porcelain is now displayed on the walls of these structures. There are literally thousands of pieces, some, especially the celadon, being extremely fine. Much of the collection was found after the revolution, unused, still packed in the cases in which it had come from China a century or two previously. The Chinese porcelain was first mentioned in 1504, though most of it was obtained in the time of Suleyman the Magnificent (1520-66).

From the second court another gate led to a third enclosure known as The House of Felicity, Dar-es-Saadet, and immediately within its gate was the Throne Room (Pl. 74), a structure of the fifteenth century, but redecorated in 1716 and again in 1856. It still contains fine tile work of the sixteenth century. The throne itself was captured from Shah Ismail of Persia by Selim I in 1514. Here Ministers of State and favoured ambassadors were received, having being clothed in special robes after their reception by the Divan, and the accounts of the magnificence and grandeur of the event left by Venetian, French and English visitors alike make very impressive reading. Beyond the Throne Room no visitor could penetrate except under the most exceptional circumstances. Otherwise entrance was restricted to the Corps of Pages and the White Eunuchs.

The latter were occupied with the service of the sultan's private dwelling; the former were recruited from captured children, mostly Christian, who were given a full and special education in the palace, till they were fourteen. It included Turkish, Persian and Arabic, music and various polite sports. Thereafter they were drafted to the Army, to the provinces, or to court appointments, according to their capacity. When once they left the palace they might never return.

The actual gate of the court is first mentioned in 1561, and it was presumably first built then; it was restored in 1774 and again in the nineteenth century. It was in the charge of the White Eunuchs, while the buildings adjoining were divided between them and the palace school. Close to the Throne Room is a small mosque which now serves to house part of the superb Saray library. Farther on within the court, on the sea side, was the Treasury—still used as such, and forming a part of the Saray Museum. Originally it was under the charge of the White Eunuchs, and one of the last of them still held one of its several keys as recently as the early 1930's.

There is no marked separation between the third and the fourth courts, and the fourth was no more restricted than the third. It was in fact really the sultan's private garden, and still retains today the general plan that characterized it in the seventeenth century, though the plants are different, for there are no vestiges now of the famous tulip garden of Sultan Ahmet III (1703-30), during whose reign the passion for this flower reached its height in Turkey. The whole area was surrounded by numerous kiosks, some of which have disappeared, though others survive; most renowned are the Erivan and Bagdad kiosks (Pl. 70), built by Murat IV on his return from the campaigns in which those places were captured. Both of them are adorned with tiles of very great beauty; they are indeed the finest of the individual kiosks, though there are better tiles in the harem. The former was copied from a pavilion Murat actually saw at Erivan in 1635, though it was made more elaborate; the latter was similarly inspired by a building he admired at Bagdad in 1638. Near the former was the Kiosk of Circumcision (Sunnet Odasi) built by Sultan Ibrahim (1640-48) and beyond the latter two rather delightful smaller buildings, the Kiosk of Kara Mustapha (Pl. 71) and that of the Head Physician. The former is first mentioned in 1748 and is probably an eighteenth century structure; the latter may be earlier, though it has subsequently been considerably redecorated.

Further to the east, dominating the slope above the Marmora, is the most recent of all the additions to the Saray, a kiosk built by Abdul Mecit in 1840 on the site of two older kiosks which were destroyed to make way for it; it is in the florid style of the nineteenth century, which was given fuller expression and on a larger scale in the palaces of Çeragan and Dolmabakçe on the shores of the Bosphorus. Near to this kiosk is a final gate, through which there is access to a stair leading down to Seraglio point. This was used by the sultans when they came to the Saray by boat, and also on occasion to admit secret envoys or those engaged on special missions, among them some of the travellers who have left accounts of the palace and the life lived therein.

It was difficult enough to obtain access to the third and fourth courts, but a few intrepid travellers succeeded in doing so, either in the course of duty, like Thomas Dallam, who set up an organ in one of the pavilions in 1599—it was sent as a gift by Queen Elizabeth (*see* p. 171)—or by means of bribery and influence, like Aubray de la Motraye, who went in disguised as a clock-mender's assistant. But not all lived to tell the tale, and in 1680 a man was put to death for gazing at the harem through a telescope. Two other sections of the palace which adjoin one another on the north-west side were even more sacred, the harem and the Pavilion of the Holy Mantle; the one reserved as scene of the sultan's pleasure, the other as shrine of the Faith of Islam.

The Pavilion of the Holy Mantle (Pl. 73) was constructed to house the insignia of the Prophet—his mantle, staff, sword, seal and a portion of the beard—which were brought from Egypt by Selim I in 1517, when he assumed the dignity of Caliph of Islam. The Prophet's standard remained in Damascus till 1595, but was then added to the collection, to be brought out and exhibited whenever holy war was declared; the last occasion was in 1915. The Pavillion itself was reconstructed by Mahmut I (1730-54), and contains an inner sanctuary where the relics are preserved, two other chambers and a stone-paved court. The relics were tended by a special group of guardians, whose duty included continuous reading of the Koran by night and day alike.

The harem—the most romantic and enthralling section of all the vast complex of the Saray—occupied a comparatively small area along the north-west side of the Saray, limited at one end by the Pavilion of the Holy Mantle and at the other by the Divan and the present arms museum, in the second court. The main entrance was situated there, and was guarded by the Black Eunuchs; indeed it was impossible to penetrate into the Harem from the second court without passing first through the so-called hall of the Black Eunuchs, repaired after a fire in 1665. On to this their living quarters opened, and thence a passage called the Golden Road led to the Harem (Pl. 76. 77) itself. It is decorated with some of the finest tile-work in the whole of Turkey, the glazes flawless, the colours rich and pure. Originally designed simply as guards for the harem, the importance of the Black Eunuchs gradually increased, till by the seventeenth century their chief had become almost the most important person in the state, subordinate only to the sultan and to the sultan's mother. Near to the Hall of the Eunuchs was the room where the young princes were educated—they remained in the harem till they were eleven.

At the end of the Golden Road a maze of small rooms opens up, some adorned with exquisite tile-work, some with painted decorations and some with panelling. Even today it is uncertain if all its nooks and crannies have been planned, and it is far from easy even now to obtain permission to visit it, though parts of it were at one time open to the public. Reasonably full accounts have, however, been published by Dr Miller (*Beyond the Sublime Porte*, 1931), who made a reasonably comprehensive plan between 1916 and 1919 and N. M. Penzer, who published a full and complete account in 1936, under the title of *The Harem*. He gives a summary of previous accounts made by the few who penetrated there, notably Nicolas

59. Mihrab of the Mosque of Sokollu Mehmet Pasha. The mihrab is constructed with tiles which represent some of the finest work in the city. The mosque was built by Sinan.

de Nicolay in 1551, Domenico Hierosolimitano between 1580 and 1590, Thomas Dallam in 1599, Ottavio Bon between 1604 and 1607, Edmund Chichull in 1701, Aubray de la Motraye between 1699 and 1717, Jean-Claude Flachat between 1740 and 1755, Sir Adolphus Slade in 1829 and Maxime Du Camp in 1844 or 1845. After that date visitors became more numerous, for the harem of the reigning sultan was transferred to one of the new palaces on the Bosphorus, and the old building in the Saray was used only to house the widows of his predecessors. Even before that a new summer harem had been built by Ahmet III in 1709 on the low ground near Seraglio point. It remained in use till 1862 when it was totally destroyed by fire.

The harems of the earlier sultans had actually been housed in the Old Saray which stood on the site of the university, near the Mosque of Bayazit. The first to move to the New Saray was Roxelana, who apparently persuaded Sultan Suleyman to allow to her to join him there sometime between 1541 and 1545; the fact that the Old Saray was damaged by fire in 1540 or 1541 perhaps served as an excuse. She took one hundred ladies in waiting with her, as well as eunuchs and domestics, so the buildings made available for her must have been fairly extensive. The rest of the harem—comprising about 1200 women—was moved there under Murat III (1574-95), and he undertook a great deal of building to make room for it. Even so conditions must have been terribly crowded, for though it is a labyrinth of small rooms, the actual surface area of the Harem is comparatively small, and in addition to the wives, servants and eunuchs there must have been many young children.

It is hard to picture today the lives led by these unfortunate women, cooped up together in so small an area, waiting for something which for the majority of them never came, under the eye of jealous favourites who resorted to any means, fair or foul, to retain the eye of the sultan, and under the care of eunuchs whose characters had been warped both by their condition and even more by the nature of their employment. And, if they did chance to catch the sultan's eye and produce a male child the chances were that, if it succeeded in surviving the jealousies of other mothers in the Harem, it would be slaughtered the moment a new sultan came to the throne. Such thoughts as these strike one most forcibly as one walks through the harem today, in spite of the delightful decorations of so many of the rooms, with their lovely tiles, marble fountains or charming painted woodwork—but one must remember that the women's lot here was perhaps better than that of many, for they lived in great comfort, and the seclusion of the harem had by the fifteenth century become universal for all but the wives of peasants, even if, little more than a century before, the women of the upper classes had been virtually free. As late as 1333 the sultan's favourite wife had entertained the Arab traveller Ibn Batutah when he visited Asia Minor.

Though a few travellers had penetrated into the second and one or two into the third court, the first European to enter the precincts of the actual Harem was apparently the physician Domenico Hierosolimitano between 1580 and 1590, who had on occasion to tend some of the inmates. The account he has left however does little more than mention the existence of the Golden Road and the rooms beyond it. Dallam in 1599 saw " thirtie of the Grand Sinyor's concubines " through a grille when he was setting up the organ sent by Queen Elizabeth somewhere in the third court. Aubray de la Motraye was taken into the hall of the Harem in the guise of a clock-mender's assistant during the sultan's absence in Adrianople. He described it as a domed chamber with a superb fountain in the middle and fine tile-work on the walls. On the way out he was taken past " several little chambers with doors shut, like the cells of monks or nuns." He saw inside one of them, which was richly adorned with paintings and gilding; the windows however were placed high up in the walls and were filled with painted glass, so that it was impossible to see out of them.

60. Fountain of the Library of Ahmet III. The library forms a part of the vast complex of buildings which constitute the Saray, or Palace of the Ottoman sultans.

149

A much fuller description was given by Jean-Claude Flachat who spent fifteen years in Constantinople between 1740 and 1755. During that time he succeeded in striking up a friendship with the chief Black Eunuch, who in return for presents of mechanical dolls introduced Flachat into the Saray among workmen engaged in setting up some new French mirrors. Flachat wrote a very full description of the Saray, discussing it court by court and pavilion by pavilion, and describing several of the rooms in the Harem, especially those looking on to the gardens, where the women sat behind grilled bars and watched what going on outside without being seen. He also described the women's bath, with its large marble plunge-bath and marble basins; the women of lesser rank and the eunuchs, he wrote, had separate baths. At the end of his visit he was shown the *cafes* or " cage " where the sultan's sons who might aspire to the throne were kept in luxurious seclusion. It was, he says, like a strong citadel, with a high wall around it. There was a pretty garden and the princes had fine rooms and baths in a detached building; they were cared for by a large number of eunuchs. Sometimes he adds they were taken to other palaces—but always they were kept in seclusion.

No other visitors seem to have penetrated to the harem thereafter till it was made accessible after the Young Turk Revolution in 1912. Even Gurlitt, who was allowed to plan the second, third and fourth courts in 1910, was not permitted to enter the Harem and it was left a blank on his plan. The first person to investigate it at all thoroughly indeed was the American, Dr Miller, who first made a tour of some three hours, as a guest. At the first visit she was given coffee served on diamond studded trays, for the Saray was still maintained as a palace. Only with the final exile of the sultan in 1922 did it become a museum, parts being thrown open to the public soon after. Today nearly all of the Saray can be visited in the normal way except of course for the Pavilion of the Holy Mantle and, at the moment, the Harem— though there was a time, around 1930, when that also was open.

THE ARCHITECTURE OF THE TURKISH PERIOD

AS WE HAVE SEEN, Sultan Mehmet started on the process of rebuilding the city very soon after the conquest. The Old Saray, near the site of Bayazit's mosque, was built almost at once, the New Saray on Seraglio point was begun, and within a few years the Church of the Holy Apostles, where the Byzantine emperors were buried, was pulled down to make way for a new mosque, the Mosque of the Conqueror, Fatih, which was the first in a long line of major religious structures. However, it was by no means the first mosque to be built in the city, for there had apparently been one in Galata since the time of the Arab attack in the eighth century, and in mid-Byzantine times one had been set up at the expense of the state for the use of Moslem subjects of the Byzantine empire—it was burnt by the Latins in 1204. Churches had of course also been converted immediately after the Conquest, while a mosque perhaps already existed at Eyub, on the Golden Horn, since it was the reputed burial place of the standard bearer of the Prophet who had been killed during the first Arab attack on Constantinople in 673. It was certainly rebuilt immediately after the Conquest.

Work on the Mosque of Fatih, as it was usually called, began in 1463, to the designs of a Greek architect called Christodoulos. It was finished in 1469, much of the building material being reused from the church. We know very little about it, however, for it was seriously damaged by an earthquake in 1509 and again in 1765, and was entirely rebuilt around 1771 with a great central dome on four columns in a style which had then become classical for the great mosques, following the inspiration of Byzantine Agia Sophia. So far as can be gathered, it would seem

61. The fountain of Ahmet III, with Mosque of Sultan Ahmet in the background. Fountains, important as the source of communal water supply, were set up by numerous benefactors throughout the city.

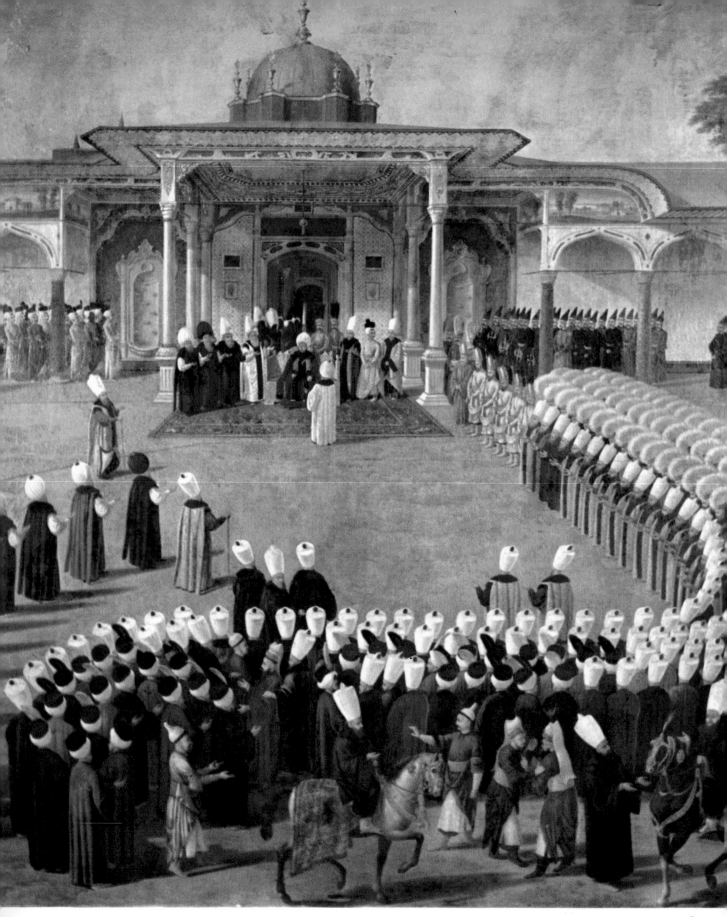

that the original building consisted of a rectangular chamber with a central dome, flanked on each of three sides by a row of five smaller domes over square chambers, while there appears to have been a semi-dome over the mihrab on the fourth side. It thus belonged to a type which had first been evolved by the Seljuks and was then taken over and further transformed by the Ottomans at Bursa. It was copied very closely in the Selimiye mosque at Konia.

Quite a number of variants on the plan are to be found in Istanbul; indeed nearly all the earlier mosques belong to it and their number serves to illustrate the activity both of the sultans and of their richer subjects as patrons of architecture. The most important examples are Mahmut Pasha Camii, built in 1464, Murat Pasha Camii, 1466, Daoud Pasha Camii, 1485, Atik Ali Pasha Camii, 1497 and Sultan Selim Camii, 1520. The first of these has two domes over the main area; the pendentives below them are probably later additions. There are three small domes along each side and four over the vestibule. Murat Pasha Camii also has two main domes, but only two at the sides, and five over the vestibule. Daoud Pasha Camii has a single central dome, two on each side, and five over the entrance, which is in the form of a projecting porch upheld on antique columns. Atik Ali Pasha Camii is closer to Fatih, for it has one central dome with a semi-dome over the mihrab. Sultan Selim's mosque represents an enlarged elaboration of the basic theme; the central dome is larger and there are nine small domes along each side; moreover it is preceded by a forecourt which must have been inspired by the atrium of Agia Sophia or one of the larger Byzantine edifices.

In his analysis of the mosque plans of Istanbul in which he distinguishes five principal types, Gabriel assigns to a different group a number of other mosques with a square central chamber, but without the flanking chambers at the sides, though there is usually a portico roofed with small domes on the side opposite the mihrab. The earliest example he cites is Firuz Aga Camii, built in 1491, but the type was popular for smaller mosques in the fifteenth century and was still followed not infrequently in the eighteenth and even in the nineteenth century, as, for example, in the large and rather impressive Nur Osmaniye Mosque close to the main entrance of the bazaar.

Gabriel's third group is distinct, for here the prototype is to be found not in Bursa or the Seljuk world, but at Byzantine Constantinople, in the great church of Agia Sophia. The essential of the plan is a greatly enlarged central area roofed by a single dome, extended into a rectangle by the addition of semi-domes at each end. The first to exploit the idea was apparently the architect Kemal ed-Din, who built the Mosque of Bayazit between 1501 and 1507; the idea was carried further by his successor, the great Sinan. Byzantine influence had only partially affected the Mosque of Bayazit, for there were no side or western galleries, as in Agia Sophia, but flanking aisles as in the previous group, each roofed by four domes. There was a great cloistered court at the west, as in earlier Byzantine buildings, and the idea was followed in most of the other large mosques of the group. The Mosque of Bayazit was however unique in the wide separation of its twin minarets, standing not in a line with the north and south aisles, like the towers of Western churches, but well outside the line of the main structure, at the very limits of the western façade.

The next mosque of the group, that of Sultan Suleyman (Pl. 48), was built between 1550 and 1557 by the architect Sinan. It is certainly the finest of the mosques in the city, though many would regard the great mosque at Edirne (Adrianople) as Sinan's masterpiece. Both are original, in that they have four minarets, but at Edirne they mark the four corners of the building, whereas in the Mosque of Sultan Suleyman there are two at the western end of the building itself and two rather smaller ones at the extremity of the court or atrium. The lighting is effective, for the drum

62. Painting from a manuscript in the Saray, showing a ceremony enacted during the religious festival of Bayram.

Fig. 12. The Architect Sinan. From *The Generall Historie of the Turkes* by R. Knolles, 1638. Photo: *British Museum*.

of the central dome is pierced by thirty-two windows and there are thirteen windows in each of the semi-domes below. However, it is the proportions of the interior that especially distinguish this building and best illustrate the genius of Sinan. The Mosque of Bayazit is, in contrast, somewhat clumsy; Fatih, as we know it today, lacking in balance; while the other great mosques, fine though they often are, lack something of the perfection and beauty of that of Sultan Suleyman. The tombs of the Sultan and of his consort Roxelana (Pl. 53. 54) to the east of the mosque are also noteworthy, both for their proportions and the lovely tiles of their interiors.

The same themes of large scale, a great central dome and semi-domes to east and west, were to be exploited in several other mosques, notably Kilic Ali Pasha Camii, built by Sinan in 1580, and the plan was also elaborated, to include additional semi-domes to north and south also. This idea was first adopted by Sinan in his Shah Zade Camii, begun in 1548; he called it a work of his apprenticeship. But it was developed by a number of later architects for example in the Valide Yeni Camii (1614), in Sultan Ahmet (Pl. 49. 51. 55. 58) (1608-14), and in the eighteenth century reconstruction of the Conqueror's mosque, Fatih. In the Iskele Camii at Scutari, built in 1547, the western semi-dome was omitted, so that the plan is virtually a trilobe. Of all these mosques the finest is probably that of Sultan Ahmet.

63. Miniature representing Sultan Mehmet II the Conqueror, also known as Sultan Fatih.

Inside the four piers that support the dome are perhaps over massive and heavy, but outside the way in which the semi-domes carry the line of the dome downwards is outstandingly lovely, while the six minarets, four taller ones at the corners of the building and two smaller ones at the extremity of the court, are again most effective, both with regard to their disposition and in their wonderfully thin, pencil-like proportions. The Valide Yeni Camii (Pl. 52) close to the head of the old bridge across the Golden Horn is also very fine and on a very large scale. It was begun for the wife of Ahmet I and completed by the mother of Mehmet IV some years later.

Sinan's experiments embraced various other types of plan and other new conceptions. In the mosque of Sultan Selim, on a large scale, the main dome was supported not on columns or piers, but on the four outside walls. Much smaller, but exquisite in its detail and especially famous for its tiles, was the mosque he built for Rustem Pasha, Suleyman's grand vizier, near the bridge over the Golden Horn. Here the body of the building is rectangular, with aisles on the north, south and west. It is one of the most lovely of the smaller mosques in the city, and the plan is one which Sinan favoured, for it is reproduced with little variation in several other mosques, notably Miramar Camii (Pl. 56), founded by Rustem Pasha's wife, Bali Pasha Camii, Ibrahim Pasha Camii, and Zal Mahmud Pasha Camii at Eyub, built in 1551. Most enchanting of all his work on a small scale, however, is the Sokollu Mehmet Camii, built in 1572, with a rectangular chamber roofed by a dome supported on six pendentives, preceded by a porch with seven small domes. Its proportions are perfect, its cloistered court, with chambers around for the guardians, a haven of peace, and its tile work inside even finer perhaps than that of Rustem Pasha Camii. It is disposed in one great panel framing the mihrab (Pl. 59), with smaller horizontal panels over each of the windows, and represents the very acme of the ceramic worker's art.

Essentially Turkish though it is, this mosque and others of its type ultimately represent variations on the Byzantine theme of dome over square, but there is little that is Byzantine in another group of which Piyale Pasha Camii is the most outstanding example. It dates from 1573, and has six domes, a sort of portico all round the outside, and a minaret at the middle of the façade, so that it looks rather like a ship with a central mast. Its patron, Piyale Pasha, became high-admiral under Suleyman the Magnificent and is said to have dictated the nature of the building himself, so it may be concluded that the similarity to a ship was intentional. The multiplicity of domes that we see here was not unusual in the seventeenth century, when variations of plan became very numerous. But even then the square chamber with a single large dome was preferred, and plans tended to remain conservative, though the carving and decoration became more ornate and more baroque as time went on, and painted adorments replaced tilework. At first the designs were delicate and the colouring restrained, but during the nineteenth century the designs became coarse and tasteless and the colouring garish. Though it is quite fine as a building, the Miramar Mosque (Pl. 56. 57) near the Adrianople gate has thus been redecorated with singular tastelessness; founded by the widow of Suleyman's grand vizier Rustem Pasha, its interior offers a striking contrast to that of Rustem Pasha's own mosque close to the head of the old bridge. Nevertheless, some of the later mosques were extremely attractive; one of the most notable is the Laleli Camii near Aksaray, built for Mustafa III between 1760 and 1763. Its decoration is wholly Rococo, and there is much Western influence with regard to detail though the general result is wholly Turkish.

A striking feature of all these mosques, large and small alike, is the excellence of the craftsmanship. The old Byzantine use of brick—nearly all the later churches were in that material—was entirely cast aside so far as the Ottoman religious build-

64. The Tophane fountain.

ings were concerned; all the mosques were built of neatly worked and carefully squared stones, usually a fine hard limestone, though marble was also used for more important details. Columns from Byzantine churches and occasionally capitals too were normally re-employed; otherwise the carving was in a truly Turkish style, in very low relief using floral and vegetable motifs in a fluent manner; it is much lighter, more delicate and more linear than Seljuk work but owes an indirect debt to the earlier art. The love of building in stone is perhaps also to be regarded as a debt due to Seljuk influence.

In secular work on the other hand brick was used a good deal, sometimes alone and sometimes in association with stone. The technique was however quite distinct from the Byzantine; the bricks were smaller, more like tiles, and the arrangement of a number of courses of brick, usually five, alternating with a number of stone ones, was given up in favour of one where one course of brick would alternate with one or two of stone; sometimes the bricks were also set vertically, between the stones.

Of the secular buildings of early date that survive the most important are the baths and the hans. The finest of the baths is one in two sections, one for men and one for women, which stands just to the south of Agia Sophia; it is now no longer in use as a bath, but has been kept in good repair. The technique of its construction is wholly Turkish and it is probably to be dated to the early sixteenth century. The plan however was no doubt derived from a Byzantine prototype, for the idea of the " Turkish bath " was, like so much else, taken over from the Byzantines with little change. There is a representation of a Byzantine bath on a famous Byzantine ivory depicting the Forty Martyrs at Berlin, and the close similarity that the Turkish examples bear to it is very obvious. Once these structures, with their brick domes pierced with small glass windows or steam vents, just as depicted on the ivory, were very numerous throughout the city. With modern plumbing they have tended to fall out of use and today few are still in operation and many have been destroyed.

Another type of structure which was very common throughout the whole Turkish period and which again must have been very similar to predecessors of the Byzantine period were the hans or caravanserais for the use of merchants and travellers. They were usually more or less square on plan, with an open court in the centre and chambers all around, usually on two floors, below depots or stables, above rooms for sleeping, opening on to wooden galleries. At first glance these hans appear somewhat forbidding from outside, especially as regards the lower storey; up above the walls were often revetted at an angle, so that each room had a view up the street from a small narrow window, as well as across it from a larger one. These old hans are rapidly tending to disappear with the modern passion for " improvements ", but happily some of the finest were recorded by de Beylie in a supplement to his book *L'Habitation Byzantine*.

If some idea as to the nature of the larger buildings of late Byzantine times can be gathered from those of early Turkish date, it may well be that the old houses of the city which in the nineteenth century were apparently well nigh identical with those of the sixteenth or seventeenth, also reproduce types that were first used in Byzantine times and then passed over to be developed by the Turks. Pococke described them in 1745; they were made of wooden frames, filled in with unburnt brick, exactly similar to those that survive in the poorer quarters of the city today. Houses of another type were similarly wooden framed, but instead of the mud brick they were made of boards. These probably represent a newer and more advanced type, introduced perhaps in the early eighteenth century. They were no doubt more comfortable and made the construction of larger rooms easier, but they were even more liable to destruction by fire than those of wood and mud brick. Even

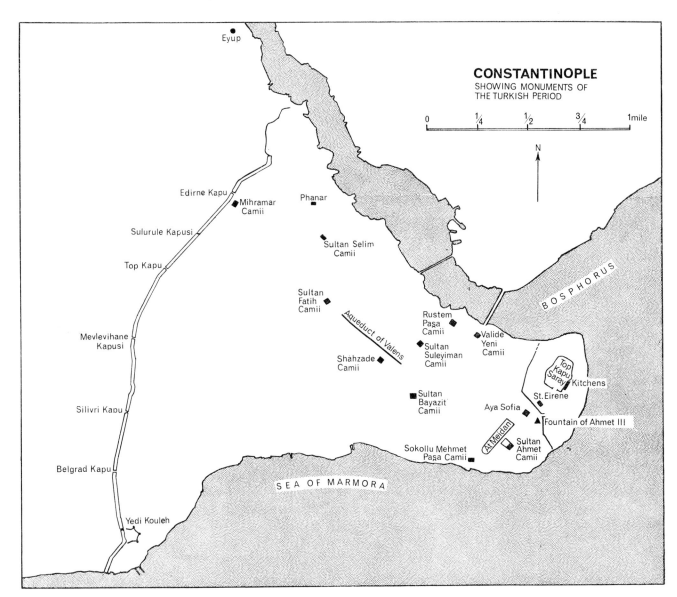

Map. Constantinople: showing monuments of the Turkish period.

so, if the larger houses of three or more storeys are omitted, the streets of Istanbul in the sixteenth century must have been very similar to those of the poorer quarters today. Even in the eighteenth century Pococke notes that they had a raised pavement at each side. He also states that they were clean, and in 1767 Lord Baltimore said the same. That is not always the case today, but perhaps the standards of the eighteenth century observers were less exacting than ours.

Another feature of Turkish times was the popularity of fountains (Pl. 60. 64). Once again the various sultans and a mass of individuals sought to benefit the town by erecting them, and they vary from small marble slabs simply decorated, with a single tap below and an inscription praising God and giving the name of the donor, to structures of considerable size with numerous sources of water, providing the passer-by not only with the possibility of obtaining water, but also of finding a shady seat or shelter from the rain. The most impressive of these larger structures is probably the fountain of Sultan Ahmet III (Pl. 61) which stands to the east of Agia Sophia, close to the main entrance to the first court of the Saray. It was finished in 1728. It is square on plan, with a basin on each side and at each corner a niche protected by a grille, through which goblets of pure fresh water were handed to passers by. The main façades are adorned with inscriptions in golden letters from the verses of the poet Wehbi, comparing the water to that of the fountains of Paradise. Its roof is surmounted by five small domes which give it a rather Russian appearance.

In addition to the public fountains in the streets, there is invariably one associated with each mosque, for the washing of hands and feet before prayer was a very essential part of the Moslem faith. Sometimes these take the form of fine great taps of brass in the lower part of the façade of the mosque itself, as at the side of the Valide Yeni Camii, but where the mosque has a forecourt there are usually quite elaborate circular or multi-side structures at the centre of it.

Once more the idea must have been derived from that of the phiale which occupied a similar position at the west end of the larger churches. But the regular use of the fountains for ritual washings was a Turkish addition; similar rules for cleanliness were never a dictum of Christian teaching, and the anchorites seem to have preferred dirtiness.

Last but not least among the products of Turkish architecture were the castles, and three important ones survive in or very near Constantinople, Rumeli and Anadolu Hissar on the Bosphorus and Yedi Koule or the fortress of the Seven Towers, built as a sort of adjunct to the Byzantine Golden Gate. There are others on either side of the Bosphorous where it debouches into the Black Sea, but both are in part Byzantine and in part Genoese.

Anadolu Hissar is the oldest, for it was built by Yilderim Bayazit as a stronghold about 1390 and enlarged by Mehmet Fatih in 1452 before he set siege to the Byzantine capital. The castle—together with that of Rumeli Hissar (Pl. 47) on the opposite shore—commanded the passage of the Bosphorus and was intended to aid in enforcing a blockade on the city in case of necessity, as well as to serve as a centre from which a tax might be levied on all shipping passing along the water way. Its position is not very impressive, for it stands close to the shore. Rumeli Hissar, on the other hand, occupies high ground, obviously chosen for its defensive possibilities, and there can be little doubt that its rather unusual plan was dictated by the lie of the land, in spite of a picturesque legend that it reproduced the form of the first letter of Mehmet's name in the kufic script. Nor can much faith be put in the legend that the Byzantine emperor gave Sultan Mehmet permission to build a pavilion on the European shore as long as it did not exceed the size of an ox-hide; Mehmet, as the story has it, cut the ox-hide into thin strips and used them to enclose a considerable area of land. There can be no doubt but that the reason for the construction of the two castles was aggressive. Yilderim Bayazit was called away before he could follow up his advantage; for Mehmet Fatih it was the first move in his plan of capturing the city. Rumeli Hissar was completed in less than four months—a remarkable achievement, typical of the Conqueror's insistence and energy, but in spite of the hurry the work was well done and the fortress is today outstandingly impressive. Its strength was however never to be put to the test, for once Constantinople had been taken the Turks remained in absolute control of the city's hinterland. It had also been admirably restored and is today one of the most impressive monuments of the Turkish period.

The fortress of the Seven Towers—two bastions of the Byzantine Golden Gate and two of the towers of the Byzantine city walls make up four of the seven—was built as a sort of citadel or keep just within the Golden Gate, and was equally protected from and equally accessible to both the open country on one side and the city on the other.

65. Gateway and old houses adjoining Agia Sophia.

160

It was constructed, except of course for the portion already existing, between
1457-58 first to serve as a treasury, though very soon it became a prison. Like the
castles on the Bosphorus it was never called on to withstand a siege, but as a prison
it attained considerable fame, for one sultan, several grand viziers and a whole
number of Western sea-captains, traders and even ambassadors were at one time
or another confined within its walls. The French ambassador was imprisoned there
in 1660 and 1661, the Venetian in 1668, the Russian chargé d'affaires soon after;
in 1670 one of the secretaries at the French embassy who was imprisoned there
succeeded in escaping. Some of these, and many others, left inscriptions on the
walls recording their sojourn in the prison; the longest of them was left by the
Venetian ambassador Domenico Franceschi who was arrested in December 1714
when Turkey and Venice declared war and, after a period of confinement in a
house, was moved to the Seven Towers in March 1715 with most of his staff. It
was still in use in the early nineteenth century when certain prisoners taken at the
battle of Navarino were incarcerated there; one Frenchman even wrote, " Vive la
République Française " on the walls in 1801. There was apparently a chapel there
for the use of Christian prisoners and in the seventeenth century Capucin monks
were permitted to hold services and conduct confessions.

The castle was more or less star-shaped, the longest side with four towers consisting of the city wall with the Golden Gate at its centre, while the four other sides
were Turkish, each built with an indentation at the centre so that the whole wall
could be easily commanded from the towers at either end. There was, however,
neither keep nor moat, so that from the first severe attacks can never have been
expected.

The masonry of the walls of the Turkish period is rather rough and poor in
contrast to the Byzantine—indeed in no other place in the city is it so easy to
contrast the methods of construction, not only of the Turkish and Byzantine periods,
but of the various phases and styles of both. When its towers were furnished with
tiled roofs it must have been attractive and impressive; today the interior is ill-kept
and dirty and has a very neglected appearance.

One last building—or series of buildings—may be mentioned, not so much because of any architectural distinction, but rather because it is one of the first places
that the casual visitor to Istanbul is likely to seek and because it still retains to a
considerable extent a wholly oriental atmosphere; it is the bazaar. It consists of a
central area, the bezestan, with a more extensive shopping area concentrated in a
mass of small streets arranged in a square around it. Bazaars of the same type, where
the various trades are collected together in particular areas, constitute an essential
part of most oriental towns, and it would seem that a bazaar quarter was one of
the things that were instituted in Constantinople immediately after the conquest.
Sultan Mehmet in any case built a bezestan in 1461 and the larger bazaar around
it was built by Sultan Suleyman. Both structures were in wood, and were destroyed
to make way for more durable ones of masonry under Mehmet IV in 1651 and
several following sultans. The buildings they set up were seriously damaged by an
earthquake in 1898, but repairs followed the same lines and to all intents and
purposes the visitor to the bazaar today may with no great effort of the imagination
recreate in his mind's eye the atmosphere of sixteenth century Turkey. The idea
of grouping the various trades together goes back to Byzantine times, but then the
booths where each group carried on its business were situated along particular streets,
many of them indeed along the line of the main street, the Mese. The idea of collect-
ing them in a centralized area under a single roof would seem to be distinct—it is
something that the Turks brought with them from the East and today the bazaar
quarter of Istanbul is the sole example of this wholly Eastern idea to be found on
European soil.

DURING THE LATTER days of the Byzantine empire, the Levant trade had been mainly in the hands of Venice although Genoa was at times a serious rival. It had been conducted in a series of large, well equipped vessels known as the Argosies, the name being taken from Ragusa, where most of them were built. The vessels had called regularly at London, Sandwich, Southampton, and Bordeaux as well as at many ports in the Mediterranean. With the rise of Turkish power however the trade had been interrupted not so much because of Turkish antagonism as because of the increase of the Barbary pirates whom Turkey did very little to control, and Venice had concentrated her efforts on guarding her most essential routes to Constantinople, Smyrna, Alexandretta and Alexandria and allowed the sea-borne trade with the West to lapse. The last of her Argosies actually reached London in 1500.

Though Venice was to maintain important trading colonies in the Eastern ports for many centuries to come and though the Republic remained the principal entrepôt in Europe, the interruption of the voyages of the Argosies farther west induced the traders of Bordeaux, London and Bristol to tackle the problem and early in the sixteenth century both France and England started to develop the Eastern trade for themselves. Soon after both countries had established missions in a number of Eastern cities and more especially in Constantinople, and from about the middle of the sixteenth century Venice, France and England were vying with one another to obtain most favoured terms from the sultan. Indeed as early as 1466 a merchant of Bristol, Robert Sturmy, had set out for the East, staking his whole fortune in a single vessel. It was, alas, destroyed in a storm, and a second vessel sent out by him eleven years later was sunk off Malta by the Genoese. But Sturmy's efforts had inspired others, and in 1510 a private syndicate for trading with Turkey was formed in London, while in 1536 capitulatory rights were granted to the French by Suleyman the Magnificent, and soon after one Anthony Jenkinson obtained permission from Sultan Suleyman for the English to trade anywhere in Turkey on the same conditions as the French. The Venetian Bailey, as their representative at Constantinople was called, seemed to be in the most favoured position.

At first the trade was mainly with Greece—wine seems to have played a large part in it—and the first trading representatives were established in Chios. But for some reason no advance was made by England for the next twenty years or so and it was not until the defeat of the Turkish fleet at Lepanto in 1571 that English merchants attempted to push farther into Turkey, and a certain William Clement was despatched in 1575 to Constantinople to procure from the sultan a safe conduct for William Harborne to follow him there as resident English representative at the Porte. Queen Elizabeth had agreed to his appointment as her " messenger, depute and agent, her true and undoubted orator ", but she refused to allow him the title of her ambassador—a typical half-measure which was to give rise to considerable complications in the future.

Harborne set out from London in 1578 and began to trade under the French flag. His gay friendly personality seems to have endeared him to the Turks, and within a few months he obtained from Sultan Murat III (1574-95) capitulatory rights for the English similar to those which had been granted to the French some forty years earlier. These capitulatory rights were important, for they virtually gave the foreign merchants extra-territorial status. Having set affairs on what he hoped was a sound footing, Harborne returned to England in 1580, but no sooner had he left than the French ambassador started to undermine the English position in the belief that it would decrease the value of the French trade, and on his representations the sultan revoked the grant of capitulations to the English saying that such favours could

67. The chimneys of the great kitchens of the Saray. There are ten double-domed chambers, and they constitute one of the most striking features in a distant view of the city. The kitchens were built by Sinan.

only be ceded to a fully accredited ambassador. Elizabeth refused to meet the expense of such an appointment, but on the merchants agreeing to deal with this aspect of the matter she agreed to grant the title and Harborne returned, a fully accredited ambassador, but paid by the merchants, whose organization soon after took to itself the title of the Turkey Company. But though it was to prosper considerably there were always difficulties with regard to paying the ambassador's salary and in this respect Harborne and his successors were constantly at a disadvantage vis-à-vis their French and Italian colleagues. In 1593 for example the English ambassador complained that the French received between 8,000 and 10,000 crowns of gold and the Italian 8,000 ducats whereas he only got 3,000 ducats. In addition their task was a difficult one, for they had to combine the posts of trade representative and diplomatic ambassador, whereas the Frenchman's duties were mainly diplomatic. It was not till as late as 1792 that the duties of the two posts were finally separated. The company however always enjoyed royal support and in 1605 was granted arms by James I.

When Harborne returned as ambassador he came equipped with suitable presents—a wonderful clock, some dogs and other treasures. The clock was much appreciated, for the Turks always enjoyed mechanical devices and it was very elaborate, representing a silver mine with people at work digging and drawing water, while on the other side men were shown hunting with dogs and shepherds with their flocks; it was made of silver and precious stones and was intrinsically of very considerable value. The dogs were also well received, for the sultan was a collector of sporting dogs which he kept in a huge imperial kennel in the Top Kapu Saray. Indeed several travellers commented on the value set on dogs, and the Frenchman Bellon was surprised to find that dogs were fed even if they had no particular masters; they were not however permitted to enter the houses.

On this occasion Harborne was well prepared, but the problem of presents was one which caused repeated difficulties, for people at home were very loath to agree to the necessary expenditure or even to realize that value was set on such things in the East. Sandys, who went to Turkey in 1610, wrote with considerable annoyance about the custom, and both the Crown and the Turkey Company totally refused to accept the reports sent home by the ambassadors as to the necessity of expenditure on such things. But the ambassadors were not exaggerating when they ranked the power to offer a fine gift as one of their most valuable assets, for the sultan gauged the importance and goodwill of the donor by the rarity and value of his presents.

Although the sultan was delighted with the clock which Harborne took, he was soon ready for something more, and it was hard to persuade the queen to follow up the advantage which had been acquired. Her attitude placed Barton, Harborne's successor, in a difficult predicament. His personal prestige depended to a considerable extent upon his ability to offer the sultan a token of regard no less magnificent than the most handsome object presented by his predecessor. But in London financial difficulties rendered an immediate outlay inconvenient, regardless of whether its cost was born by the crown or the Company. As a result Barton's entreaties were disregarded and either inadequate presents were sent out or even worse, the complete absence of any present placed him at a real disadvantage.

Barton's requests for presents make pitiful reading. As early as 1592 we find him writing home begging for a present for " the Grand Signior and Beshaw (to the value of £ 2500) ", and entreating for its early despatch " lest (the English) at the instigation of their opponents lose their privileges in the Levant seas." He chafed against the inadequacy of the gift that had arrived " a thing—which Your Highness pardon be it spoken—more becoming merchants than so mighty a prince as Her Majestie, for what delight has the Grand Signior in cloth, who never weareth

68. Gateway of the first court of the Saray.
The Saray was divided into four courts; the first was accessible to all, but after that access became progressively more difficult.

167

any, being so mightie an Emperor and yet in the said present is nothing but quarters of pieces of cloth, and a little gilt plate, and which is no small harm and consideration, the cloth cut in remnants, which coming as from Her Majestie, it cannot be imagined a thing done by her or by her order ...   I humbly require your Lordship ... to procure some rare thing for the Grand Signior ... some rare clock, though small, or other fine device, in silver gilt ...   Mr Harborne brought a clock worth all the rest of the presents ... it were good reason that the present were more royall than that of Mr Harborne."

Little notice was taken of his plea, although in the following year, when returning to Turkey from leave, he was allowed to bring Murat III " twelve goodly pieces of plate, thirty-six garments of cloth in all colours, twenty garments of cloth of gold, ten garments of satin, six pieces of fine Holland and certain other things of value ". In addition he carried a present for the Sultana. It consisted of " a jewel of Her Majestie's picture, set with some rubies and diamonds, three great pieces of gilt plate, ten garments of cloth of gold, a very fine case of glass bottles, silver and gilt, with two pieces of fine Holland."   In 1599 this elicited an exquisite acknowledgement, the Sultana assuring the queen that " I send your Majestie so honourable and sweet a salutation of peace that all the flocke of Nightingales with their melody cannot attain to ye like, much less this simple letter of mine. The singular love which we have conceived one towards the other is like a garden of pleasant birds: and the Lord God vouchsafe to save and keep you, and send your Majestie an happy end, both in this world and the world to come."   The letter was accompanied by a gift, which the Company valued at £ 240.   It consisted of

" first two garments of cloth of silver, might cost	£ 68
more one girdle of cloth of silver, might cost	£ 10
more two handkerchiefs wrought with massy gold	£ 22
more, one shell of gold which recovered the seal of her letter	£ 20
to Your Majestie upon which was set all small sparks of dyamondes	
and all small sparkes of rubies, might be worth	£ 120

The ball had now been set rolling in earnest, and it could not be allowed to rest. The Company advised the queen that " in return for this present " it had despatched " a watche rechelye furnished " and " craved Her Majesty's answer (if your Honour so think meete) to the Sultana herself". However, the queen seems to have tired of the game. Two years later Barton was again writing to beg " Her highness make some princely resolution to ease the burden and charge of the merchants ... by adjoining of her princely beningnity to the Sultan his pencion a clock in the form of a cock which I hear Her Highness hath in one of her palaces, or some other princely gift in room thereof, and to remember the Old Empress with some princely token which may both show Her Highnes's bountifulness and conserve her friendship for future good occasion."

Barton alas failed to secure the clock he coveted for the Sultan, and he never ceased regretting his inability to present him with one, for in the sixteenth no less than in the seventeenth and eighteenth centuries the Turks set great store on English clocks. Indeed, they were so highly esteemed in the Seraglio that, according to a report which the Governor of Corfu despatched in 1612 to the Doge and Senate of Venice, special servants were entrusted with handling them. The governor describes the arrival in his castle of a man in Turkish dress, who claimed to have escaped from the Seraglio. He affirmed that his " father is a Spaniard from Madrid, his mother from Palermo. He is a nephew of the Admiral of the Neapolitan Squadron—the Marquis of Santa Cruz ...   About four years ago, he ... was captured off Majorca by three Barbary pirates manned by Turks and English ...   Within

69. Miniature from a manuscript in the Saray library depicting a firework display. Such displays were very popular during Turkish times and have been described by numerous Western visitors.

fifteen days he was made a Turk by order of the Grand Signior ... and taken to lodge in the Sultan's Seraglio, and there he stayed two years and eight months ... He was educated in the Seraglio by Turkish masters and had the duty of bringing the clock to the Sultan when he wanted to know what time it was."

English timepieces retained their popularity in Turkey well into the nineteenth century. In 1682 the sums which the Company's agents expended on buying clocks and watches as presents for Turkish notables reached such a serious proportion that the London headquarters felt obliged to remonstrate with John North, their agent in Smyrna and they wrote telling him that " we observe by our accounts ... that many clocks and watches are presented to great men and charged to us at excessive rates, which we would have forborne as much as may be ". As late as 1797, Dallaway was still writing from Constantinople that " English watches, prepared for the Levant market, are more in demand than those of other Frank nations, and are one of the finest articles of luxury that a Turk purchases or changes if he has money to spare."

Although Barton was unable to add to the sultan's collection of watches and mechanical contrivances, his successor Lello fared so well that it rather looks as though he reaped where Barton had laboriously sown. There seems no other reason to account for the truly magnificent present that was despatched to the Sultan during Lello's ambassadorship. It took the form of a full-sized organ which could either be played in the ordinary way or else be set so that it worked mechanically. Furthermore it was embellished with some fascinating mechanical devices, and the whole was surmounted by a clock with chiming bells. In its final form it was a novelty even in England; an ordinary organ would no doubt have come as an equal surprise to the Turks who were unacquainted with this instrument. Its maker, Dallam, was sent out with it to set it up, and he has left us a detailed account of his instrument and a vivid description of his journey to Constantinople and his experiences there.

Before embarking for Constantinople Dallam assembled the organ at Whitehall, and the queen came personally to inspect it. She pronounced herself well satisfied. Thereupon Dallam dismantled the instrument and proceeded to pack it up and embark with it for Constantinople in one of the Company's vessels. He was accompanied by his mate " Harvie, who was an engineer, Mr Reginald Buckett the paynter, and Nyghell Watson, the joiner." They reached Constantinople safely in September 1599, and were installed in the embassy. Lello had been anxiously awaiting their arrival, and it must have been a relief to him to be able to report that " the Signior is so great content as seldom hath been seene that he hath made soe greate a demonstration of the pleasure as by the same he showed to have conveyed. The day before he brought out all his women supposing the ship (bearing Dallam and the organ) should enter, which by reason of a contrary wynde did not, the next day he came again in person with all his courte to a house of pleasure upon the water side, purposely to see the shippe at her salutation made with ordinance and the sounde of our English trumpettes which gave him so greate contente as those about him say they have not seen him so delighted in any Christian prince's strength and defence."

The organ was carefully unloaded and reassembled in the embassy so that Dallam might see whether it had been damaged in any way on the journey. A number of repairs were required, and when these had been completed the leading notables were invited to the embassy to inspect the instrument. Their reaction was not encouraging and London was disappointed by Lello's report that " though at first (the organ) was thought of small esteem, yet it was generally considered that the Sultan would be pleased with it if any of his people can maintayne the use thereof."

After this a dragoman was attached to Dallam, " a Turke but a Cornishman

70. The Baghdad kiosk.
The Saray was not a palace in the Western sense,
but consisted of a number
of more or less isolated structures.
The Baghdad pavilion is one
of the best known of these
buildings.

171

borne ", and the Englishmen anxiously started on the work of reassembling the instrument in the Saray. The rest of the story is so interesting and vivid that it may best be told in Dallam's words. " When I had sett al my worke in good order ", he wrote, " the jemyglanes which kepte that house espied the Grand Sinyor cominge upon the water in his goulden Chieke (caique) or boate, for he cam that morning six miles by water; whear I stoode I saw when he sett foote on the shore.

" Then the jemyglanes tould me that I muste avoyd the house, for the Grand Sinyor would be there presently. It was almost halfe a myle betwyxte the water and that house; but the Grand Sinyor, haveinge a desire to see his presente, came thether wythe marvalus greate speede. I and my company that was with me, beinge put forthe, and the Dore locked after us. I hard another Dore open, and upon a sodon a wonderfull noyes of people; for a little space it should seme that at the Grand Sinyore's coming into the house the dore which I hard opene did sett at libertie four hundrethe persons which weare locked up all the time of the Grand Sinyore's absence, and just at his coming in theye weare sett at libertie, and at the firste sighte of the presente, with great admyration did make a wonderinge noyes.

" The Grand Sinyor, beinge seated in this Chair of estate, commanded silence. All beine quiett, and no noyes at all, the present began to salute the Grand Sinyor; for when I lefte it I did alow a quarter of an hour for his cominge thether. Firste the clocke strouke 22; than the chime of sixteen bels went of, and played a songe of 4 partes. That being done, two personagis which stood upon two corners of the second storie, houldinge two silver trumpetes in there handes, did lifte them to thiere heades, and sounded a tantarra. Then the muzicke went of, and the orgon played a song of 5 partes twyse over. In the tope of the organ, being 16 foute hie, did stande a holly bushe full of blackbirds and thrushis, which at the end of the musick did singe and shake their wynges. Divers other motions thare was which the Grand Sinyor wondered at. Then the Grand Sinyor asked the Coppagawe yf it would ever doo the lyke againe. He answered that it would doo the lyke againe at the next houre. Cothe he: I will se that. In the meane time, the Coppagaw, being a wyse man, and doubted whether I hade so appoynted it or no, for he knew that it would doo of it selfe but 4 times in 24 houres, so he cam unto me, for I did stand under the house sid, wheare I myghte heare the organ goo, and he asked me yf it would goo againe at the end of the nexte houre; but I tould him that it would not, for I did thinke the Grand Sinyor would not have stayed so longe by it; but yf it would please him, that when the clocke had strouke he would tuche a little pin with his finger, which before I had shewed him, and it would goo at any time. Than he sayde that he would be as good as his worde to the Grand Sinyor. When the clocke had strouke 23, he tuched the pinn, and it did lyke as it did before. Than the Grand Sinyor saied it was good. He satt verrie neare unto it, ryghte before the Keaes wheare a man should playe on it by hande. He asked whye those keaes did move when the organ wente and nothinge did tuche them. He tould him that by those thinges it mighte be played on at any time. Than the Grand Sinyor asked him yf he did know any man that could playe on it. He sayd no, but he that came with it hether, and he is heare without the dore. Fetche him hether, cothe the Grande Sinyor, and lett me se how he dothe it. Than the Coppagaw opened the Dore, which I went out at, for I stoode neare unto it. He came and touke me by the hande, smylinge upon me; bit I bid my drugaman aske him what I should bow or whiether I should goo. He answered that it was the Grand Sinyor's pleasur that I should lett him se me playe on the orgon. So I went with him. When I came within the Dore, that which I did se was verrie wonderfull unto me. I cam in directly upon the Grand Sinyore's ryghte hande, some 16 passis from him, but he would not turne his head to louke upon me. He satt in greate state, yeat the sighte of him was nothinge in Comparison of the traine that stood behinde him, the sighte whearof did make me almoste to thinke that I was in another worlde. The Grand Sinyor satt still, behouldinge the presente which was befor him, and I stood daslinge my eyes with loukinge upon his people that stood behind him, the which was four hundrethe persons in number. Two hundrethe of them weare his princepall padgis, the youngest of them 16 years of age, som 20, and some 30. They were apparled in ritche clothe of goulde made in gowns to the mydlegge; upon their heads little caps of clothe of goulde, and some clothe of Tissue; great peecis of silke abowte theire wastes instead of girdls; upon their leges Cordivan buskins, reede. Their heades wear all shaven, savinge that behinde Their ears did hange a locke of hare like a squirrel's taile; their beardes shaven, all savinge their uper lips. Those 200 weare all verrie proper men, and Christians borne.

" The thirde hundrethe weare Dum men, that could nether heare nor speake, and they weare likewyse in gouns of riche Clothe of gould and Cordivan buskins; bute theire Caps weare of violett velvett, the croune of them made like a lether bottell, the brims devided into five picked corners. Some of them had haukes in their fistes.

" The fourthe hundrethe weare all dwarffs, bige-bodied men, but verrie low of statue. Everie Dwarfe did weare a simmeterrie by his side, and they weare also apareled in gowns of Clothe of gould ...

" When I had stode almost one quarter of an houre behouldinge this wonder full sighte, I harde the Grande Sinyore speake unto the Coppagaw who stood near unto him. Than the Coppagaw cam unto me, and toukemy cloake from aboute me, and laye it Doune upon the Carpites, and bid me go and playe on the organ; but I refused to do so, because the Grand Sinyor satt so neare the place wheare I should playe that I could not com at it. But i muste needes turne my backe Towardes him and touche his kne with my britchis, which no man, in paine of deathe, myghte dow, savings only the Coppagaw. So he smiled and lett me stand a little. Than the Grand Sinyor spoke againe, and the Coppagaw with a merrie countenance, bid me go with a good curridge, and thrust me on. When I cam verrie neare the Grand Sinyor, I bowed my head as low as my kne, not moving my cape, and turned my backe righte towardes him, and touched his kne with my britchis.

" He satt in a verrie ritche Chaire of estate, upon his thumbe a ringe with a diamon in it halfe an inche square, a faire simeterie by his side, a bow, and a quiver of Arros.

" He satt so righte behinde me that he could not se what I did; tharfore he stood up, and his Coppagaw removed his Chaire to one side, wher he myghte se my handes; but, in his rising from his chaire, he gave me a thruste forwardes, which he could not otherwyse dow, he satt so neare me; but I thought he had been drawinge his sorde to cut my heade.

" I stood thar playinge suche thinge as I coulde untill the cloke strouke, and than I boued my heade as low as I coulde, and wente from him with my back towardes him. As I was taking my cloake, the Coppagaw came unto me and bid me stand still and let my cloake lye; when I had stood a little whyle, the Coppagaw bid me goo and cover the Keaes of the organ; then I wente close to the Grand Sinyor againe, and bowed myselfe, and then I went backewardes to my Cloake. When the Company saw me do so theye seemed glad and laughed. Then I saw the Grand Sinyor put his hande behind him full of goulde, which the Coppegaw receved, and broughte unto me fourtie and five peecis of goulde called Chickers (sequins), and than was I put out againe wheare I came in beinge not a little joyfull of my good suckcess."

The Sultan endeavoured to persuade Dallam to stay on in Turkey, and on the latter's refusal, he tried to detain him, but eventually Dallam succeeded in getting away. He sailed from Constantinople in November 1599, reaching Dover in the following March, thus ending not the least strange or adventurous undertaking of the Elizabethan age.

With the turn of the century, and the great queen's death, England lost some of her exuberant inventiveness, and the official gifts despatched to the Porte reflect this loss in their lack of originality. However the custom of sending presents to the Sultan persisted well into the nineteenth century, as did the reluctance of those at home to provide adequate gifts, and in 1741 we find the ambassador, Fawkener, demanding some spectacular gift as insistently as Barton had done a century and a half earlier. He too tried to goad London into sending something suitable by reporting that, at a recent ceremony the Persian gift " consisted of seven elephants and a quantity of fine jewels. There were several rings of value, amongst which one stone computed at £ 20,000. The Muscovite ambassador's present consisted of fine furs, than which there is nothing more acceptable here and of china ware, some pieces of Lyons brocade and parcels of tea and rhubarb. The French ambassador's present consisted chiefly of Goblins carpets and Lyons stuffs ". Nevertheless, London remained impervious and it would seem that the best that the ambassador could obtain were a few wholly conventional and unimaginative gifts, the banal character of which in no way compensated for the infrequency of their presentation.

In addition to the difficulty of coaxing adequate presents out of the authorities at home the British representatives were beset by another problem which no doubt bothered their other European colleagues equally—namely the mistrust with which they were often regarded by the Turks. Not being Moslems and not knowing the language they inevitably lived in a very restricted society, for as unbelievers they were looked down on. Few Turks would consent to serve them and as a result they were forced to depend on Levantines or Italian renegades, men who were in constant danger of arrest or enslavement by the Turks and who were thus out to feather their own nests at every opportunity, resorting to prevarication and intrigue in order to do so. The French ambassador in the seventeenth century sought to solve the problem by sending home a batch of youths to train as interpreters, but the scheme proved a failure. No greater success greeted the despatch in 1692 of a batch of Greek youths for training at Oxford, for the boys were extremely reluctant to return to their native land, and proposals for further efforts in this direction were turned down by the Turkey Company. The appointment of an Englishman who knew Turkish as interpreter in 1647 proved more successful, and thereafter the post proved to be almost as regular as that of chaplain. There were chaplains associated with all the foreign missions, and the Turks never objected to their presence for the religious minorities within their realm were always allowed freedom of worship. Many of the chaplains were scholars of repute, and we are indebted to them not only for much of our knowledge of Turkey at the time but also for the assembling of important collections of manuscripts, both Greek and Oriental.

Though at first the majority of Westerners who went to Turkey were merchants or official representatives connected with the missions, it was not long before others started to visit the country through curiosity and for the sheer delight of travel. Fynes Morrison, who set out for Turkey about 1597, was not only intrigued by Turkey's political ascendency but also by her cooking; Blount, who went there around 1630, wanted " to see what lay behind the forbidding façade of catamites dressed in scarlet velvet and holding gilt scimitars "; in 1608 Coryate visited Constantinople in the course of a journey on foot to India; in 1661 a Quaker called John went there with the express purpose of converting the Sultan and was almost at once installed in a mad-house; it took the ambassador six months of hard work to get him out. Other travellers, though perhaps less tiresome, nevertheless sometimes proved something of an ordeal to the ambassadors, though with the eccentrics there were mingled men of learning like John Greaves who went to Turkey in 1638 to collect manuscripts and on his return published a Turkish grammar written in Latin as well as two books of travel about the country and a description of the Saray. He was to be followed by quite a number of other learned travellers in the

71. The Kiosk of Mustapha Pasha. Like the Baghdad Kiosk, this formed a part of the Saray. Such pavillions were added by many of the Sultans and named after themselves or their ministers.

174

later seventeenth or early eighteenth century, such as Dr Covell, later Chancellor of Cambridge, George Wheeler and Jacques Spon who in addition to making a renowned archaeological journey in Greece, also gathered together much interesting information about Constantinople.

The first history of the Turks was compiled by Richard Knollys in 1603; it was followed by a fuller and more authoritative one by the Fleming, Paul Rycaut, published in 1668, which was for long regarded as a standard work, and writings on the country in English, French and German thereafter became quite numerous. Few however succeeded in acquiring as intimate a knowledge of the country and its customs as Lady Mary Wortley Montague, whose husband was appointed British ambassador there in 1716. Though their stay was comparatively brief she penetrated into the Saray and into the Harem of the grand vizier and learnt much about the home life of Turkish women; more important she observed that the Turks were in the habit of vaccinating their children with cow pox against the dreaded disease of smallpox and decided to have her own son treated. She found out the nature of the vaccine and on her return to London she set out to persuade people to let her vaccinate them also, and though many treated her with derision her discovery was welcomed with approval in the Gentleman's Magazine for 1724, and was eventually perfected into the system of vaccination we know today.

As one looks back it is surprising how readily people were prepared to make the journey to Turkey, which was at best long and arduous and at worst dangerous. When Harborne went there in 1578 he had travelled overland, going first to Poland. There he donned Turkish costume, and joined the caravan of the Turkish ambassador to Poland, who was returning home. They went by way of Moldavia, Wallachia and Bulgaria, the whole journey taking some three months and proving both hazardous and expensive. Had the Argosies still been in service he would no doubt have gone by sea—or he might have travelled overland to Venice and gone on a Venetian vessel from there, for Venice was still the main centre of the Levant trade in Europe. A few other travellers, notably those in search of information, also followed the land route, but when once a more or less regular service had been established by the Turkey Company, most travellers, and certainly all the Company's officials, made the journey by sea.

The sea journey, though more comfortable, also had its hazards, for from about 1580 Algiers had become a centre of renegades and pirates, and there was always danger of an attack by sea, for their boats were fast and well armed and their reputation for daring considerable. So great was the menace, indeed, that from about 1590 it had proved necessary for the merchant ships to go in convoys, often of as many as twenty at a time. The number seems to have increased as time went on, for the Turks did little to curb the power of Algiers which was virtually a free and independent state, though nominally under Turkish control. When Blount sailed from Gallipoli in the 1630s a convoy numbering eighty-five vessels was assembled, many of them of as much as 500 tons. Even so, and in spite of protective action by the navies, the pirates continued to prove a menace, raiding as far afield as Ushant and even it would seem as far west as Plymouth, for in the first half of the seventeenth century there were continued reports of Turkish pirates threatening shipping in the Channel. The Moslem pirates were it seems often joined by renegade Englishmen, Latins and Dutch, and in the archives of Venice and Genoa there are a number of complaints of the actions of these men; the names of some of them, notably a certain Captain Ward, are recorded. In addition to the danger from pirates was that of enemy action, especially around 1700 when England and France were at war.

In spite of all the difficulties and dangers the English ships proved reliable and began to attract the cream of the passenger traffic as early as about 1600—so much so that the Italians sought to entice English crews and vessels into their service.

72. Miniature from a manuscript known as the Surnama of Murad III.

177

Taken as a whole the travellers from the West tended to like and appreciate Turkey, and the earlier visitors took a great interest in the country and its way of life; even the most jaundiced of visitors found much to admire. The pomp and circumstance of the court was remarked on with wonder by all, and many of those who were admitted to audience by the sultan have left descriptions of their reception. Either a Sunday or a Tuesday was the day chosen for an ambassador to be presented to the sultan. According to Withers, at the appointed time, " the vizir sendeth the Chiaush Bashaw, with many of his Chiaushes on horse-bak, to accompany the Ambassador: who, being come to the Divan, is set face to face, close before the chief Vizir, upon a stool covered with cloth of gold. Having for a while complimented and used some friendly discourse together, the Bashaw commandeth that dinner be brought: the which is done after the same manner as upon other Divan days; only the round plate, on which the meat is set, is of silver, and the victuals are more delicate and in greater abundance ... They having dined, the Vizir entertaineth the Ambassadour with some discourse, until such time as the Ambassadour's followers have dined also, who I can say are fed after a very mean fashion; and then the Ambassadour, together with his own attendants, retire themselves into a certain place near the King's gate: where he must stay till such time as all the orders of the Divan (Council) have had audience with the King, who being dismissed do all depart, the Bashaws excepted, who for the Grand Signior's honour are to stay, and attend in the room upon his Majesty." Meanwhile the Ambassador's present had been displayed to the people and then carried into the second court and placed before the Sultan. The Ambassador was in his turn presented with a gift of vests from the Sultan and, robed in one, he was then conducted to the second court. Winchelsea reported that " within, it was paved with white marble, where attended some forty eunuchs all clothed in divers colours of silke and satin vests; coming near ye presence door, we made a pause just unto ye porch (where was a pleasant fountain of water) and trod very softly so as not to disturb with ye least motion that Great Majestie, where was so profounde a silence that nothing was heard, more than ye murmurings of ye fountains. Just at ye entrance hung a ball of gould studded with diamonds and precious stones and above it chaines of rich pearle. The chamber where ye Grand Signior set was covered with carpets and crimson velvet and embroidered with gold wire, and so likewise was an open gallery before ye entrance, through which we first passed, and many of them set with small seede pearles." The Ambassador and his staff were then permitted to kiss the Sultan's sleeve, whereupon the ambassador would present his letters of credence, the Dragoman proceed to explain the Ambassador's mission, and the audience draw to an end.

This ceremonial lost none of its elaboration or magnificence with the passing of the seventeenth century. If anything it gained in elegance during the first half of the eighteenth, when adoration of the tulip kindled a radiance that was reflected in the life of the capital. During this period, which has gone down in Ottoman history as the Tulip Age, or the Lâle Devri, Turkish poets broke free from Persian tutelage, and Turkish taste and manners reached their highest refinement. The imperial display, whilst still retaining its earlier splendour and pomp, acquired an additional polish, and every move in the elaborate ceremonial now added another sparkle to the customary magnificence. The whole ritual evolved to a cadence that seemed attuned to the slow and delectable stages that mark the exquisite unfurling of a tulip bud.

It was customary for the Sultan to present ambassadors from minor powers with vests which were as valuable as those destined for the envoys of important states; yet, according to Withers, these less important personalities did not come " to the Divan in that pomp, neither are they feasted as the others are, but go privately."

73. The Pavilion of the Holy Mantle in the Saray. When the Ottoman Sultan Selim conquered Egypt in 1517 he brought back the garments of the Prophet which were preserved there and installed them in this pavilion in the Saray.

Fig. 13. The Aga of the Janissaries. From *Pérégrination Faites en Turquie* by Nicolay, 1567. Photo: *British Museum.*

North disclosed the reason for the difference by relating that several " petit mon-archies " send ambassadors occasionally, and they are entertained as such, though their business is little else but selling slaves. He reported that a Mingrelian am-bassador had recently been to Constantinople with a great retinue of two hundred; but he sold them all one after another, and his secretary last; after this his embassy was at an end, and he returned home.

Both in Constantinople and in Adrianople great pageantry marked the Sultan's ceremonial Bairam visits to the mosque. Until the dissolution of the Janissary Corps this spectacle was considered the finest sight in Europe. Every traveller of note endeavoured to see the march past at some time or other. The procession included every high officer of the realm and detachments from every regiment of the Sultan's bodyguard. The splendour of the uniforms, the intricacy and variety of the turbans and the magnificent colours and furs of the robes left the onlookers

74. Entrance to the throne room (Arz Odassi) in the Saray. It was here that ambassadors from the West were received by the sultans with the greatest pomp.

181

spellbound. The greatest thrill was provided by the beplumed Janissaries, for each of the feathers in their turbans indicated a victim killed in battle. The Sultan's place was towards the middle of the procession where he appeared surrounded by the highest officials of the realm and the personnel of his immediate entourage, all wearing resplendent robes. The crowd, which was always immense, contributed to the splendour of the scene by the variety and beauty of its dress. Nothing as elaborate could be seen in Europe. Yet this extraordinary pageant even surpassed its own magnificence and beauty on the occasion of the celebrations organized at Adrianople in May 1675 to mark the circumcision of the heir to the throne, Mustafa Effendi, the eldest son of Mehmet IV.

Covell, Cook and Dudley North all accompanied their Ambassador, Sir John Finch, to Adrianople to witness the scene. They found the streets lined with people, the women ranged on one side, and the men on the other. Covell relates that " the women of quality came coached, and the chief had stands, or shops, or chambers, on purpose provided ". Most people taking part in the procession were " excellently horsed ... Most were in rich furre vests, the outside cloth ... some the outside silk, satin, velvet, cloth of gold and silver. The horse-trappings extream rich; the buttock cloth embroyder'd with gold, silver, pearles, etc., at the meanest wrought with silk; the saddles in like manner; the stirrups, many of silver, some guilded; the bridles plated with gold, or silver and bars; and many set with good stones and pearl, especially the peak on the forehead, and at each ear."

The Janissaries marched first; they were followed by the Vizier's pages, dressed " in crimson velvet floured Delaman's ... with very large silver gilt embost girdles ". The Armourers came next wearing green caps " edged with gold or silver ... victuallers with red caps like Janizares, only the flap stands higher above the head pieces ". They were succeeded by the judges, men of law and their clerks all dressed in " lawyers' gowns, without a cape, short sleevs, and of severall colours and stuffs, richer or baser according to their ability, silk, satin etc. all fur'd ... Then followed the Vizir's Guards in green vest and caps; their vest was closed together with monstrous great buttons and tassels." Finally the Mufti appeared " in a white cloth vest and ermine furre; on the right hand the Vizir in a white satin sable furr'd vest; on his left hand the Mosaif, the Favourite, in a green sattin sable vest."

The procession of dignitaries was broken up and enlivened by the inclusion of some curious decorations. Covell's description is immensely intriguing: " there were caryed 40 Naculs ", he wrote, " 20 on a side, which are devices made upon a large pole in forme of a pyramid or cone (rather) of wire, painted paper, beggar batten (such as we trim hobby horses withall) and flowrs and fruit of wax work and painted paper etc. It was continued in quite another kind of frolick upon a large mast of a ship; it was 27 yards long, and the lower part was 5 or 6 yards diameter; the ornaments of it were much like this here described, only between every sphere were large square cubes furnisht out with the same fancyes, especially wax work. Now you will say: How could this colussus be moved? At the bottom were eight or ten large bars of wood fastned parallell (as the strings or bars of a sedane) and betweene these were harnest about 100 slaves; and before it (upon these bars) stood (or road) a master of a gallet, who managed the Slaves, they resting and reering it up and down at the noyse of his whistle. Now, for fear it should overset and topple down, there were four long pikes of wood fasten'd about half way up, and as many ropes came from the top, by which other slaves (taking hold of the lower end) guided the top and kept it always right up. To let these walking timber-trees pass by the streets of the city many houses were untiled, and some in part pul'd down."

It was only after these objects had passed that the young prince appeared. He was " surrounded on every side, before and behind, with a brave troop of Cherbugées

75. Miniature from a manuscript in the Saray library. **Festivities on the water.** These vivid views of contemporary events are characteristic of Turkish art of the sixteenth and seventeenth centuries.

(Collonels), all on foot, in their caps and feathers. The Prince himself was mounted upon a lovely beast, which was, in a manner, nothing but jewels, pearls, gold and silver from head to tayle, and led by two mighty, lusty Cherbugées richly clad, on each side one; two more in like manner went fanning him all the way and shadowing him (for it was about ten oclock, and a most excessive hot day). They have large fans made here on purpose for great personages of bustards' feathers, contrived from one and a half to two or three foot wide... (The Prince) had a plain Turbant on, like a common Turk, and a black single feather on the left side, at the bottom of which was a diamond of about 40 (or as they say 43) carats, sent home from the King of Persia of old to a young prince of this Empire. He had likewise two others, very large, on each side his vest, to clasp it before, and instead of buttons were large pearls set al down the edge. His Delamon under his vest was cover'd all before (instead of buttons and loops) with broaches of rubyes and emeralds; his vest was a white cloth of silver sabled; his delamon purple cloth of gold." The procession closed with a band consisting of ten pipers, six drummers, four trumpetters, two kettledrums, and four tamburs or tympanums, " like sives cover'd with parchment at bottome " explains Covell.

The splendour and orderliness of these official celebrations deeply impressed the foreigners who were present, and the reports they sent home contributed in no small measure to maintaining the Sultan's prestige long after his power had in fact passed its heyday.

Yet there were occasions when the attitude of the Turkish crowd differed completely from that of the spectators watching a ceremonial procession — this at the very time when the sultans were in truth omnipotent in their own land and when their festivities unrolled with the utmost decorum. Thus Dallaway was startled to discover that, if the Sultan came to watch one of the great fires which so often broke out in Constantinople, ravaging the city, the women would " assemble in a group near the Sultan (who generally stood close to the firemen) and unmercifully load him with the bitterest revilings, particularizing his own crimes and the errors of his government, and charging him with the cause of their calamity. At such encounters no crowned head need envy Sultan Selim his situation. As this is the only privileged time of conveying the voice of the people to his ears, and as women in Turkey say anything with impunity, it is presumed that many of the fires are not accidental."

This, however, was the single exception to the rule whereby, on all his other appearances, the Sultan remained beyond reach, moving amidst unapproachable pomp and glory. Sanderson watched him depart from Constantinople " toward the (Balkan) warrs surrounded not only with the panoply of war but also by a great number of doggs led after him, well manned and in their best apparell; cloth of gold, velvet, scarlet and purple cloth; his haukes by horsemen carried in great number; tame lions and oliphants, with other beasts of many sorts, but especially the jaraff... being prince of all beasts, was led by three chaines of three sondrymen stalkinge before him. For it is the custome that, the Great Turk in person going on warfare, most or all in generall the cheafe men and beasts attend him out of the citie."

On the whole the Sultan's camping tents were rather less elaborate than might have been expected. He had three for his personal use, all of them surmounted with golden balls at the corners and with one ball in the centre at the top. One of the tents was circular, the other two rectangular, their floors covered with what Covell described as " a thick sort of coarse Yorkshire or Kidderminster woollen cloth ", over which were spread either valuable carpets or sumptuous brocades.

The sultan's caiques were showier than his tents and fascinated visitors from Western Europe. They were some sixteen feet long, with eighteen banks on which were ranged the oarsmen, who had been specially trained to row standing. According to Withers, the poop, which was very sumptuous " was covered with crimson

76. One of the most important sections of the Saray was the Harem. It is a rambling complex of rooms; two known as the Ocakli Sofa and the Cameli Sofa (room with a hearth and room with a fountain) are shown here.

velvet richly embroidered, under which he himself sits, and none but he, upon cushions of velvet, and cloth of gold; his Aghas standing all on their feet, holding with one hand by the side of the Kaik, and only the Bostangee Bashaw (or Head Gardener) who steers the barge, may now and then sit down, that he may handle the helm better." The caique advanced to the distressing sound of the howling of the mute oarsmen who were expected to ensure the secrecy of their monarch's conversations by muffling it from others with the only sound that it lay in their power to make. Withers compared this dreadful noise to the howlings of little dogs.

TURKISH ENTERTAINMENT

THE TURKS ARE by temperament a tranquil and sober people, and in that leisurely age they were content to spend their time at games of chess or else sitting in their gardens contentedly admiring a flower and listening to the slow babbling of some fountain; often they sat for hours quietly pulling at a nargilch, and carrying on a slow almost wordless conversation with their friends. The women, confined as they were to their own quarters, idled their leisure away gossiping, eating sweatmeats, making delicate embroideries and singing snatches of plaintive little songs. Special family festivities were celebrated by more formal singing and dancing, as well as by feasting, and it was only on national holidays that the people as a whole expected some more elaborate form of organized amusement. On such occasions it was always forthcoming. Its character surprised most of the English visitors, for swinging and firework (Pl. 69) displays provided the mainstay of the entertainment. Swinging had from a relatively early date been a favourite pastime and whereas in England swings still consisted for the most part of a plank suspended from two ropes, in Turkey they had attained a much more considerable degree of elaboration. Peter Mundy, who visited Constantinople at the turn of the sixteenth century, was fascinated by some which he watched being erected in preparation for the Bairam festivities. He made several drawings of them which he supplemented with lengthy descriptions. One type of swing he compared to an exceedingly high pair of gallows. Indeed its posts reached to the house tops. Three ropes were suspended from the summit and a triangular board fastened to them at a height of three feet from the ground. The person to be swung seated himself on this board. If a young boy, he was generally strapped in, but older people were expected to hold themselves fast. Then four or five men would come forward and start the swinger off. As he gained impetus, bands of webbing placed in front of him were used to pull him on his backward journey, the pulling being continued until he had attained a very great height. Men often dispensed with the aid of pushers or pullers and attained a tremendous height simply by swinging themselves. Music played throughout the operation.

Mundy considered these swings most dangerous and preferred some of a type that clearly foreshadowed the Great Wheel of Vienna or that erected earlier in this century at the White City in London. On the Turkish prototype children sat on little seats which retained their vertical position when the wheel revolved, so that the children always sat upright (Pl. 75). Another machine which enthralled Mundy foreshadowed our own merry-go-round. The Turks adored every type of swing, and in one of Mundy's sketches he included a dense crowd of onlookers sedately lining the street, gazing admiringly at those on the swings as they patiently awaited their turn. The amusement was cheap enough for all to participate in, for three aspers sufficed to provide an adequate spell on any swing, irrespective of type.

During Bairam, according to Covell, every shop was decorated with laurel flowers, " candle machines with pretty figures... and old mystical figures of health ". Bands consisting of trumpets, pipes, great drums, kettle drums and cymbals played in the streets, and dancers often performed before large crowds. These performers were all young men, generally of Greek origin, but occasionally Turks, Armenians and Jews joined their ranks. When the Sultan was present, the dancers were splendidly attired, wearing either cloth of gold or silver garments or shimmering silk. Under a surcoat of these materials they wore a kind of petticoat, very large and full, reaching to their ankles. It cannot have been an easy garment to dance in, especially as it was generally made in a heavy stiff material, such as velvet or brocade, but it was always of a light and glowing colour, and the whole effect must undoubtedly have been extremely decorative.

Actors were almost as popular with the crowd as were the dancers, and many gathered to watch with fascination as they performed little plays and interludes. They had no scenery but they generally wore Persian costumes, partly because the majority came from Kurdistan, and partly because the Osmanlis preferred to see the plays performed in the ornate robes of the Eastern regions rather than in the local dress.

Even more popular than the actual theatrical performances were the Karagöz shows. These took the form of shadow puppet plays, the brightly coloured figures being made of camel hide. These plays were generally extremely ribald, but were performed with such consummate skill that their popularity has survived even to the present day. The figures too were often extremely well made and constitute real works of art in themselves. Acrobats and tight-rope dancers were also popular, and there were booths with jugglers and wrestlers performing for the benefit of the public. All had their devotees. Covell was impressed by the acrobats, but he considered the jugglers less proficient than many he had seen in England, and he thought the wrestling a " nasty sport at best." As it seems to have resembled the all-in-wrestling of today Covell was probably justified in his view, but Fynes Morrison was anxious to emphasize that the wrestlers " bee such as doe it to delight the people and doe make it their profession."

Yet of all these entertainments it was the firework displays which gave the greatest delight. They continued late into the night, often over long periods, and their variety and elaboration amazed the foreign visitors. Sandys was so enthralled by the fireworks that he attempted to record their beauty in drawings, and although there is nothing so transient as the effervescence of rockets, he did to a certain extent succeed in capturing something of their glamour.

A decade or so earlier Edward Webb was tremendously impressed by the display which accompanied the festivities (Pl. 72) arranged to celebrate the Circumcision of Murat III's son, Mehmet. The festivities lasted for seven weeks, with displays of acrobats and jugglers by day and fireworks at night. His description of the whole affair is vivid and intriguing. " On Saturday the 7th there were some fine doings in the Hippodrome as festivities were going on within, the son as I had it on a trustworthy report, having to be circumcised. Mehmet Pasha, formerly Beylerbey of Greece, was summoned, who being a favourite with the prince, came to him and brought him into a chamber, entertaining him with pleasant words. Then he asked his leave to perform a duty necessary for the performance of the laws, and for the satisfaction of their Majesties his parents; and making him say the Alla illah la, uncovered him before, and it is said with a knife that he had ready for the purpose dexterously and promptly circumcised him, three persons only being present to testify to the circumcision. He shed a few tears though they say it was without pain; but he was placed on a superb bed under the care of his confidential people and the Pasha went to kiss the Signior's hand and give him the good news of the success. The Signior immediately gave him 20,000 sequins, his own robe which he was then wearing and twenty other robes very superb. The Pasha then sent the bloody knife to the Sultana Mother in a golden cup, who sent him back the cup with 10,000 sequins. In like manner the Sultana Consort presented him with 4,000 sequins and ten most honourable robes.

"This evening the Signior has thrown to the people 4 loads of aspic and many silver cups. The four wax lights which I mentioned in my former letter were lighted and burnt all night and fireworks without and were let off, with a great uproar of drums, trumpets and similar instruments and this lasted all night." They comprised elaborate set pieces, one of which was described as "a cunning piece in a form like ye Ark of Noy, being 24 yards high and 8 yards broad, wherein was placed 40 men, drawen on 6 wheeles, yet no man seene, but seemed to go alone as though it were onely drawen by two fiery dragons, in which shew or arke there was thirteen thousand pieces of fire worke" (Pl. 69, 78).

The Turks were indeed far in advance of Europe in this art, and in any case in England fireworks of such elaboration were entirely unknown. By 1594 however Whitehall had become sufficiently interested in fireworks for Barton to think it, worth while to report from Constantinople that certain "engines" had been taken from a drunken engineer who had formerly served at the Spanish court. Barton was tempted to get hold of the man and send him back to England, but at the same time he feared that the drunkard might already have turned Turk and divulged his secrets to the Osmanlis. However the man eventually himself asked to be sent to England and Barton despatched him to London as "in ingenery making artificial fireworks with powder and curious for the mind." Unfortunately that is the last we hear of him. However it may not be a mere coincidence that the publication in 1615 of Sandy's travel book, containing enthusiastic descriptions of Turkish fireworks, was followed in 1616 by a magnificent firework display on the Thames. When Covell's descriptions of the firework displays held at the Adrianople festivities of May 1675 appeared in print in England they were keenly noted by the appropriate artificers.

Writing of these fireworks Covell abandoned his customary reserve and his tendency to carp and frankly admitted that the displays "very much delighted him." He asserted that two foreigners, a Venetian and a Dutchman, had been responsible for the more elaborate items, but stressed the great variety of the fireworks. Thus there were "several figures of monstrous giants, many-headed and deformed. They were hollowed and framed with little hoopes, and paper'd over. These were hang'd all over with crackers, serpents, sausissons, etc., and after these were fired (which alwayes was done with excellent time), out of their heads, eyes, nose, eares, flew severall rockets, and, last, out of their mouths gushed streams of fire. Some had charges in their hands, which fired in the last place, and the armes being continued loose, swung them about very dexterously. Severall of these machines were contrived to turn upon the pole or spindle on which they hung, and were caryed round by a blind rocket attacht to the hem of their garments, for you saw no leggs — nothing but a long coat covered their lower part. What was burnt of the frame was infallibly repair'd by next night."

There were also some pyramid-shaped frames ten or twelve yards high hung with rockets, crackers and various other types of fireworks, as well as some tall, hollowed stands, which were filled with blazing matter that outlasted the others by a good quarter of an hour. Some castles, similarly filled and covered in fireworks, produced a splendid blaze, whilst spectacular fountain-like effects were achieved by firing fireworks from carefully placed pipes.

The star turn consisted of "a very large castle, intended to represent the castle at Candia. After an infinite of fireworks discharged from it, and God knows how many guns fired from within (by men on purpose, who withdrew afterwards from a porthole), it took fire at last (designedly) in so admirable a manner as no naturall fire could seem more reall. The combustible matter was made with so exquisite a

77. View of another of the rooms in the Harem. All were comparatively small but were luxuriously decorated with tiles, painted panelling or silk hangings.

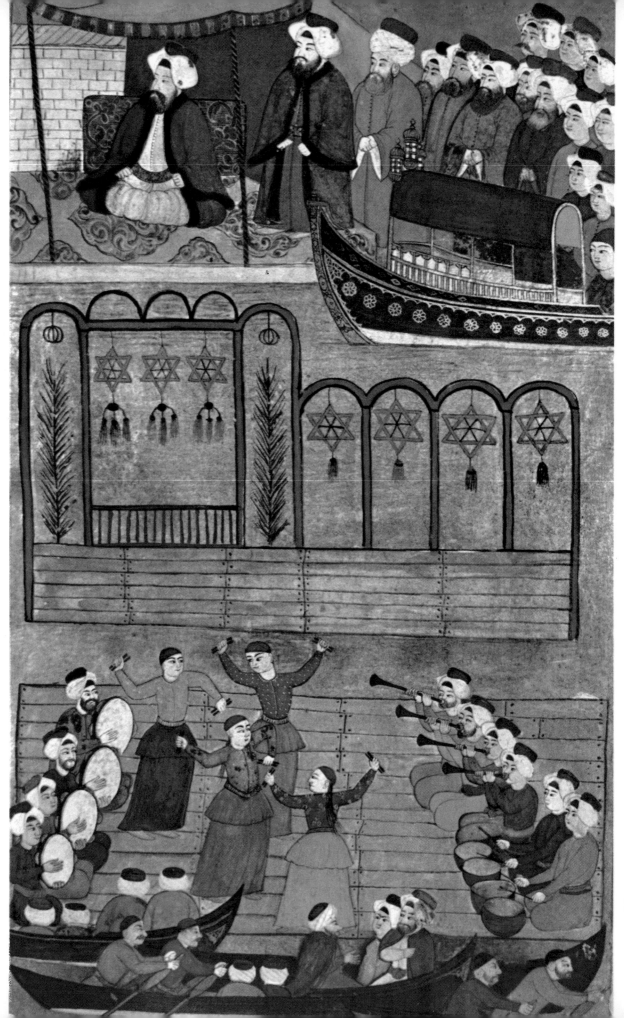

composition, and the ribs so well contrived, as though the flames burst out in many places about the bottom of the roof; yet the top took fire in due time and burnt with the body, and dropt down first, piece by piece. Then the sides began to let the fire break out through them, and by little and little the top parts of them fell down first, and then the walls wasted in order, till all was dropt down in one heap of fire. All this was done with that leisure, as it lasted at least an hour, and made the goodlyest bonfire that ever I saw."

Finally Covell mentions " several men with hobby horses about them, and other figures, cover'd all over in like manner with fireworks, which taking fire, ran up and down and encounter'd one another bravely. There were great timbers placed up like gallowes, and to one another were fastened ropes in such manner as upon them were hanged little ships, galleys, etc. able to hold two or three men, (but many, made of paper, and the like stuff, represented a whole ship's crew), who managed the guns and fireworkes within, contrived most dexterously; and with other ropes pulling the vessels backwards and forwards, they represented a sea fight very naturally."

Even the Italian onlookers were impressed by the spectacle, and although Cook, who was of the party, maintained that some fireworks which he had seen in Rome on his outward journey surpassed certain of those fired at Adrianople, he nevertheless admitted that he had never seen anything to equal one of the Turkish inventions. It consisted of " a great bason, like a mortar-piece, which sent out a violent stream of fire, with a hideous noise, to a great height." He found it " an object equally terrible and delightful."

The official entertainments to which Franks were invited were much more formal affairs, consisting for the most part of well nigh interminable banquets. Those held in the summer were more agreeable affairs than the winter ones, for they generally took place outside Constantinople, either in one of the lovely wooden houses, the local konaks, overhanging the Bosphorus, or in an exquisite kiosk set in some verdant glade, within earshot of running water. Withers described a kiosk as " a room with a fine prospect ", but it is more than that. As in a hunting lodge, so in a kiosk, the interior does indeed generally form only one room, but, in addition the building itself has to combine the sumptuous and the exquisite both externally and in its interior. In a kiosk the chamber was generally domed, and the building itself was sometimes surrounded by a moat or else encircled by streams of pellucid water. The konaks, on the other hand, were large country houses with deep eaves and overhanging balconies draped in the spring with wisteria and plumbago. Here from the early eighteenth century onwards the reception rooms were wainscotted with small, diversely shaped panels adorned with painted fruit and floral motifs. In the older ones splendid wall tiles were assembled into a large panel to form compositions of great loveliness, whilst the ceilings displayed intricate geometric patterns or flowing arabesques. The windows looked onto beautiful landscapes, for the shores of the Bosphorus and the Marmora provided glorious ever-changing vistas, while the countryside is at most seasons of the year rich and luxurious.

Whenever possible, visitors went to these receptions in caiques, and in the gentle calm of a Constantinople summer this form of travel was deliciously agreeable. In and around Constantinople the caique fulfilled much the same service as does the gondola in Venice, but, although equally delightful, it provided a far swifter form of transit, for the average private caique was manned by sixteen oarsmen. The Turks loved its silent, rapid motion, but Greeks, then as now, preferred to advance to the sound of gay music, and Lady Craven noticed that they generally took with them musicians who played the lyre, fiddle and guitar.

In 1740 Fawkener was invited to dine with the Vizier at his kiosk in the forest of Belgrade, some twelve miles to the north of Constantinople. He tells us that the dinner consisted of over a hundred dishes served simultaneously, except for the first

78. Miniature from a manuscript known as the Surnama-i-Vehbi of Ahmet III (1703-1730) from the Saray library.
It shows festivities on the water.

191

and last courses. The first course was made up of five dishes, four of which were of different varieties of melons neatly sliced. The melons stayed on the table until the last course was served, which in its turn consisted of five varieties of rice. A silver dish of roughly four feet in diameter set upon a low stool served as a table. Fawkener was seated at it beside the grand vizier. They were both given a cloth of gold to spread over their knees and an embroidered muslin towel to drape over themselves, " from the right shoulder over the breast ". The rest of the diners had to content themselves with a small muslin towel for their knees and a little muslin napkin to wipe their fingers on. The vizier and Fawkener were also each handed a silver plate into which their food was ladled by a sort of server who stood behind them holding a dish. The others helped themselves direct from the dish either with their fingers or a spoon. The plates were not changed for the different courses, but now and then they were wiped. Fawkener was provided with a gold knife, fork and spoon studded with jewels, and a cushion to sit upon, but the other guests sat cross-legged on the floor. There was music and singing both before and during the meal, but the banquet only lasted for about an hour and the entire visit for three. Conversation was stilted throughout and, notwithstanding the host's marked cordiality, the proceedings remained purely formal. Similar reserve persisted whenever foreigners were entertained, but in 1811 Lady Hester Stanhope succeeded in breaking through it when she wheedled the commander of the Turkish fleet into permitting her to go aboard his flagship, the Sultan Selim. She had to wear men's clothes for the occasion, but — perhaps precisely because of this — the visit was a great success, unmarred even by the death of the admiral's wife earlier that day. Undeterred by his loss the bereaved host gave Lady Hester a splendid dinner, and it is quite obvious from her account that the evening was gay and completely informal.

She does not unfortunately tell us much about the ship, but it was no doubt a very gorgeous affair, for many of the ships in the Sultan's navy were extremely ornate. Their fighting fitness seems to have been a secondary consideration, and Evliya Effendi was anxious to stress that the fleet of eighty ships specially commissioned by Murat at a cost of a million piastres for his abortive expedition to Malta was such that " even Noah might have considered himself secure in them." The flagship had only three decks instead of the customary five, but each was " as large as a caravanserai." In 1621 Roe was invited aboard the prince's galley as it lay at anchor at Messina. It had cost the Porte 3200 ducats, largely because it was lavishly gilt and profusely decorated with silver inlay. It had six chambers below deck, all " richly and curiously gilt. The awning over the poope was of cloth of gold, and the whole gally, from sterne to sterne, covered with damask, red and yellow."

Taken as a whole however, life aboard ship was of very small significance in Turkey, and nautical festivities were never of very great importance. Sometimes the fireworks were let off from barges, but that is as far as things went in that direction. Nor have many of the travellers had much to say about boats, other than the caiques, whether in earlier times or later, in the eighteenth and nineteenth centuries.

TURKISH GARDENS

THE TURKISH APPROACH to nature surprised the Westerners almost more than did any of the sights, customs or opinions they encountered on their travels. It was based on a regard for all growing things which was so contrary to anything experienced in Europe in the sixteenth and seventeenth centuries that Westerners found it wholly incomprehensible. In the seventeenth century the formal garden was very fashionable in the West and even in the eighteenth century when it had at last become the custom to enjoy a fine prospect, Europeans as a whole still did not set

79. Dolmabagtche Palace. Early in the nineteenth century, with the progress of Westernization, the old Saray was deserted and new palaces, in a florid Western style, were built on the shores of the Bosphorus.

80. A street scene. In the distance is the Church of St Theodosia, now known as Gul Camii. It was there that the Christians took refuge last at the time of the Turkish conquest in 1453.

79

80

81   83

82

much store by nature itself, considering it perfectly desirable that gardeners should improve upon a natural landscape by uprooting trees, levelling inclines, raising hillocks and altering the course of rivulets. Such intransigeance was in complete contrast to the Turkish attachment to the natural and even more their intense sensitivity towards plant life. Indeed the Ottoman's respect for natural beauties was so great that Lady Craven noted with amazement that if they found it necessary to build a house where a tree stood, they left a large hole for the tree to pass through, with room for it to increase in size, maintaining that its branches formed a delightful ornament for the top of a house.

Fynes Morison was one of the first to call attention to the Turkish love of nature and to their preference for having their meals by the banks of rivers or in gardens rather than in a house, and he notes also that they derived as much pleasure from tasting a spring of good water as do Franks from drinking a vintage wine. Withers affirmed that " never indeed doth a Turk, at any time, show himself to be so truly pleased and satisfied in his senses as he doth in the summer when he is in a pleasant garden: for he is no sooner come into it (if it be his own, or where he thinks he may be bold) but he pulls off his uppermost coat, and lays it aside, and upon that his Turbant, then turns up his sleeves, and unbuttoneth himself, turning his breast to the wind, if there be any; if not, he fans himself, or his servant doth it for him. Again, sometimes standing upon a high bank, to take the fresh air, holding his arms abroad (as a Cormorant sitting upon a rock doth his wings in sunshine after a storm) courting the weather and sweet air, calling it his soul, his life, and his delight, ever and anon showing some notable sign of contentment; nor shall the garden (during his pleasant distraction) be termed other than Paradise, with whose flowers he stuffs his bosom, and deketh his Turbant, shaking his head at their sweet favours, and sometimes singing a song to some pretty flower, by whose name peradventure his mistress is called; and uttering words of as great joy, as if at that instant she herself were present."

Purchas was irritated because, throughout Bairam, whenever he set foot in the street, he was followed by dervishes and Janissaries pressing tulips and other flowers upon him and expecting a gratuity of some sort in return. Although this was undoubtedly in part a trick to make a little money, the habit nevertheless also reflected the Turks' genuine love of flowers.

" No one ", wrote the Frenchman Bellon, " takes such intense delight in wearing flowers as do the Turks; when they see a beautiful gilly flower or any other pretty blossom; even one lacking scent does not lose favour in their sight. But whereas we love posies made up of various flowers intermingled with sweet smelling grasses, the Turks are not desirous of seeing them so blended, and have no wish to wear more than one, and even when they are able to collect flowers of various sorts, yet, in contrast to the general usage, they continue to wear them singly, tucking each one into a different fold of their turbans."

Though it was the individual tree or flower that most attracted the Turks, they were also ardent admirers of gardens as such. Most of those who penetrated to the Saray commented on the lavishness and beauty of the gardens there. Withers writing in 1650, states that they were " very faire, with all sorts of flowers and fruits that are to be found in those parts, with many very pleasant walks, inclosed in high Cypress trees on each side, and marble fountains in such abundance that almost every walk hath two or three of them; such great delight doth the Grand Turk and all the Turks in general take in them." Penzer has shown that Withers' work was really a translation of that of Ottavio Bon written half a century earlier, but this in no way detracts from the value of what is said on the subject of gardens. Other sources tell that they were planted with 20,000 cypresses and many hundreds of fruit trees. These seem to have formed a sort of aviary, the birds being virtually a part

195

of the garden. By the seventeenth century, if not before, the tulip parterres formed one of the chief wonders. A vast number of gardeners were required to maintain them, and Dallam noted that in the sixteenth century there were at least one thousand; " no garden ", he said, " was so well kepte in the worlde." A century or so afterwards Evliya Chelebi described them as " the threshold of the Abode of Felicity, the veritable counterpart of the gardens of Irem ", the legendary pleasure grounds which lie hidden in the deserts of Arabia.

It is however no easy matter to learn how the Turkish gardens were laid out. Water, as always in the Near East, had an important role to play and fountains and streamlets were always present. The best idea is probably that given by Lady Mary Wortley Montague, who penetrated into quite a number. She thought them most attractive and always suitable to the house to which they belonged. Arbours, fountains and walks were, she says, thrown together in agreeable confusion. Usually the gardens were enclosed by high walls and there were masses of tall trees which gave agreeable shade. Even so, she gives us very little detail.

The scarcity of information regarding Ottoman gardens becomes all the more tantalizing when we read that, in the seventeenth century, portable models of gardens were specially made in Turkey for processional purposes. Covell relates that at weddings it was customary for the presents made by the bridegroom to the bride to be carried through the town. As Covell watched the procession formed for the Favourite's wedding he noticed that the presents included three or four artificial gardens, each about three yards square, with pretty little mounds and walks. They were full of flowers and trees covered with fruit, all skilfully modelled in wax. One contained a kiosk standing in the centre of its grounds, with birds and beasts placed amongst the flowers and trees; two had artificial fountains which were supplied with water by a clockwork engine. The gardens were carried on slings by slaves. Watching another procession Dudley North noticed a similar garden, with trees laden with fruit, all made of sugar.

Something of the sort seems also to have existed in Vienna late in the sixteenth century, but in this particular instance the garden contained earth and grew real plants. It must therefore either have resembled a miniature Japanese garden, or else it must have been a real garden, however tiny its scale. All we are told about it is that when Clusius visited Vienna he was taken to see a model of a Constantinopolitan garden and that, to his delight, he found growing in it the first double yellow rose he had ever seen. Parkinson was undoubtedly referring to the same rose in the passage in *Paradisi in Sole*, in which he wrote that " the double yellow rose, which was first procured to be brought into England by Master Nicholas Lete, a worthy merchant of London, and a great lover of flowers, from Constantinople (as we heare) was first brought thither from Syria; but perished quickly both with him and with all other to whom he imparted it; yet afterwards it was sent to Master John de Franqueville, a merchant also of London, and a great lover of all rare plants, as well as of flowers, from which is sprung the greatest store, that is now flourishing in this kingdom."

Although Parkinson then went on to relate that " the miserably infatuated Turks ", as he called them, would not allow a rose leaf to remain lying on the ground for fear that it might be trodden on, believing that the flower had sprung from the Prophet's sweat, he made no mention of the custom of distilling syrup and rose water or making jam from the rose. Nor was he aware that the rose had been cherished for centuries throughout the Middle East, that the greatest poets of Persia and Arabia had found their finest inspiration in the flower, and that the Turks delighted in quoting the verses in which Hafiz, Sadi and Firdausi had immortalized its beauty.

The introduction of new plants and flowers from lands with which they were becoming familiar was a matter of real importance to the Elizabethans. They considered that every facet of their lives had been marvellously enriched by new discoveries and Hakluyt commented gratefully on numerous benefits that the travellers had conferred on England. " It is reported at Saffron Waldon ", he wrote in 1582, " that a Pilgrim purporting to do good to his countrey, stole a head of Saffron, and hid the same in his Palmer's staffe ... If he had bene taken, by the law of the countrey from whence it came, he had died of the fact ... And if this care had not been heretofore in our ancestors then had our life been savage now, for then we had not had Wheat nor Rie, Peaze nor Apple, Vine nor many other profitable and pleasant plants, Bull nor Cowe, Sheepe nor Swine, Horse nor Mare, Cocke nor Hen, nor a number of other things that we injoy, without which our life were to be sayd barbarous: for these things, and a thousand that we use more, the first inhabitants of the land found not here. And in time of memory things have been brought in that were not here before, as the Damaske rose by Doctor Linaker, King Henrie 7 and King Henrie 8 Physician. Turkey cocks and hennes about fifty years past, the Artichowe in the time of King Henrie 8, and of later time was procured out of Italy the Muske rose plant, the plum one called Perdigwena, and two kinds more by Lord Cromwell after his travell, and the Abricot by a French priest, one Wolfe, Gardiner to Henrie 8; and now within these foure yeares there have been brought into England from Vienna in Austria, divers kinds of flowers called Tulipas, and those and others procured thither a little before from Constantinople, by an excellent man called Mr Carolus Clusius."

It is curious that the tulip should not have been known in England, or in fact in Europe, until this late year, but it is even more surprising to find that its fame was of surprisingly slow growth even in its native land. Though indigenous to the Middle East, no gardeners prior to the Emperor Babur appear to have been attracted by it, and no artists other than the Byzantine mosaicist who was responsible for the lovely decorations in the basilica known as the Acheiropoietou at Salonica, ever reproduced the tulip in art. The Turks were in fact the first to do so, but not until the late fifteenth century, when they had succeeded in fully consolidating their gains in Anatolia and were free to devote their attention to other things beside warfare.

The Emperor Babur had been able to collect thirty-four varieties of tulips in Afghanistan; these flowers, like those which the Turks discovered in Anatolia, were of the short-stemmed, pointed-petalled varieties of the species plant. The Osmanlis patiently cultivated them in their gardens, and as the quality of the blooms improved, so did their interest in the flower develop into an enthusiasm. Within a surprisingly short time the flower came indeed to exercise a veritable fascination over them, inducing their artists to embark upon the endless variations, elongations and stylizations of the tulip motif, which culminated in the elaborately formalized yet impressionistic versions of the flower which, today, still continue to delight us with their rare beauty and sensitivity. In fact, the establishment of the tulip motif with its pointed petals clearly distinguishing it from the rounded Egyptian lotus, must be considered a major contribution to decorative art, and it is one for which the Ottomans were largely responsible.

Peter Angeli was probably the first European to notice the tulip. By birth an Italian, by temperament a poet of some accomplishment, he was by profession a diplomat. It was in this capacity that he accompanied an envoy of Francis 1 of France to Constantinople, Greece and Asia Minor. At some point on his travels he became sufficiently charmed by the tulip to refer to it in his verses, but it never occured to him to try to introduce the bulb into Europe. It remained for Busbequius to prove more practical if less poetic, and, on the completion of his mission to the Porte, it was the ex-ambassador who brought some tulips back with him to Vienna.

In *Paradisi in Sole*, published in 1604, Parkinson ranked the tulip as one of the finest of flowers. He recognized its Anatolian origin and proceeded to list the varieties which were at that time in cultivation in England. His list is a surprisingly long one, comprising forty-nine flowers of the praecox group, fifteen of which were albas, sixteen purpureas, eleven rubras and seven lutaes. Parkinson also mentioned thirteen more early varieties, including the Tulipa Byzantina Duabas Floribus, which he ascribed to the Constantinopolitan region, a Tulipa Cretice and an Armeniaca. In addition he named another fifteen albas. It was however the painter Rubens who made the flower more generally famous by depicting a tulip bed in some detail in one of his most charming pictures—that where he and his second wife are shown walking together in their garden.

Whilst Rubens was at work on this evocative picture Europe succumbed to a veritable mania for tulips. Collectors committed the wildest follies to satisfy their craving for rare bulbs, and whereas, in the 1620s, the absence of tulips from a garden had denoted little more than the rusticity of the owners, ten years later their presence now became indispensable to any person of standing, and served as a hallmark of elegance and breeding. Whilst the craze lasted artists and craftsmen turned to the flower for inspiration and, in textiles, the tulip motif became of the utmost importance, not only in Turkey and Italy, where the design was a basic one in the finest velvets and brocades, but equally so in English needlework. In France even the iron workers succeeded in handling the motif with felicity as, for example, at the Chateau de Wideville, Seine et Oise, where François Marchant combined tulips and martagon lilies in the design of a truly superb pair of gates.

Throughout the period that this frenzy dominated in the West affection for the flower continued to follow a more or less normal course in Turkey, and it was not till a hundred years or so later that a similar enthusiasm for the flower began to develop there. Even so there was a difference for, in Turkey, the passion for tulips did not lead to extravagant excesses. Instead, under the aegis of Sheik Lalezari, it inspired so exquisite a creativeness both in poetry and craftsmanship that the period has gone down in history as the Lâle Devri, the Age of the Tulip. Many of the Turkish customs which had charmed the earlier English travellers in the Levant matured during this period, to wane, like a veritable tulip, with the passing of the tulip age that had brought them to flowering. Thus, the close of the Lâle Devri acts as a dividing line between two epochs in Turkish life; the earlier, which for all its underlying grimness, yet possessed elegance in living and delicacy in the arts, and the later, when periods of stagnation alternated with those of attempted reforms. The final stage in the history of the Ottoman Empire produced a society which belongs to modern times rather than to the picturesque age that formed the Osmanli community which the Elizabethans and Jacobeans had contemplated with such lively interest and curiosity.

THE LAST PHASE

THE BEGINNING of the eighteenth century marks the opening of a new phase in Turkish history. The empire, which had reached its widest extent at the time of the second attack on Vienna in 1683, thenceforth began to disintegrate. True, the process was a very slow and gradual one, but the apex had undoubtedly been passed by around 1700; Austrian expansion was already beginning to make itself felt and with the Treaty of Karlowitz in 1699 Transylvania and most of Hungary passed out of Turkish hands; and soon after the cession of the Azov area and parts of what is now Roumania to Russia marked the beginnings of Russian ascendancy. At the same time the nature of affairs was changing at the Turkish capital. Though for a brief period in the first and second decades of the eighteenth century Venice obtained control of the Morea and Dalmatia, the age of her glory was almost at

84. Musicians from a Turkish manuscript of the sixteenth century. Such musicians might have entertained the Sultan in the Saray, though they also performed in public, for example in the Hippodrome.

85. Miniature of a dancer from a manuscript illustrated by the painter Leoni in the Saray library.

84   85

an end and thereafter the influence of the Venetian bailey, as her ambassador at Constantinople was called, became insignificant. The role of the other Western representatives was also changing and they gradually became less significant as the heads of trading enterprises and more important from the political point of view. By about 1750 the trade of the Turkey Company had seriously declined and by the end of the century it had almost ceased. But on the other hand the role of the heads of missions gradually became more and more active and by around 1800 the French, British and Russian ambassadors were to be numbered amongst the most important figures in Turkey. Depending on the position of their respective countries and their individual personalities they alternated with one another in exercising a leading influence on the conduct of affairs. In fact the age of European diplomatic action was dawning, and nowhere was it to be given a freer rein than in Constantinople.

At the same time the attitude of the Western representatives in and visitors to Turkey also began to alter. Originally it had been one of sympathetic wonder, and a tone of awe and admiration had distinguished all the reports that were sent home in the sixteenth and seventeenth centuries. With the eighteenth the observations tended to become more critical, and the expression of admiration for what seemed strange and impressive gave way to a more reasoned evaluation which was a great deal less tolerant. The Turks and their customs indeed ceased to impress, and even if they did awake feelings of curiosity, the Western attitude became distinctly superior. This new approach is admirably represented by some remarks made by Lord Baltimore in 1767. He commented somewhat ruefully that " the religion, the laws and customs of the Turks are as much as they can make them, in direct opposition to ours; they eat, write, sleep and sit low, we high; their dead they carry out head, we feet foremost; their cloaks are long, ours are short; they have many wives and mistresses allowed by law, we only one; they have few wh..., we a multitude; they believe in one God, we in the Trinity; they believe in predestination, we do not; our potentates send ambassadors to each other, the Grand Signior sends none; ... The Turks make great use of baths, we do not." In the following century Lord Broughton added to this disconcerting catalogue. " The Turks ", he wrote, " not only differ, but are just contrary to ourselves. They turn in their toes, they mount on the right side of the horse, they put their guests in a room first and out of it last, serve themselves at table first, take the wall and walk hastily in a sign of respect, they think beheading disgraceful in comparison with strangling, they cut their hair from their head and leave it on the chin, they invite with the hand, by throwing it backwards, not drawing it towards them, their mourning habit is white." Yet even these long lists failed to include all the points of difference and omitted perhaps the most obvious of them all—that whereby in direct contradiction to the European, the Osmanli script read from right to left instead of from left to right.

This difference of outlook towards Turkey was to a great extent inevitable. In Europe a new age was dawning and change was in the air; in Turkey the attitude of the palace hierarchy and the religious leaders was wholly retrogressive; the country was poor, much of it even in a deplorable state, the army was ill-trained and disorganized and the government machine totally inefficient, and it was not till the nineteenth century that any attempts were made at reform; by then it was too late.

The decline in Turkey was nowhere more discernible than in the Corps of the Janissaries. Once they had constituted some of the finest fighting troops in the world; by the eighteenth century they were no more than a vast disorderly body of reprobates battening off the state and threatening not only the Sultan but also the peace of the realm; they even started fires in the city so that they could have an excuse for looting. They married and brought up children, demanding that the state

86. Decorative element from the battle standard of Suleyman the Magnificent now in the armoury of the Saray.

should support their wives and families also, and all vestiges of discipline had been lost. Soon after the middle of the century they presented a very sorry spectacle, as a report sent to the foreign secretary by the British representative in Constantinople serves to show. " On Thursday ", he writes, " the Janissaries marched out to a number of 103 ortas, 76 others remaining at Court; they were of all ages, from children of 8 to old men of 70. They made a very bad appearance, without regiments, many of them very ill clothed, with bad muskets of various sorts and bores, some with swords and pistols and some without, the old men were decrepit and many of the young men sickly and infirm. There were near 11,000, but deducting the old men, children and infirm there seemed to be not more than 8 or 9 thousand fit to serve. In addition there were about 2,000 cooks. The officers made a fine appearance, especially the Janissary Aga who had 8 led horses with superb furniture. His guards and retinue, who were clothed in an uniform and well armed, amounted to about 600 men. Each orta had two, three or four fools or buffoons. On Friday the Armourers marched out and next day the Topgi (artillery) and the Arabegis or wheelwrights, which corps made altogether about 5,000 men."

These were the troops which had once struck terror into Europe, and on the basis of this description alone it is not in the least surprising that Turkey had assumed for the Europeans the character of an outmoded curiosity which might be exploited rather than a vital power which had to be taken into serious account.

The new attitude towards Turkey was also intensified by events in the political field. Austrian and Russian expansion had begun, a desire for freedom and autonomy among the numerous minorities contained within the vast Turkish empire was rising up, and Russia soon assumed the role of protector of the Christian, and especially the Slav, minorities—a role which was more or less officially sanctioned by the Treaty of Kutchuk Kainardgi in 1774. The treaty further gave the right to Russian shipping to navigate and trade freely in all Turkish waters—an important concession, which tightened the economic stranglehold under which the empire struggled. The treaty also ensured a position of leading importance for the Russian embassy in Constantinople and marked the end of Turkish hegemony northward of the Black Sea.

All through the seventies the struggle for freedom among the minorities in the empire—Christians in the Balkans, Moslems in North Africa and Egypt—was going on, and revolts were suppressed with ruthless ferocity. In 1778 for instance visitors to Constantinople were regaled with the sight of thirty-nine heads of Greek insurgents from the Morea implanted at the entrance to the Saray. But that the revolts would ultimately be successful already appeared as a possibility, and in the 1780s Russia even conceived a plan in collaboration with Austria for the partition of the Turkish empire. The scheme collapsed partly owing to Austrian incompetence and partly as a result of Pitt's policy of maintaining the balance of power in Europe, but thereafter Turkey virtually became a pawn in the game of European high politics. First Napoleon's attack on Egypt automatically brought her into the coalition against France; then, with the re-establishment of peace in Egypt, France sought to regain the position of most favoured friend which she had previously held, and Turkey was drawn to her side by Napoleon's victories around 1805. Encouraged by this the Sultan dismissed the hospodars of Walachia and Moldavia without consulting Russia, which was in breach of an agreement made with Russia in 1802; Russian troops therefore invaded the area and Britain, at that moment an ally of Russia against France, sent a fleet through the Dardanelles to threaten Constantinople. The French however helped the Turks to prepare the defence of their capital and the fleet withdrew without accomplishing anything.

The next few years were marked by a general dissolution of the power of the monarchy in Turkey and the whole state would have been in danger of collapse had not Sultan Mahmud come to the throne in 1808 determined to reform the government. Although the state survived, the surge of movement was not to be stopped. First Montenegro, then Serbia and Greece and finally Bulgaria were in revolt, supported to some extent by Russia officially and in the case of Greece privately by Britain. Mahmud's reaction was virtually to countenance a series of terrible massacres of Christians which included one in Constantinople itself in which the Patriarch was torn from his church and murdered in public. Europe was greatly shocked by these events and in 1827 a treaty was drawn up between Britain, France and Russia by which the three powers agreed to guarantee the rights of the Christian minorities. The immediate outcome was the battle of Navarino, in which the fleets of the allies totally destroyed those of Turkey and Egypt, a country which was by now also independent, but had come to Turkey's aid. A change of government in Britain however reversed the anti-Turkish policy, and in 1828 Britain withdrew, leaving Turkey and Russia face to face. Russia continued the attack; Adrianople was captured the next year and the threat to Constantinople seemed so serious that Sultan Mahmud asked for an armistice. One of its results was independence for a part at least of Greece and soon after, in 1835, for the establishment of an independent principality in Serbia. At much the same time the Egyptian ruler Mohammet Ali succeeded in obtaining control of Syria. And scarcely had the problem of Arab desire for independence been arranged when Russia forced on Turkey the acceptance of the Treaty of Hunkiar Skelessi, which reduced the Ottoman empire almost to a state of vassaldom and even more important transferred the control of the straits to Russia. Both England and France refused to recognize the treaty and thereafter they worked together to diminish Russian influence, France becoming the sponsor of Mohammet Ali in Egypt and England of the Sultan at Constantinople. This dual role, allied with the innate enmity of England and France, proved to be a root of cause of disagreement between the two, and Russia naturally did her best to exploit the situation. At first events moved against Russia and a new Straits Convention was agreed in 1841, but around 1850 she made new claims on Turkey and in 1853 Turkey declared war in resistance against them. England and France came to Turkey's help in the Crimea till hostilities were ended by the Treaty of Paris in 1855. The many British who died of wounds in the campaign are buried in a sad little cemetary at Scutari, close to the hospital where Florence Nightingale worked.

During the next twenty years the process of liberation continued, for in 1876 a *coup d'état* had removed the incompetent Sultan Abdul Aziz from the throne and had granted a constitution at home, while in the Balkans movement towards independence had been intensified. But the new sultan was soon in a madhouse, and had within a few weeks been replaced by Abdul Hamid whose attitude towards constitutions was not quite what the ministers had expected. He soon took up a stronger line, and in 1877 a second war had broken out between Turkey and Russia, though this time Turkey was on her own.

After preliminary Turkish successes the Russians advanced almost to Constantinople and imposed very severe terms on Turkey at the Treaty of San Stefano in 1878, and had it not been for the timely despatch of the British fleet, theoretically to protect her nationals, the key to the Bosphorus might well have fallen into their hands. As it was Abdul Hamid took advantage of the occasion to put an end to the Constitution and though the Christian minorities in the Balkans achieved a greater degree of freedom little of the praise for this redounded to the credit of Russian victories, for the terms of the Treaty of San Stefano had been considerably revised the next year at Berlin. At much the same time Cyprus had been ceded to Britain in return for her guarantee to assist in halting Russian aggression against Turkey.

Encouraged perhaps by the humiliation that had been brought on Turkey by the San Stefano treaty the Armenians now made a bid for independence; the idea of an independent Armenia was fostered by Russia and a clause was inserted into the Berlin Treaty giving the powers the right to superintend the reforms which Turkey agreed to carry out in Armenia. But the Turkish reforms amounted to little and a minority of enthusiasts was driving the generally peace-loving Armenians to take violent action. Simultaneously the warlike Kurds were turning to revolt, and as these were Moslems and presented a more serious problem the local authorities preferred to lay the blame for disturbances on to the Armenians, and reports of Armenian revolutionary activities began to pour in at Constantinople. Affairs reached a head in 1894 when a series of bloody massacres began, which culminated in a mass destruction of Armenians even in Constantinople. The event not only inflamed the fury of Europe but also encouraged a general mistrust of the sultan, and a crisis which might have been final was only arrested by the fact that in 1897 Greece attacked Turkey. The Turkish army won a series of victories over the insurgents and faith in the sultan was re-established. But the last years of Abdul Hamid's reign were not tranquil, for to the revolts of the minorities was now added that of the liberal movement among the Turks themselves. The " Committee of Union and Progress " had been constituted, and in 1908 a new constitution was forced upon the old autocracy. This time it was to be lasting—in spite of setbacks— and, if there were to be changes they were all to be in the direction of greater liberalism.

This brief survey of the history serves to show that the eighteenth century was primarily a period of inaction in Turkey, the nineteenth one of action, in which Russia and the European powers were the prime movers. The architecture of Constantinople reflects the character of the history in a most interesting way. In the eighteenth century little was done; what there was, on a small scale and though it shows hints of the influence of the styles dominant in Europe at the time, Turkish elements were more to the fore than purely European ones. In the nineteenth century on the other hand European styles were adopted universally and the old city which had been Constantinople and which had by then become more or less generally known as Stamboul ceded place to the new Europeanized town of Pera to the north of the Golden Horn or for the shores of the Bosphorus. There activity was considerable, though the most important buildings of the age were not so much mosques or religious colleges as in the past, but rather the great embassies of the foreign powers or the palaces of the sultans, where they could to some degree follow the manners and customs of the West and conduct the game of diplomacy at least on an equal footing so far as the surroundings were concerned.

Of the great embassies the first to be built was the British, on a magnificent site at the summit of Pera which was presented by the sultan in thanks for assistance given in resisting Napoleon's attack on Egypt in 1798. The impressive embassy built soon after was destroyed by fire in 1870 and was replaced by the present Italianate structure during the next two years. Designed by Barry, architect of the Houses of Parliament in London, it is vast and impressive, a monument wholly in keeping with a period in which the British ambassador lived as a prince, surrounded by an army of retainers and kavasses, and at times dictated the policy of the empire. The French embassy was built in the Louis Philippe style between 1838 and 1845. The Russian is perhaps more interesting, for it was designed by the Italian Gaspare Fossati who had trained in Russia and went to Constantinople expressly to build the embassy in 1838. When the work was completed the architect entered the service of the Turkish government and for the next twenty years was responsible for a large number of designs, which included several massive buildings in the Renaissance manner. His most important work however was the restoration of Agia Sophia for

Sultan Abdul Mecit in 1846. The structure had fallen into disrepair owing to neglect and the effect of earthquakes and Fossati was commissioned to recondition it from floor to ceiling. The work was carried out most thoroughly and there can be no doubt that what he did was in the main wholly beneficial. In the process of the work part of the old mosaic decoration was discovered; Fossati was instructed to examine it all and then to cover up again the parts depicting figural subjects. This was done, but he and his brother Giuseppe made a number of sketches and others were done by an Austrian, Salzenberg. Now, most of the mosaics that survive have once more been uncovered, but it would seem that in the interval some have perished, for some of the panels to which the Fossatis referred are no longer there.

The most spectacular buildings that belong to this age were the vast palaces which the sultans built to replace the Saray. The first of these more Western dwellings was quite a small palace beside the Sweet Waters of Asia; it was built by Mahmud I in 1740 but restored by Selim III in 1795 and again in 1815; it still remains the most elegant and attractive of the palaces on the Bosphorus. Dolmabagtche (Pl. 79), built by the architect Balian for Sultan Mecit in 1853 is on a much more grandiose scale. Though heavy and overcharged with decoration, it is none the less impressive, to a great extent because of its position on the shore of the Bosphorus, and serves more than any other building to recall the somewhat hollow magnificence of its age when, in spite of territorial losses and economic decline, Turkey was still playing a leading role in the game of Balkan politics, a game in which at times she succeeded in out-witting her opponents even when she was at a distinct material disadvantage.

One might have thought that one such palace on the water's edge would have been enough, especially for an empire in so parlous a financial condition, but within little more than twenty years a new edifice had been begun, only a few hundred yards away; it was the Palace of Çeragan, now a fire-blackened ruin, for it was burnt in 1910. It was built for Sultan Abdul Aziz and was apparently the most luxurious of all the palaces; the luxury was perhaps some slight compensation to Sultan Murat V who was shut up there by Abdul Hamid for twenty-seven years of his rather miserable life. Abdul Hamid himself preferred to live on a more modest scale in a palace, or rather almost a pavilion, at Yildiz, on the slope over-looking the Bosphorus a few miles farther to the north. But if he spent less on building, this eccentric figure did not spare expenditure on the problem of lay-out, and his dwelling at Yildiz consisted of a large park, beautifully planted, lovely gardens, a zoo, and a series of independent pavilions. The whole complex was surrounded by a double wall with an open area in between, guarded by ferocious dogs, so that it was virtually impossible to penetrate. Today it still remains difficult to obtain access, though one of the pavilions, the Jale Kiosk, was at one time open to the public. It is sad, for the age of Abdul Hamid was in its own way little less curious and romantic than that of the sixteenth century, and though the Top Kapu Saray could by then be visited occasionally as a special favour, the complex of Yildiz was guarded by its dogs and soldiers no less securely than the Saray had been by its Janissaries. But within, instead of the terrible sultan, commander of armies, whose word was law over much of three continents, and who was surrounded by hosts of court officials and eunuchs in gorgeous costumes, there was a nervous, lonely man in a frock-coat, bargaining for his existence and that of his empire with the skill of a stock-exchange manipulator. And with the abdication of Abdul Hamid in 1909 the days of the autocratic sultanate were really at an end, for though two more sultans and a third of the line, who was only Caliph, were to follow him, the power passed into other hands with the Revolution of 1908 and in 1923 Turkey became a Republic.

Soon after the Greeks living on Turkish territory were exchanged for Moslems from the lands which had become independent—Greece, Yugoslavia and Bulgaria.

But the Greeks on the European shores in the region of Constantinople were allowed to remain, a last vestige of the old Byzantine population; it may even be that some of them still have the blood of the old colonisers from Megara in their veins. They have lived through many vicissitudes, but there are certainly some of them still alive today who look back with considerable nostalgia to the days before the First World War, when Constantinople—still very largely a Greek city—was at the height of its prosperity. Trade was active, business flourishing, life comparatively easy especially for the more wealthy classes, while Greeks who were loyal subjects of the sultan might rise to the highest positions in the state. Coal wharves and petrol depots had not as yet begun to disfigure the Bosphorus; steam ships that were still things of exquisite beauty anchored in the roads; caiques, with their coloured sails and beautiful curving lines sailed the waters, while picturesque rowing boats, with their cargoes of tittering ladies of the harem, dignified men in fezes going to their offices, or local fishermen at their trade moved along near the shore. And on land, though in the towns men favoured the sombre frockcoat of the west, countrymen still wore local dress, while the large brown eyes of the ladies peered romantically over the yashmaks and long robes of fine silk served to disguise the rather full lines and dumpy proportions of their figures. Nor was the fate of the working class so very disagreeable in contrast with that in other parts of Europe, even if for the Armenians the situation was more painful owing to the fears of the sultan that members of that race were planning his murder. It must not be forgotten that until the middle of the nineteenth century the lot of the Christians had not been much more severe than that of many of the Moslem inhabitants of the great Ottoman empire. Neglect by the central government, extortions by the tax collectors, the rule of weak officials who were incompetent and dishonest had been the lot of all, whether Christians or Moslems, and it was really only in comparison with recent times that the Christian minorities within the realm had come to be looked on with hate and treated with cruelty—a cruelty which was intensified by fear as the state became weaker and the minorities began to assert their independence.

With the establishment of the new republican regime, the centre of control was, in 1923, transferred to Ankara, and the city, which for some 1600 years had been one of the world's greatest capitals, was reduced virtually to the rank it had occupied when Constantine weighed its claims as superior to those of so many rivals shortly before 330. Yet the city still has the air of a capital; still it is revered in the hearts of Greeks and Turks alike; still it is coveted by the Russians as guardian of the straits; still it remains one of the great historical cities of the world, and even if its role in politics and public affairs is now comparatively insignificant, it remains nevertheless in the minds of all a queen among towns. It was, in the days of its glory, known as the New Rome, and only by Rome was the significance of the role it played in the history of Europe surpassed. Today it is only the second city of Turkey. Yet it has a future. With the need for wide roads, modern sanitation and up-to-date facilities much that was picturesque and attractive is inevitably doomed. New buildings are rising up, new streets being cut. May those on whom the responsibility of reconditioning the city rests remember that the past has its claims as well as the present, in addition to the future. Though we admire the magnificent architectural heritage left by the Turks, we nevertheless regret the mass destruction of so much of what went before. One can hardly hope that what the twentieth century has to add will equal in value what was given in the fifteenth. One can hope however that the destruction of what is of value and interest will be less universal, conducted without chauvinism and with respect for all that is good regardless of its age or origins.

Bibliography

Texts of the Byzantine period are comparatively numerous; the most important of them are summarized by J. P. Richter, in *Quellen zur Byzantinischen Kunstgeschichte* etc., Wien, 1897. From the time that Peter Gyllius visited Constantinople in 1561, books by Western writers became increasingly numerous. A full bibliography of the latter will be found in Arif Müfid Mansel, *Bibliografya*, published by the Turkish Historical Society in 1948. For general reading the following may be recommended:

Byzantine History and Civilization.

Baynes, N. H., and Moss, H. St. L. B., *Byzantium: An Introduction to East Roman Civilization.* Oxford, 1948.

Ostrogorsky, G., *History of the Byzantine State.* Oxford, 1956.

Vasiliev, A. A., *History of the Byzantine Empire.* p. 324-1453. Oxford, 1952.

General books on the City.

Diehl, C., *Constantinople.* Paris, 1924.

Jalal, Asad, *Constantinople, de Byzance à Stamboul.* Paris, 1909.

Ebersolt, J., *Constantinople Byzantine et les Voyageurs du Levant.* Paris, 1918.

Janin, R., *Constantinople Byzantine.* Paris, 1950.

Mamboury, E., *Byzance - Constantinople - Istanbul; Guide Touristique.* Istanbul, 1930.

Schneider, A. M., *Konstantinopel.* Mainz und Berlin, 1956.

Young, G. F., *Constantinople.* London, 1926.

Byzantine Buildings.

Ebersolt, J. and Thiers, A., *Les Eglises de Constantinople.* Paris, 1913.

Fossati, G., *Aya Sofia of Constantinople.* London, 1852.

George, W. S., *The Church of Saint Eirene at Constantinople.* Oxford, 1912.

Lethaby, W. R. and Swainson, H., *The Church of Sancta Sophia.* London, 1894.

Salzenberg, W., *Altchristliche Baudenkmäle von Konstantinople vom V bis XII Jahrhundert.* Berlin, 1854.

Schneider, A. M. and Meyer B., *Die Landmauer von Konstantinople.* Berlin, 1929-33.

Strzygowski, J. and Forcheimer, P., *Die Byzantinischen Wasserbehälter von Konstantinopel.* Wien, 1893.

Van Millingen, A., *Byzantine Constantinople. The Walls of the City and adjoining historical sites.* London, 1899.
Byzantine Churches in Constantinople. London, 1912.

Wulzinger, K., *Byzantinische Baudenkmäler zu Konstantinople.* Hannover, 1925.

Zaloziecky, W. R., *Die Sophienkirche in Konstantinopel und ihre Stellung in der Geschichte der abendländischen Architektur.* Città del Vaticano, 1936.

Account of the more important Excavations.

British Academy, *Preliminary report on the excavations carried out in the Hippodrome in 1927 and 1928.* Oxford, 1927 and 1928.

Demangel, R. and Mamboury, E., *Le quartier des Manganes et la Ière région de Constantinople.* Paris, 1939.

Mamboury, E., " Les fouilles à Istanbul en 1936-37 ", in *Byzantion.* 13, 1938.

Walker Trust, *The Great Palace of the Byzantine Emperors.* First report, 1935-38. Oxford, 1947. Second Report, 1951-54. Edinburgh, 1958.

The Great Palace.

Ebersolt, J., *Le Grand Palais de Constantinople et le Livre des Cérémonies.* Paris, 1910.

Mamboury, E. and Wiegand, T., *Die Kaiserpaläste von Konstantinopel zwischen Hippodrom und Marmara Meer.* Berlin-Leipzig, 1934.

Vogt, A., *Le Livre des Cérémonies.* 2 vols of text and 2 of commentaries. Paris, 1935-39.

BYZANTINE ART.

EBERSOLT, J., *Sanctuaries de Byzance*. Paris, 1921.
RICE, D. TALBOT, *The Art of Byzantium*. London, 1959. Also in French and German.
WHITTEMORE, T., *The Mosaics of St Sophia at Istanbul*. Oxford, 1933, 1936, 1942, 1952.

TURKISH HISTORY.

GIBBON, H. A., *The Foundation of the Ottoman Empire*. Oxford, 1916.
HUBBARD, G. E., *The Day of the Crescent*. Cambridge, 1920.
MAYES, S., *An Organ for the Sultan*. London, 1956.
PALLES, A. A. (Ed.), *In the Days of the Janissaries*. London, 1951.
PENZER, N. M., *The Harem*. London, 1936.

TURKISH ARCHITECTURE.

GABRIEL, A., "Les Mosquées de Constantinople", in *Syria*, VII, 1926.
GLUCK, H., *Die Bäder Konstantinopel*. Wien, 1921.
UNSAL, B., *Turkish Islamic Architecture in Seljuk and Ottoman Times, 1071-1923*. London, 1959.

Other Books by David Talbot Rice

Byzantine Glazed Pottery. Oxford University Press, 1930.
Byzantine Art. Oxford University Press, 1935.
The Great Palace of the Byzantine Emperors. Excavations by the Walker Trust. Edinburgh University Press, 1958.
The Art of Byzantium. Thames and Hudson, 1959.
The Byzantines. Thames and Hudson, 1962.
Art of the Byzantine Era. Thames and Hudson, 1963.

Index